# CRITICAL INSIGHTS

## Mario Vargas Llosa

# CRITICAL INSIGHTS

## Mario Vargas Llosa

Editor
**Juan E. De Castro**
*Eugene Lang College, The New School for Liberal Arts, New York*

SALEM PRESS
A Division of EBSCO Information Services, Inc.
Ipswich, Massachusetts

**GREY HOUSE PUBLISHING**

∞ The paper used in these volumes conforms to the American National Standard for Permanence of Paper for Printed Library Materials, Z39.48-1992 (R1997).

**Library of Congress Cataloging-in-Publication Data**

Mario Vargas Llosa / editor, Juan E. De Castro, Eugene Lang College, The New School for Liberal Arts, New York.

pages : illustrations ; cm. -- (Critical insights)

Includes bibliographical references and index.
ISBN: 978-1-61925-401-5

1. Vargas Llosa, Mario, 1936---Criticism and interpretation. 2. Peruvian fiction--History and criticism. 3. Spain--In literature. I. Castro, Juan E. De, 1959-. II. Series: Critical insights.

PQ8498.32.A65 Z6394 2014
863/.64

Cover image : Quim Llenas/Getty Images


First Printing


PRINTED IN THE UNITED STATES OF AMERICA

# Contents

**Resources** _____

# About This Volume

Juan E. De Castro

Novelist, essayist, playwright, pundit, politician, political and cultural agitator, and, in recent years, also actor, Mario Vargas Llosa has long occupied a central position in Latin American and Spanish culture. The importance of the Peruvian novelist, also a Spanish citizen, was reaffirmed and brought again to the attention of international readers and critics by the Nobel Prize in Literature he received in 2010. *Critical Insights: Mario Vargas Llosa* studies the works of this central figure in Hispanic letters.

The volume opens with a reflection on Vargas Llosa's career, its evolution, and his position in Latin American and world literature and culture. It is followed by a biographical essay that traces Vargas Llosa's personal story, from his traumatic childhood to his consecration as a central writer of 1960s "Boom" of the Latin American novel to his conversion to free-market policies in the 1980s to the present. Both are written by the editor of this volume.

Composed of four essays, the section "Critical Contexts" attempts to situate the novels and essays of Vargas Llosa within their personal, social, cultural, political, and historical contexts. The first of these is "Authoritarianism, Rebellion, and the Father Figure in the Fictions of Vargas Llosa" by Carlos Granés. In this essay, Granés presents an overview of the evolution of the Peruvian's narrative that not only takes into account the author's biography—he had an abusive father—but also the political evolution of Peru and Latin America. According to Granés, the figure of the abusive father finds its representation in the public sphere in that of the dictator, who also exemplifies and expresses patriarchal values at their most brutal. Vargas Llosa's celebration of individual freedom and his opposition to all dictatorial governments is, therefore, rooted in his biography. The evolution in Latin America from dictatorships—best represented in Vargas Llosa's life by that of Manuel A. Odría, who governed Peru in the 1950s—to liberal democracies can be seen as a liberating influence on the Peruvian novelist. His early novels, as in the case of *La ciudad y los perros*, 1963 (*The Time of the Hero*, 1966) present individuals trapped by social iniquity.[1] These give way to stories of successful resistance to social constraints, best exemplified by *La tía Julia y el escribidor*, 1977 (*Aunt Julia and the Scriptwriter*, 1982) the fictionalized version of his years as apprentice writer and of his courtship of Julia, his aunt by marriage. Vargas Llosa's evolution concludes in his most recent novel, *El héroe discreto*, 2013 (*The Discreet Hero*), in which parents are benign, and society, though flawed, presents opportunities for those willing to take chances.

This historical and biographical overview is followed by "Reading Vargas Llosa: The Ups, Downs, and Ups of a Literary Career." In this essay, the editor provides a survey of the reception of Vargas Llosa's novels in Spanish and English. While Vargas Llosa achieved literary stardom with his first novel, the reception of his novels has been affected by English language resistance towards narrative experimentation, the preference for "serious" topics among some Latin American critics, and the positive and negative impact of his political evolution on critical and public opinion. Nevertheless, despite these ups and downs, Vargas Llosa is now generally considered to be the greatest active novelist in the Spanish language.

Raymond Leslie Williams' "Natural and Built Environments: Toward an Ecocritical Reading of the Novels of Mario Vargas Llosa" interprets Vargas Llosa's novels from an eco-critical perspective. What makes Williams' approach so innovative is that the Peruvian's novels have generally had urban settings. Moreover, Vargas Llosa's critical work has denigrated the value of the so-called *novelas de la tierra* (novels of the land)—realistic narratives that stressed the determinant influence of rural or natural landscapes—and which, before the rise of the "Boom," had been considered the region's most characteristic novels. However, in addition to stressing the importance of natural settings in many of the Nobel Prize winner's novels, Williams notes the manner in which built environments, such as cities or neighborhoods—the characteristic settings of Vargas Llosa's novels—can be analyzed through an eco-critical framework.

In "Disentangling the Knots: Vargas Llosa and José María Arguedas in *La utopía arcaica*," Sara Castro-Klarén studies Vargas Llosa's 1996 monograph, *La utopía arcaica: José María Arguedas y las ficciones del indigenismo* (*The Archaic Utopia: José María Arguedas and the Fictions of Indigenismo*), in order not only to establish the Nobelist's intellectual and emotional relationship with Arguedas, the other great Peruvian novelist, but also with his native country's intellectual tradition as a whole. Before Vargas Llosa, Peruvian narrative, as well as intellectual life, was dominated by *Indigenismo*, a literary and social movement that not only attempted to defend the indigenous population from exploitative social practices and institutions—such as the serf-like conditions they experienced in the *latifundios* (large estates)—but also vindicated the social and political potential found in existing indigenous institutions. Underlying Vargas Llosa's critique of Arguedas and his rejection of Indigenismo are profound disagreements not only about literature, but also regarding the political and social futures of Peru. However, as Castro-Klarén notes, Vargas Llosa is unable to fully shake-off the national and personal questions raised by the novels of Arguedas.

"Critical Readings," the second section of the book, presents studies of specific topics in Vargas Llosa's narrative and essays. In "Charisma and the Structures of Power: Vargas Llosa's Early Short Stories," Nicholas Birns presents a detailed reading of Vargas Llosa's short fiction. Written during his first decade as a professional writer—they include the short story collection titled *Los jefes,* 1959 ("The Leaders") and the novella *Los cachorros,* 1967 ("The Cubs"), jointly translated as *The Cubs and Other Stories* in 1979. These are, as Birns notes, case studies of adolescence. However, in these, Vargas Llosa exhibits his characteristic preoccupation with power, as expressed not only at the national or institutional level, but also at that of the family and of personal interactions. These short narratives show Vargas Llosa at the start of his career, not only as a student of international writers, such as Ernest Hemingway, but also a careful observer of his own life and his Peruvian surroundings.

In "*The Time of the Hero*: The Moral Itinerary," Alonso Cueto, himself a major Peruvian novelist, studies *The Time of the Hero,* the novel that made the then twenty-seven-year-old into a writer celebrated throughout Latin America and Spain. Cueto analyzes how the different characters in the novel rebel against the Leoncio Prado Military School's oppressive structures and the society it faithfully replicates. He concludes that, despite their failure to change the institutional and social circumstances that stifle their individuality, the novel is ultimately an optimistic and romantic paean to human freedom. Gene H. Bell-Villada's "From *Conversation* to *Feast*: Vargas Llosa's Bookend Novels of Dictatorship" reads jointly *Conversación en La Catedral*, 1969 (*Conversation in The Cathedral*, 1976), often considered to be Vargas Llosa's greatest novel, jointly with his last widely recognized masterpiece, *La fiesta del Chivo*, 2000 (*The Feast of the Goat*, 2002). Both novels deal with Latin American dictators—*Conversation in The Cathedral* depicts Peruvian society during the reign of General Manual A. Odría, while *The Feast of the Goat* portrays Dominican dictator Leonidas Trujillo's brutal regime—but were written during two very different moments in his political evolution. The first was published when Vargas Llosa was a public supporter of the Cuban Revolution, the second when he had become Latin America's best-known neoliberal. For Bell-Villada, the excellence of *The Feast of the Goat* is proof that his political evolution has not affected his ability to craft sophisticated, lucid, and moving masterpieces.

In "From Parable to Pedagogy: Mario Vargas Llosa's War on Fanaticism," Jeffrey Browitt looks at the manner in which Vargas Llosa's political ideas of the 1980s—classically liberal politically and skeptical epistemologically—are represented in *La guerra del fin del mundo*, 1981 (*The War of the End of the World*, 1984) and *La historia de Mayta*, 1984 (*The Real Life of Alejandro Mayta*, 1986). Contradicting the usual consideration of *The War of the End of the World* as one of the summits of Vargas Llosa's narrative, Browitt argues that these novels are marred by the interference of political ideas and values, both in the characters' dialogues and in the development of the plot. However, like Bell-Villada, Browitt sees *The Feast of the Goat* as the instance in which Vargas Llosa's political ideas and narrative verve successfully come together.

---

x

Jean O'Bryan-Knight's *"The Real Life of Alejandro Mayta and The Storyteller*: Success at Last for Mario Vargas Llosa's Professional Narrators" deals with the two Vargas Llosa novels that include, among their central characters, professional narrators who are fictionalized versions of the author himself: *The Real Life of Alejandro Mayta* and *El hablador*, 1987 (*The Storyteller,* 1989). The essay links these fictionalized versions of the author with other narrator-characters in Vargas Llosa's novels, including *The Time of the Hero, Conversation in The Cathedral, Pantaleón y las visitadoras*, 1973 (*Captain Pantoja and the Special Service*, 1978), *The War of the End of the World* and *Aunt Julia and the Scriptwriter*. According to O'Bryan-Knight, beginning with *Aunt Julia and the Scriptwriter,* but in a much more clear and developed manner in *The Real Life of Alejandro Mayta* and *The Storyteller*, the professional narrator is shown as having liberated himself from the shackles of national failure.

*¿Quién mató a Palomino Molero?*, 1986 (*Who Killed Palomino Molero?*, 1987), Vargas Llosa's first full-blown incursion into the detective genre, is the topic of Miguel Rivera-Taupier's "Pessimism and Detection in Vargas Llosa's *Who Killed Palomino Molero?*" For Rivera-Taupier, this novel expresses the social chaos into which Peru had descended by the mid 1980s as a result of the internal conflict unleashed by the Maoist terrorist group the Shining Path. Instead of the coherent social structure that permits the classic detective, by means of the solution of the crime, to reinstate order, the novel presents a situation, in which there is no order to which it is possible to return. Vargas Llosa's other detective novel, *Lituma en los Andes*, 1993 (*Death in the Andes*, 1996), is studied by Haiqing Sun in "Reflections on the Absurd: A Comparative Reading of *Death in the Andes* and *The Time of the Hero*." Both novels—*Who Killed Palomino Molero?* and *Death in the Andes*–share a key character, Lituma, a policeman who also appears in other novels by Vargas Llosa. But *Who Killed Palomino Molero?* and *Death in the Andes* are also connected in that both depict the social decomposition caused by internal conflict, though only in the latter does the Shining Path figure as a central element of the plot. Sun also sees in *Death*

*in the Andes* the end of the period that began with *The Time of the Hero*—a novel she also analyzes as incorporating aspects of the detective genre—in which Vargas Llosa's narrative was primarily the expression of his concerns with the social, political, and cultural realities of Peru. The following period in Vargas Llosa's narrative, prefigured by *The War of the End of the World* set in nineteenth-century Brazil, would be characterized by novels based on the author's research rather than his experience.

This period is exemplified by *El sueño del celta*, 2010 (*The Dream of the Celt*, 2012), which depicts the life and death of the controversial Irish independence leader Roger Casement. This novel, coincidentally published at the time Vargas Llosa was awarded the Nobel Prize, is studied in detail in Ignacio López-Calvo's "Colonialism as a Smoke Screen: Anti-Nationalist Discourse in Vargas Llosa's *The Dream of the Celt*." According to López-Calvo, despite Vargas Llosa's explicit opposition to colonialism and imperialism, *The Dream of the Celt* does not contradict his liberal (or neoliberal) beliefs. Underlying his sympathy for Casement's anti-imperialist and anti-colonial activity is a paradoxical—given the role belief in the nation has played in anti-colonialism—opposition to nationalism, an idea that has, at least since the 1980s, been central to Vargas Llosa's thought.

Vargas Llosa's thinking about literature and culture is spotlighted in the last two essays in this collection. In "Dissonant Worlds: Mario Vargas Llosa and the Aesthetics of the Total Novel," Mark D. Anderson studies the Peruvian Nobelist's concept of the total novel. The phrase total novel has been widely used as a descriptor of key Latin American modern novels, such Vargas Llosa's own *Conversation in The Cathedral*, Gabriel García Márquez's *One Hundred Years of Solitude*, and more recently, Roberto Bolaño's *The Savage Detectives* and *2666*. Anderson traces the intellectual sources that inspired Vargas Llosa's use of the concept; studies the contradictions in the Peruvian novelist's simultaneous stress on the fictional and mimetic aspects of the total novel; and ultimately vindicates the total novel's political relevance. The section concludes with "Mario Vargas Llosa and his Discontents," in which Will H.

Corral looks sympathetically at Vargas Llosa's most recent book-length essay *La civilización del espectáculo*, 2012 (Civilization of the Spectacle). For Corral, Vargas Llosa's essay—generally received as a jeremiad about postmodern decay in artistic and literary quality—has been misread. Instead of a clichéd lamentation over the loss of cultural standards, *La civilización del espectáculo* is perfectly compatible with his long-standing belief in cosmopolitanism, the possibility of cultural development—individual and communal—and with his classically liberal, not conservative, politics.

While no volume can fully encompass the oceanic totality of Vargas Llosa's works—for instance, no essay deals with his theatre, or with his political activity—it provides a solid introduction to the novels and essays of one of the major writers and cultural figures of the twentieth- and early twenty-first centuries. Moreover, the diversity of positions regarding Vargas Llosa found in these essays—ranging from celebration of his novelistic genius or cultural significance, to critical analysis of the political valences found in his works—faithfully represents the reactions that the Nobel Prize winner has generated, not only with academics, but also among general readers. The one common underlying trait of all the essays is the acknowledgement of Vargas Llosa's importance as one of the Spanish-language's greatest writers and one of the main shapers of Hispanic public opinion.

## Note

1. The essay will use the titles of existing translations after the first mention of a Vargas Llosa novel.

# THE BOOK
# AND
# AUTHOR

# On Mario Vargas Llosa

Juan E. De Castro

An unsigned editorial in the November 12, 2008 issue of *N+1*, the trendy New York cultural magazine reads: "Foreign writers are like our own candidates for President: it helps to have been a prisoner of war or at least to have grown up poor. (Poor Mario Vargas Llosa, preppy and smooth with excellent hair, is the John Kerry of Latin American letters.)" (*On Bolaño* 11). Although obviously mistaken regarding U.S. politics—only one presidential candidate has ever been a prisoner of war—this statement belittling Mario Vargas Llosa reflected the consensus among the literati regarding the Peruvian writer at the time. Although, with Gabriel García Márquez, Carlos Fuentes, and Julio Cortázar, widely acknowledged as one of major figures of the Latin American novelistic Boom of the 1960s, with his novels long a staple in Spanish-language literature courses in the United States, Vargas Llosa's reputation had, like Kerry's in electoral politics, somewhat faded by the time of the article's writing. For the hip, Vargas Llosa was, at best, the runner-up to Roberto Bolaño in the race for canonical glory: the *N+1* article in question dealt with the U.S. reception of the Chilean novelist. Of course, for an earlier generation of readers, Vargas Llosa, and all other Latin American writers, had been measured against Gabriel García Márquez and found wanting. Needless to say, on October 7, 2010, a call from the Nobel Committee to Vargas Llosa, ironically then living in Manhattan and teaching at Princeton, upended the narrative proposed by the (relatively) youthful Brooklyn intellectuals of *N+1*.

Of course, in Latin America and Spain, this relative loss of prestige had never taken place, even if his political evolution from supporter of the Cuban revolution to apostle of the free market and liberal democracy had given rise to discussion and, in some quarters, animosity. Not only had he never stopped being seen as a major creative force—having published at least one masterwork in the new century, 2000's *La fiesta del Chivo* (*The Feast of the*

*Goat*, 2001), as well as several novels and plays, all critical and market successes—but by 2008 was long established as arguably the most influential public voice in the Hispanic world, not only regarding literary and cultural issues, but also political matters.[1] The Nobel, which brought Vargas Llosa back to the literary forefront in the United States, simply cemented his position at the core of Latin American and Spanish literary, cultural, media, and even political networks.

Underlying Vargas Llosa's eminence is the excellence of his novels. As we have seen, he was one of the central figures of the Boom of the Latin American novel that brought the literature of the region to the attention of readers world-wide. But even among this august group, he occupies a special position. As Alberto Manguel notes about his first novel, *La ciudad y los perros*, 1963 (*The Time of the Hero*, 1966):

> There had never been anything like it in Spanish-language fiction before. A fierce indictment of Peru's military system, incandescent with rage against the hypocrisy of the established order as mirrored in Lima's most prestigious military academy (which the author had attended), it was also the chronicle of an adolescent rite of passage into the ranks of the commanding patriarchy (109).

While Fuentes had published *The Death of Artemio Cruz* the year before, and Cortázar *Hopscotch* a few months earlier, the case can be made that Vargas Llosa's novel began the international reception of the Boom. It was a finalist for that year's Prix Formentor, losing to Jorge Semprun's *Le grand voyage*. It had, before publication in 1962, already won the Seix Barral Novela Breve award, and, in 1963, had been awarded the Premio Nacional (National Award) as the best book published in Spain. *The Time of the Hero* was acknowledged as an instant masterpiece and made its author into a pan-Hispanic celebrity and a full-fledged member of the Boom.

However, while *The Time of the Hero* brought Vargas Llosa to the forefront of Spanish-language letters, it is only the first jewel in his literary crown. Noted Spanish novelist Javier Cercas has written about Vargas Llosa's position within the Boom:

What is singular about Vargas Llosa, even in the midst of this continental flowering of talent, is that his first novel is not the only masterpiece he has written. I can count at least five more: *La casa verde* [*The Green House*], *Conversación en La Catedral* [*Conversation in The Cathedral*], *La tíaJulia y el escribidor* [*Aunt Julia and the Scriptwriter*], *La guerra del fin del mundo* [*The War of the End of the World*], and *The Feast of the Goat*. I do not know of which other novelist one can say the same. In Spanish, at least, there is no one. Even if there are in our language a handful of novels comparable to Vargas Llosa's best, as far as I can tell, no one has written a group of novels comparable to this (475).

Cercas' list of major works is also unusual in the length of years implied. Vargas Llosa's first major novels were written in the 1960s, in addition to *The Time of the Hero*, *The Green House* (1966, trans. 1968) and *Conversation in The Cathedral* (1969, trans. 1975); continued in the 1970s with *Aunt Julia and the Scriptwriter* (1977, trans. 1982) and the 1980s with *The War of the End of the World* (1981, trans 1984); and, until now, concluded in the 2000s with *The Feast of the Goat* (2000, trans. 2001).

Unlike other Boom authors, who became identified with specific styles or topics, such as García Márquez and magical realism, Fuentes and Mexican history, or Cortázar and the fantastic or metafiction, Vargas Llosa's novels have a wide thematic and stylistic range. Limiting oneself to the masterworks identified by Cerca, one finds novels dealing with life in a military boarding school (*The Time of the Hero*); Peruvian society during the Manuel Odría dictatorship from 1948–1956 (*Conversation in The Cathedral*); and a fictionalized version of the young author's romance with his former aunt by marriage and of his friendship with a Bolivian radio soap opera writer (*Aunt Julia and the Scriptwriter*). Moreover, if the novels of the 1960s, as well as, to a lesser degree, the later *The Feast of the Goat*, are characterized by what Sara Castro-Klarén calls a "cinematic take and cut assemblage procedure" (11), he will experiment with other styles and narrative procedures in his later work. For instance, *The War of the End of the World*, his first novel set outside Peru, in late nineteenth-century northeast Brazil—*The*

*Feast of the Goat* is set in dictator Rafael Leonidas Trujillo's early 1960s Dominican Republic—is narrated in the grand realist style of a Balzac or Tolstoy.

As mentioned above, despite the continued importance of Vargas Llosa as a cultural figure in Latin America, one can identify a clear dividing political line in his work and life: his break with the Cuban government in 1971 over the censorship and jailing of poet Heberto Padilla. Vargas Llosa wrote an open "Letter to Fidel Castro," decrying the "the use of repressive measures against intellectuals and writers who have exercised the right of criticism within the revolution" (250). It gathered the backing of many of the best-known progressive intellectuals—the signers claimed to be "supporters of the principles of the objectives and principles of the Cuban Revolution" (250)—including, in addition to Vargas Llosa, the other three major Boom writers, as well as Susan Sontag, Jean-Paul Sartre, and Simone de Beauvoir. Despite the common assertion of leftist beliefs, the "Padilla Affair" would lead to the break-up of the Boom. García Márquez and Cortázar reconciled with the Cuban government. However, Fuentes evolved into an independent leftist and later liberal, while—after a brief social-democratic period— Vargas Llosa became a believer in free-market solutions to the region's economic and political problems.

While one can clearly map Vargas Llosa's political evolution, the relationship between his ideas and his literature is less clear. His narrative before 1971, which, in addition to the novels, includes his early (1959) collection of short stories *Los jefes* ("The Leaders") and the novella *Los cachorros* ("The Cubs," 1967)—singled out by Bolaño as a "brilliant exercise in speed and musicality" (321)— has been described by Efraín Kristal as comprising Vargas Llosa's "socialist period" (xiii).[2] Kristal notes that, in these novels, "upward mobility is unthinkable without moral degradation, and thoughtful individuals realize that society is corrupt through and through. Vargas Llosa's literary themes were therefore in harmony with his conviction that capitalist society was too corrupt for reform" (xiii). For Kristal, as for many during the 1960s, Vargas Llosa's negative portrayal of Peruvian society implied the need for a revolution.

However, as Kristal also notes, not all critics were convinced that the connotations of Vargas Llosa's narrative were particularly radical (67–68). One can add that if anything defines socialism, particularly Marxism, it is not a negative view of contemporary society, clearly found in Vargas Llosa's narrative before 1971, or the celebration of anti-capitalist individuals or groups, which some critics, such as Gene H. Bell-Villada, find in the portrayal of the student rebels in *Conversation in The Cathedral*. Instead, what defines socialism, especially Marxism, is the belief that society possesses structural elements, that is, social groups, which, in their evolution, have the potential to undermine society and lead to a modification in its class structure. This, for instance, explains why Karl Marx could celebrate the novels of Balzac, despite the author's explicit monarchism. Seen from this perspective, it is clear that Vargas Llosa's novels are not necessarily leftist, even if the author was personally supportive of the Cuban Revolution and revolution in general.

One can read in Vargas Llosa's 1967 reception speech for the Rómulo Gallegos Award—one of the most important awards available to a Spanish language writer and granted to *The Green House*—a clear statement of the role he assigned to socialism at the time: "I want for . . . Latin America to enter, once and for all, a world of dignity and modernity, and for socialism to free us from our anachronisms and horror" (*Literature Is Fire* 73). In 1967, Vargas Llosa identified in socialism the means for social modernization, the same goals he would later progressively identify with the free market and capitalism. Vargas Llosa's diagnosis of the root of Peruvian and Latin American problems—the existence of pre-modern social relations, which ultimately led to indignity and horror—has remained the same, even if the solutions proposed have changed: from revolution to the free market and liberal democracy. As Carlos Granés perceptively notes about Vargas Llosa's views after his break with socialism: "The diagnosis has not changed. To this day, Vargas Llosa understands that one of the worst problems facing Peru is the exploitation and misery of the indigenes and peoples of the Andes; together with . . . the corruption, hypocrisy and opportunism of public life" (57). This consistency explains why, unlike others who evolved from radicalism to what has been called neoliberalism, like the Brazilian sociologist and later president of Brazil, Fernando Henrique Cardoso, Vargas Llosa has never reneged on his earlier work. In fact, Vargas Llosa's personal webpage— www.mvargasllosa.com—foregrounds passages from "Literature Is Fire," the Rómulo Gallegos reception speech.

That said, the texts of the 1960s are characterized by an attempt at reconciling modernist literary techniques, borrowed from Flaubert, Faulkner, and Sartre, with a realistic depiction of Peruvian society, worthy, in its complexity, of the great realist novelists of the nineteenth century. The result is that *The Time of the Hero*, *The Green House*, and *Conversation in The Cathedral* can be described, in Vargas Llosa's own terminology, as "total novels." In his foundational book on *One Hundred Years of Solitude*, *García Márquez: Historia de un deicidio* (García Márquez: Story of a Deicide, 1971), Vargas Llosa argues that a total novel "puts into practice the utopian design of all imposters of god: describe a total reality, present before reality and image that is both its expression and negation" (533). "However," as Mark D. Anderson notes, "the author of a novel does not live in a vacuum, and this fictional 'total reality' is not constructed from nothingness. Rather, the referents that form the fictional world reflect the world outside the novel. The act of creation lies in constructing a novelistic system from a preexisting set of elements" (61). One can add that, in the specific case of Vargas Llosa, the acknowledgment of the artificiality of literary creation, its status as an alternative reality, is woven with the simultaneous aim to realistically represent in the text the key elements that characterize Peruvian society.

His embrace of modernist literary techniques is linked to Vargas Llosa's desire to achieve a more accurate and complete representation of Peru's tense multicultural and multiracial reality. The Peru of his youth was experiencing the complete breakdown of traditional agrarian structures—with their semi-feudal haciendas and exploited Amerindian peons—and by the mass migration of indigenous and provincial men and women to the capital city of Lima, which also saw its neighborhoods, class divisions, and traditions turned upside-down. Castro-Klarén correctly notes that before writing *The Time of the Hero*:

> he needed a narrative structure capable of encapsulating realistically, not the nostalgia for a beautiful though departing rural order, but rather the velocity of change in the everyday life of common individuals journeying from an unacceptable old order into the terrifying and relentless mixes of the cosmopolis (5).

The montage of dialogues, the internal monologues, the crisscrossing of locales and times, serve the function of representing a social reality that, at least in Vargas Llosa's mind, could not be adequately captured by the methods of traditional realism and naturalism used by most earlier Peruvian novelists.

The "Padilla Affair" and Vargas Llosa's progressive disenchantment with the Latin American left did not lead him to disown his early works because in them, as in his later works, there is a consistent concern with individual freedom, even if the former stress the social constraints that make it impossible. However, the novels he published in the 1970s—*Pantaleón y las* visitadoras, 1973 (*Captain Pantoja and the Special Service*, 1978) and *Aunt Julia and the Scriptwriter*—change their focus on the corrupt and corrupting social "totality" and instead place the stress on the individual and her capacity to resist or succumb to these negative social forces. Instead of the frescoes of Peruvian society found in the novels of the 1960s, in the 1970s and often beyond, Vargas Llosa has often preferred to proffer portraits of individuals, whether tragic or comic, in which society is often relegated to the background.

This stress on the individual in Vargas Llosa's novels is related to what Raymond Leslie Williams has called "the discovery of humor" (93). But as, Williams notes, this shift from the tragic to the comic "was not without precedents" in Vargas Llosa's novels, particularly in the case of *Conversation in The Cathedral*, since "The melodramatic elements . . . certainly would have brought a smile were it not for the dismal contexts within which they are played out" (94). Vargas Llosa has stated that melodrama is one of the social and cultural inheritances of Latin America. As he puts it: "Latin America is more melodramatic than dramatic" (Aguilar). His work moved from stressing the dramatic aspects of melodrama in the 1960s to working in a humorous vein the tensions and contrasts characteristic of the genre in the 1970s. In fact, the story of *Captain Pantoja and the Special Service*—in which Pantoja, ordered to develop a prostitute service for the soldiers stationed in the Amazon jungle, ends up ruining his career and marriage, and is exiled to an even more remote military post near Lake Titicaca—could have easily been told in a dramatic (or explicitly melodramatic) manner. While seen at the time as "entertainment," the reputation of these novels, in particular, *Aunt Julia and the Scriptwriter*, has grown through time, as evidenced by Cerca's list of masterpieces.

The second innovation introduced by Vargas Llosa in the 1970s, more specifically in *Aunt Julia and the Scriptwriter* is what Jean O'Bryan-Knight has called "the story of the storyteller," which is including the act of narration itself within the story being told. For O'Bryan-Knight, *Aunt Julia and the Scriptwriter*, together with the later *Historia de Mayta*, 1984 (*The Real Life of Alejandro Mayta*, 1986), about a failed Trotskyite guerrilla, and *El hablador*, 1987 (*The Storyteller,* 1989), about a Jew from Lima who becomes an Amazonian storyteller, would constitute a trilogy "narrated by autobiographical narrators who reflect upon their lives and literary projects in the process of writing novels" (6–7). The metafictional turn, as well as the comic turn, in Vargas Llosa's narrative has led some, including O'Bryan-Knight and M. Keith Booker, to identify the Peruvian's novels beginning with *Aunt Julia and the Scriptwriter*, if not *Captain Pantoja and the Special Service*, as postmodern. Thus the storyteller, "rather than pursuing the search for meaning, implied author is interested in examining meaning as construct" (O'Bryan-Knight 115). This view of reality as a construct, the rejection of the grand narratives of Marxism or socialism, and the embrace of humor are seen by these and other critics as marking Vargas Llosa's abandonment of high modernist literature.

One of the innovations found in *Aunt Julia and the Scriptwriter* that will become a recurring trait in Vargas Llosa's later novels is the presence of two alternating narrative lines. (The first described the young Vargas Llosa's romantic and literary beginnings. The second told the progressively more hallucinatory soap opera episodes written by Pedro Camacho). The other "storyteller novels"—*The Real Life of Alejandro Mayta* and *The Storyteller*—*El paraíso en la otra esquina,* 2003 (*The Way to Paradise,* 2003), which tells alternatively the stories of Paul Gauguin and his Franco-Peruvian grandmother, Flora Tristán; *El sueño del celta,* 2010 (*The Dream of the Celt,* 2012), which has two narrative lines, one detailing the past of human rights activist and Irish patriot Roger Casement's life, the other his "present" as a prisoner awaiting sentence; and *El héroe discreto* (The Discreet Hero, 2013), his most recent to date, which tells the parallel stories of Felícito Yanaqué, a transport entrepreneur who refuses to pay the local Piura mafia for protection, and of the elderly Ismael Carrera's marriage to his maid Armida and his struggles to avoid being declared incompetent by his sons. In fact, even his memoirs *El pez en el agua,* 1993 (*A Fish in the Water,* 1994) establish a textual counterpoint between chapters detailing his childhood, youth, and beginnings as a writer and those describing his entering active politics up to his defeat as a presidential candidate in 1990. In his memoirs, his use of contrapuntal narrative lines—presented as a depiction of reality—makes clear that this particular narrative technique is not necessarily associated with meaning, or even reality, as a construct.

Already in 1981, Vargas Llosa had written a novel that seemed, at least in principle to contradict this description of his having embraced a postmodern aesthetic: *The War of the End of the World.* This novel depicts the creation, by the Conselheiro and his poor followers in northeastern Brazil, of a town rejecting the newly implemented republican rule and its destruction at the hands of the military. Tragic, long, and serious—though without embracing the technical complexity of the novels of the 1960s—it seemed a return to the total novel. In his review of the novel, Ángel Rama, the most prominent Latin American literary critic, wrote of "Latin America having achieved its *War and Peace,* but with one hundred years of delay" (335). *The War of the End of the*

*World* would thus be the classic realist masterpiece that nineteenth-century Latin America had been unable to produce. However, for those who saw Vargas Llosa's as having experienced a postmodern turn, such as M. Keith Booker, the novel, rather than an attempt at representing a specific historical event, was mainly a rewriting of an earlier Brazilian classic, Euclides da Cunha's *Rebellion in the Backlands*. This intertextual relationship implied that Vargas Llosa's text raised "important questions concerning authorship and the relationship between history as the unfolding of events and history as the narrative inscription of those events," which would situate this novel within postmodern concerns (Booker 76).

Be that as it may, one must note, however, that Vargas Llosa has been critical of postmodernism in thought and literature, even recently dedicating a book, *La civilización del espectáculo* (*Civilization of the Spectacle*, 2012) to attacking many of the basic premises, as well as works associated with it. Whether the presence of postmodern traits in his narrative, particularly during the 1970s and 1980s, is just a temporary flirtation with a narrative tendency he would later disavow, a case of the addition of specific narrative tricks to his literary toolkit, or just another example of a writer not understanding his or her own work is something that must, by necessity, be left unresolved in a brief essay like this.

What is clear is that, to a greater degree than was the case in his novels of the 1970s, *The War of the End of the World* signals his growing distance from the Latin American left. Celebrated philosopher Slavoj Žižek sees the novel not only as predicting contemporary "self-organized collectives in areas outside the law" in Canudos, the settling organized by the Conselheiro, but also as celebrating these: "the greatest literary monument to such a utopia" (82). One can argue, however, that the novel instead presents a criticism of all social groups. For instance, the military and republican political leaders can only see British Agents in the peasants and poor led by the Conselheiro; the anarchist revolutionary Galileo Gall misinterprets Canudos as a "revolution" against capitalism; the Conselheiro and the settlers of Canudos believe the Republican government that replaced Emperor Pedro II's government is the Anti-

Christ. Even if Vargas Llosa shows compassion for the poor, who are, in the end, the victims of the novel and of the historical episode it relates, they are not only mistaken in their view of reality, but their goal, to create a theocratic utopia in Brazil, is historically doomed. In fact, the negative portrayal of Gall could very well be taken as an example of the historical inability of the left, whether international or Latin American, to understand the true meaning of the region's history and the poor and their actual goals. That said, as was the case of his novels of the 1960s, the fresco of nineteenth-century Brazil presented in Vargas Llosa's novel is harrowing. However, in this, as in much of his post-Padilla writing, the characters' narrow mindedness, dogmatism, and fanaticism are as much a hindrance to a correct action regarding political reality, as is society's opaqueness or corruption.

His later novels have also generated a similar contradictory response. While *The Real Life of Alejandro Mayta* was first received as an attack on the Peruvian left, later critics have seen the novel as a rich and complex depiction of a Latin American revolutionary. For instance, Bolaño sees in Vargas Llosa's description of the Trotskyite revolutionary, an example of "the kindness and compassion—which others may call objectivity" (324), and Marxist scholar Neil Larsen, argues that, despite any explicit intention on the part of the author, "Mayta speaks the truth and should have succeeded" (166). In this, as in the case of all his novels, one finds that, while not unideological, the complexity of his writing makes a simple political alignment of his fiction impossible.

Vargas Llosa's work as a cultural and political pundit is also of greater complexity than his critics have often asserted. As Will H. Corral has noted: "it is impossible to classify him as a slavish follower of any intellectual master, or *idée fixe*" (190). Even if since the 1980s, Vargas Llosa has been defiantly pro-free market and a defender of liberal democracy, he "has never subscribed to the radicalism of the United States followers of the socioeconomic thought of Friedrich A. von Hayek" (Corral 191). In fact, Vargas Llosa has served as a bellwether for the region's political evolution. Only a few years after Vargas Llosa came out as a "neoliberal"—in the 1986, "Prólogo" to the Spanish version of Hernando de Soto's *The Other Path*—politicians, like presidents Carlos Saúl Menem of Argentina, Carlos Salinas of Mexico, and even his victorious rival in the Peruvian elections, Alberto Fujimori, adopted free-market policies. Menem and Fujimori, as well as numerous other politicians, have been elected or reelected precisely because of their embrace of neoliberalism. Vargas Llosa's influence as a public intellectual responds, to a great degree, to the synchronicity of his ideas with the region's political evolution.

Moreover, while Vargas Llosa began publishing his Piedra de Toque column in the Peruvian news magazine *Caretas* in 1977, his bi-weekly articles achieved even greater dissemination when they began to be syndicated by *El País*, the principal Spanish-language newspaper, in 1991, after the novelist had left Peru for Spain in the aftermath of his 1990 political defeat. Vargas Llosa's growth as a public voice benefited from the expansion of Spanish capital into Latin America during the 1990s, including that of the communications conglomerate Prisa, owner of both *El País*, which became the principal Spanish-language newspaper, and Alfaguara, which published the Peruvian novelist and became the dominant book publishing house throughout Latin America and Spain. In fact, in addition to Vargas Llosa's novels, Alfaguara has also published numerous collections of his literary and political essays.

In his essays and articles, Vargas Llosa proves himself a master communicator, who exhibits an exceptional ability to summarize arguments, and, in most cases, subtly apply neoliberal ideas to specific cultural, social, and political contexts. Despite the occasional vituperative outburst against his political enemies—such as Fidel Castro, Hugo Chávez, or Evo Morales—Vargas Llosa's essays present free market-based ideas at their most expansive and least dogmatic. For instance, unlike many conservatives or neoconservatives, he is a supporter of gay and immigrant rights, of human rights in general, and is a vocal critic of the intrusion of organized religion in government.

However, in partial contradiction with these positions, the Peruvian novelist has also lent his prestige not only to free-market economic proposals, but also to culturally and socially conservative political figures, parties, and movements, such as Spain's José María Aznar and his Partido Popular or the US Tea Party. Nevertheless, Vargas Llosa has publicly expressed his admiration for those members of the "Pink Tide," like former presidents Luiz Inácio Lula da Silva from Brazil and Michelle Bachelet from Chile, who made sure that their progressive policy proposals stay within the framework of the market. In fact, to the surprise of many, Vargas Llosa supported Barack Obama's candidacy in 2008. (The articles, in which he expressed his sympathy for the candidate—"Obama y las primarias" [Obama and the Primaries] and "Obama en los infiernos" [Obama in Hell]—were promptly used by the Obama electoral team in their outreach to Latinos).

As mentioned at the start of this essay, Vargas Llosa received the Nobel Prize for literature in 2010 "for his cartography of structures of power and his trenchant images of the individual's resistance, revolt, and defeat" ("Nobel Prize"). The award was received with jubilation not only in his native Peru, his adopted Spain, but throughout Latin America, where commentators from both left and right celebrated Vargas Llosa's novels, and where the Nobel ceremony became a media event. From the Chilean Alberto Fuguet to the Argentine Rodrigo Fresán to the Colombian Juan Gabriel Vásquez to the Spaniard Cercas, the elite of contemporary Hispanic writers hailed Vargas Llosa as the most influential living Spanish language writer. A technical innovator, a writer's writer, he is also the eminently readable author of best-sellers; a defender of liberal and neoliberal policies, he is also someone committed to human and individual rights. He expresses these ideas and values not only in his essays, but also in his novels. Vargas Llosa works thus reflect, perhaps better than those of any other writer, the contradictory, ambiguous, often tragic, yet nevertheless exhilarating historical journey of Latin America during the last fifty years.

## Notes

1. The essay will use the titles of the translation after the first mention of a Vargas Llosa novel.

2.  There is no standalone translation for *Los jefes* or *Los cachorros*. The English translation of both texts is *The Cubs and Other Stories*, 1979.

## Works Cited

Aguilar, Yanet. "Vargas Llosa: 'América Latina es más melodramática que dramática'" *El Universal. Cultura.* 28 Nov. 2013. Web. 14 Dec. 2013.

Anderson, Mark D. "A Reappraisal of the 'Total' Novel: Totality and Communicative Systems in Carlos Fuentes' *Terra Nostra.*" *Symposium: A Quarterly Journal in Modern Literatures.* 57.2 (2003): 59–79.

Booker, M. Keith. *Vargas Llosa Among the Postmoderns.* Gainesville: UP of Florida, 1994.

Bolaño, Roberto. "Two Novels by Mario Vargas Llosa." *Between Parentheses: Essays, Articles and Speeches, 1998–2003.* Ed. Ignacio Echevarría. Trans. Natasha Wimmer. New York: New Directions, 2011. 319–24.

Castro-Klarén, Sara. *Understanding Mario Vargas Llosa.* Columbia: U of South Carolina P, 1990.

Cercas, Javier. "La pregunta de Vargas Llosa." *La ciudad y los perros: edición conmemorativa del cincuentenario.* By Mario Vargas Llosa. Madrid: Real Academia Española y Asociación de Academias de la Lengua Española, 2012. 473–98.

Corral, Wilfrido H. "Vargas Llosa and the History of Ideas: Avatars of a Dictionary." *Vargas Llosa and Latin American Politics.* Eds. Juan E. De Castro & Nicholas Birns. New York: Palgrave, 2010. 189–211.

Granés, Carlos. *La revancha de la imaginación. Antropología de los procesos de creación: Mario Vargas Llosa y Alejandro Restrepo.* Madrid: Consejo Superior de Investigaciones Científicas, 2008.

Kristal, Efraín. *The Temptation of the Word: The Novels of Mario Vargas Llosa.* Nashville, TN: Vanderbilt UP, 1998.

Larsen, Neil. "Mario Vargas Llosa: The Realist as Neoliberal." *Determinations: Essays on Theory, Narrative, and Nation in the Americas.* New York: Verso, 2001. 143–68.

Manguel, Alberto. "The Blind Photographer." *Into the Looking-Glass Wood.* New York: Harcourt, 2000. 109–20.

_____. "The Nobel Prize in Literature 2010: Mario Vargas Llosa." *NobelPrize.Org.* 2010. Web. 19 Dec. 2013.

O'Bryan-Knight, Jean. *The Story of the Storyteller: La tía Julia y el escribidor, Historia de Mayta, and El hablador by Mario Vargas Llosa*. Amsterdam: Rodopi, 1995.

"On Bolaño." *N+1* 7 (2008): 10–19.

Rama, Ángel. "*La guerra del fin del mundo*: una obra maestra del fanatismo artístico." *Crítica literaria y utopía en América Latina*. Ed. Carlos Sánchez Lozano. Medellin: U de Antioquía, 200. 296–343.

Vargas Llosa, Mario. "Carta a Fidel Castro." *Contra viento y marea, I (1962-1972)*. Barcelona: Seix Barral, 1986. 250-52.

_____. *García Márquez: Historia de un deicidio*. *Mario Vargas Llosa. Ensayos Literarios I*. Barcelona: Circulo de Lectores, 2006. 109–698

_____. "Literature Is Fire." *Making Waves: Essays*. Ed. & trans. John King. New York: Farrar, Straus & Giroux, 1996. 70–74.

_____. "Obama en los infiernos." *El País*. 18 May 2008. Web. 18 Dec. 2013.

_____. "Obama y las primarias." *El País*. 13 Jan. 2008. Web. 18 Dec. 2013.

Williams, Raymond Leslie. *Mario Vargas Llosa*. New York: Ungar, 1986.

Žižek, Slavoj. *Iraq: The Borrowed Kettle*. New York: Verso, 2005.

# Biography of Mario Vargas Llosa_____

Juan E. De Castro

On March 28, 1936, Peru's most famous novelist was born in Arequipa, the country's second largest city, and a bastion of Hispanic culture in the midst of the mostly indigenous Andes. He was the son of Ernesto J. Vargas Maldonado, a radio operator for the Panagra airline, and Dora Llosa Ureta. However, since the couple had divorced before his birth,[1] Mario Vargas Llosa was raised by his mother and her extended family. In fact, young Mario grew up for the first ten years of his life believing his father had died.

The Llosas were a prestigious middle-class family led by his grandfather, Pedro Llosa Bustamante. A year after his birth, escaping the scandal caused by Dora's divorce in conservative Catholic Arequipa, the Llosas moved to Bolivia, briefly to Santa Cruz, then to Cochabamba. Vargas Llosa remembers Cochabamba in his 1993 memoirs, *El pez en el agua* (*A Fish in the Water*, 1994), "as a paradise" (10).[2] In 1945, the newly-elected President of Peru, José Luis Bustamante y Rivero, an uncle of the novelist, named Pedro Llosa prefect of Piura, a department in Northwestern Peru, and Mario and his mother followed him.

The end of Vargas Llosa's happy childhood began the "last day of 1946 or the first day of 1947," when, as he narrates in *A Fish in the Water*, his mother asked the surprised child: "You already know it, of course . . . . That your papa isn't dead. Isn't that so?" (3). Without the child knowing, the parents had reconciled. Not much later—Vargas Llosa somewhat incongruously gives the date as the final days of 1946 or early 1947—he and his mother moved to Lima with Ernesto Vargas (47). A hard, domineering, and violent man, capable of physical aggression against mother and child, he became the bane of Vargas Llosa's early life: "In the years that I lived with my father, before I entered Leoncio Prado in 1950, innocence the ingenuous vision of the world that my mother, my grandparents, and my aunts and uncles had inculcated in me, vanished. In those three years I discovered cruelty, fear, bitterness. . ." (97).

With its "mechanical hierarchies . . . authorized violence" (100), The Leoncio Prado Military School proved to be no improvement on the brutal home environment. He was sent there by his father in order to eliminate any trace of sensibility and Vargas Llosa's nascent interest in literature. With the support of the Llosas, the young Mario had developed a taste for literature, even writing verses and brief narrative (13). The experience at the school, which he entered during his third year of high school, together with his traumatic relationship with his father, would later be recreated in his first masterwork: *La ciudad y los perros*, 1963 (*The Time of the Hero*, 1966). Two of the novel's major characters, the Slave, Ricardo Arana—who meets and then suffers violence at the hand of the father he had believed dead—and the Poet, Alberto Fernández—who discovers a literary vocation while in the school—present fictionalized but still identifiable versions of the young Vargas Llosa.

Unlike Alberto, however, Vargas Llosa did not conclude his studies at Leoncio Prado, but instead finished his fifth and last year of high school in Piura.[3] There, he began his literary career writing and staging a now lost play—*La huida del Inca* (The escape of the Inca). His experiences in Piura also inspired some of the best-known stories he included in his first publication, the short story collection *Los jefes*, 1959 ("The Leaders").[4]

In 1953, Vargas Llosa enrolled in San Marcos University, which, unlike the private Pontifical Catholic University, had students from all regions and classes of Peru. It was also a hotbed of agitation by Apristas[3] and Communists against General Manuel Odría's military regime. (Vargas Llosa would join Cahuide, a Communist front group). Years later, Vargas Llosa used his political experiences at San Marcos in his novel *Conversación en La Catedral*, 1969 (*Conversation in The Cathedral*, 1975), which depicts life during the Odría dictatorship.

In 1955, the budding writer married Julia Urquidi, an aunt by marriage, who was ten years older. He would later reflect on his courtship with Julia Urquidi and on his beginnings as a writer in his 1977 autobiographical novel, *La tía Julia y el escribidor* (*Aunt Julia and the Scriptwriter*, 1982). In 1958, he graduated from San Marcos, and in 1959, *Los jefes* won the Leopoldo Alas Award, which led to the publication of the collection in Spain, where Vargas Llosa has published continually from then on. He also won a scholarship to study philology at the Complutense University in Madrid. A year later, in 1960, he moved to Paris, which, in his mind, had long been the city of writers. (He would stay there until 1966, when he moved to London). His dissertation on *One Hundred Years of Solitude*, later published as *García Márquez: Historia de un deicidio* (García Márquez: Story of a Deicide 1971), is the foundational study of his great contemporary, friend, and later personal and intellectual rival. More importantly, he started writing *The Time of the Hero*, which received the Premio Novela Breve Seix Barral in 1962. With this novel begins Vargas Llosa's brilliant period of the 1960s, when the Peruvian novelist wrote four masterpieces in a row. These include— in addition to *Time of the Hero*—*La casa verde*, 1966 (*The Green House,* 1968), which would go on to win the prestigious Rómulo Gallegos Award; the novella *Los cachorros* ("The Cubs,"1967); and *Conversation in The Cathedral.*

This was also a period of personal evolution. Vargas Llosa had divorced in 1964, and married his cousin Patricia Llosa, with whom he would have three children: Álvaro Vargas Llosa (1966), today a well-known conservative political commentator; Gónzalo (1967), currently head of the Mission of the United Nations High Commissioner for Refugees in The Dominican Republic; and Morgana (1974), a photographer.

Throughout the 1960s, he had also been a staunch, though not uncritical, supporter of the Cuban Revolution. However, in 1971, the Cuban government's censoring of the poet Heberto Padilla, his successive jailing together with his close collaborators, and the obviously forced confessions they made in order to be freed, reminded many of the Stalinist show trials. In response to this so-called "Padilla Affair," Vargas Llosa wrote an open "Letter to Fidel Castro," co-signed by such well-known intellectuals as Susan

---

Sontag, Gabriel García Márquez, and Italo Calvino, demanding the reestablishment of democratic freedoms in Cuba.

In this manner, Vargas Llosa began a political evolution that took him from being a sympathizer with the Cuban Revolution to a moderate social democrat throughout much of the 1970s to—in 1986, with his preface to Hernando de Soto's "neoliberal manifesto" *The Other Path*—the best-known proponent of free-market solutions to Latin America's problems. In fact, in 1987, in response to the then Peruvian president Alan García's plans to nationalize the banks, Vargas Llosa, who had returned to Peru in 1974, founded the Movimiento Libertad (Freedom Movement). He later became the candidate for an alliance of the Movimiento Libertad and other center-right parties (Partido Popular Cristiano and Acción Popular) during the elections of 1990. Having as its backdrop an endlessly spiraling economic crisis, hyperinflation, a loss of faith in democratic institutions, and a growing insurgency by the brutally violent pseudo-Maoist group Sendero Luminoso (the Shining Path), Vargas Llosa, who was seen as the representative of the Peruvian upper classes, lost to dark-horse candidate Alberto Fujimori.

Parallel to this political transformation, Vargas Llosa's writing also experienced surprising change. While his novels of the 1960s had been characterized by an intense realism that, on occasion, veered into naturalism, they had been written in a complex style that cross-cut dialogues, points of view, time periods, and events. Starting with *Pantaleón y las visitadoras*, 1973 (*Captain* Pantoja *and the Special Service,* 1978) and *Aunt Julia and the Scriptwriter*, his novels became stylistically less adventurous—even if he could still muster the high style of his youth when needed, as in *La fiesta del Chivo*, 2000 (*The Feast of the Goat*, 2001). The two novels of the 1970s are also characterized by their humor, something obviously absent from the serious masterpieces of the sixties. Again, while Vargas Llosa would write highly serious novels after the 1970s, he was able to use humor whenever useful, as he did to great effect in *El hablador*, 1987 (*The Storyteller,* 1989); *Lituma en los Andes*, 1993 (*Death in the Andes*, 1996); and *Travesuras de la niña mala*, 2006 (*The Bad Girl,* 2007), to mention a few examples.

After his electoral defeat, Vargas Llosa left Peru and became, to an even greater degree than before, a world cultural figure. While he had always been a major public voice in both cultural and political affairs—publishing a biweekly column titled "Piedra de Toque" in *Caretas,* a Peruvian weekly magazine—starting in 1990, "Piedra de Toque" found a new home in the Spanish newspaper *El País,* which was itself beginning a process of internationalization. As of 2013, his "Piedra de Toque" column is syndicated by *El País* throughout the whole Spanish-speaking world and Brazil. His bi-weekly essays transformed the already celebrated novelist and influential public commentator into, arguably, the major political and cultural pundit in Spain and Latin America. He has become a vociferous critic of the so-called "Pink Tide" populisms, the scourge of the late Venezuelan President Hugo Chávez, whom he once offered to debate; Bolivia's Evo Morales; and Ecuador Rafael Correa, while being surprisingly supportive of those leftist leaders who stayed within democratic and free-market bounds, such as former Brazilian and Chilean Presidents Inácio Lula da Silva or Michelle Bachelet. Also belying the clichéd image of Vargas Llosa as a rigid conservative is his constant defense of human rights—especially in Peru—and his vocal support of gay rights, including the freedom to marry.

In 1993, Vargas Llosa, whose criticisms of Fujimori's constant violations of human rights and democratic institutionality had made the latter's regime threaten him with the loss of his citizenship, accepted the offer of the Spanish government and became a citizen of that country. (He retained his Peruvian citizenship, however). That same year, his novel *Lituma in the Andes* (*Death in the Andes,* 1996) won the Planeta Prize. The following year, he received the Cervantes Prize, the highest award granted to a Hispanophone writer.

Although Vargas Llosa had already written a novel about Brazil, his 1981 masterpiece *La guerra del fin del mundo* (*War of the End of the World,* 1984), perhaps reflecting his own international life and concerns, his novels were, from then on, set in international locales The Dominican Republic in *The Feast of the Goat*); Paris and Tahiti in *El paraíso en la otra esquina,* 2003 (*The Way to Paradise* 2003); and Ireland, England, the Belgian Congo, and the Peruvian Amazon in *El sueño del celta*, 2010 (*The Dream of the Celt* 2012). He would not return to explicitly Peruvian topics until 2013's *El héroe discrete* (The Discreet Hero).

Unarguably the greatest active Spanish-language novelist, Mario Vargas Llosa was rewarded with the Nobel Prize in 2010 for, in the Swedish Academy's words, "his cartography of structures of power and his trenchant images of the individual's resistance, revolt, and defeat" ("Nobel Prize"). This long-deserved award reaffirmed Mario Vargas Llosa's position as one of the major Hispanic figures of the last fifty years. In fact, he has also achieved the rather unique distinction of being the only Latin American writer to ever become a Spanish grandee, when King Juan Carlos of Spain named him the first hereditary Marquis of Vargas Llosa. In 2011, he created the Cátedra Vargas Llosa that, with the collaboration of over twenty universities in Spain, Peru, Mexico, France, and the United States, promotes the study of Spanish-language literature, and will, as of 2014, award a prize to the best Spanish-language novel published within the previous two years. Moreover, his every word is scrutinized, and as evidenced by the ballyhoo surrounding the publication of *El héroe discreto*, his books are treated as major cultural events. At an age at which most have long since winded down their activity, Vargas Llosa is still at the height of his influence.

## Notes

1.  In Spanish, the first surname corresponds to the father, the last to the mother. The essay will use the titles of the translation after the first mention of a Vargas Llosa novel.

2.  In Peru, elementary school (*primaria*) and high school (*secundaria*) each last five years.

3.  There is no standalone translation for either *Los jefes* or *Los cachorros*. Both were included in *The Cubs and Other Stories*, 1979.

4.  The Alianza Popular Revolucionaria Americana (APRA) is a populist political party founded and led by Víctor Raúl Haya de la Torre.

## Works Cited

"The Nobel Prize in Literature 2010: Mario Vargas Llosa." *NobelPrize. Org.* 2010. Web. 19 Dec. 2013.

Vargas Llosa, Mario. *A Fish in the Water: A Memoir*. Trans. Helen Lane. New York: Farrar, Straus & Giroux, 1994.

# CRITICAL
# CONTEXTS

# Authoritarianism, Rebellion, and the Father Figure in the Fictions of Vargas Llosa_____

Carlos Granés

It is not easy to know where novelists get their topics. Nor is it easy to understand why certain problems and experiences stimulate creation, while other similar events leave no imprint in an author's works. Some writers dismiss these questions and rarely address their creative process. It would seem that discovering the sources of their topics or obsessions, or the reason why they, like many others, have dedicated their lives to the creation of characters made up of words and set in worlds of their imagination, does not hold any interest for them.

This is not the case of Mario Vargas Llosa. On many occasions, the Peruvian novelist has addressed the issue of what events are incorporated into the process of writing. He has even described it as a "reverse striptease," in which authors, instead of revealing their hidden beauties, exhibit "the demons that plague and obsess them; the ugliest part of themselves, their nostalgia, guilt, and rancor" (*Historia secreta de una novela* 11).[1] Vargas Llosa has also revealed the personal experiences that have become the raw material of his fictions. These experiences share something in common. They contradicted views he had previously held about reality. For instance, the years he spent at the Leoncio Prado Military School, an institution that had students from all of Peru's geographical regions and social classes, permitted the young Vargas Llosa to get to know the deep social and racial tensions that conditioned life in his country. His trip to the Peruvian Amazon, which took place just before he began his graduate studies in Spain in 1958, brought him face to face with a Peru he had not previously known: an archaic, irrational, and savage country, in which life was not governed by modern institutions, but instead by violence.

Although these two experiences have been used by Vargas Llosa in several novels, the event that left the deepest impression

---

in his psyche and that has influenced his literature the most was the encounter with his father. This encounter is told in detail in his *El pez en el agua* (*A Fish in the Water*, 1994), the book of memoirs published in 1993.[2] Until he was ten, Vargas Llosa had believed his father, Ernesto J. Vargas, a Panagra Airlines radio operator, to be dead. However, in reality, his father had separated from his mother when she was five months pregnant and had not communicated with her for ten years. Vargas Llosa had been born in Arequipa and raised by his mother's side of the family. Afterwards, they had moved to Cochabamba, Bolivia, and finally to Piura in northern Peru. He had lived in a majority female environment, pampered and fêted as the only child, until one morning in 1946 or 1947, Ernesto J. Vargas intruded into his life.

His father was alive and had returned to take him and his mother back to Lima. He had to abandon his Edenic childhood, full of affection and care, and come to a city he did not know and face a father who soon showed himself to be authoritarian and violent. This would be the most disconcerting experience of his life. Like his time at the Leoncio Prado, or his visit to Amazonia, his relationship with Ernesto J. Vargas showed him that reality was different from what he had imagined.

*A Fish in the Water* is divided into two sets of chapters. In the uneven chapters, Vargas Llosa narrates the events that take place from the moment his father wrenches him from his childhood paradise: the moments of reclusion and terror he lived as a child, his time at Leoncio Prado and the University of San Marcos, and the beginnings of his literary vocation. In the even chapters, Vargas Llosa jumps forward to 1987 to narrate his experience as candidate for the presidential elections of 1990. He also analyzes the illusions, hopes, betrayals, and petty miseries that make up political life in Peru. It would seem these are two distinct topics—the youth of a future writer and his later decision to enter politics—but, in reality, they are both explorations of the central "demon" of Vargas Llosa's life: authoritarianism and its corollary, rebellion.

Vargas Llosa's personal and public life have both been scarred by the experience of authoritarianism. The father, whom the child Vargas Llosa met when he was ten years old, was a violent, neurotic, and despotic man, unable to enjoy life. From the start of their relationship, he attempted to frustrate the literary interests of his son. And the rival and winning candidate for the elections of 1990, Alberto Fujimori, was a democratic president for only twenty months before he decided to close Congress, the Courts, the Constitutional Tribunal, and the Superior Judicial Council, in order to lead an unusual coup against the state and govern by decree. Like Ernesto J. Vargas, Fujimori showed himself to be an authoritarian man, hostile towards democratic institutions.

As a child, when, thanks to his father, he had to face privation, caprices, and even violence, Vargas Llosa developed a strong hatred for despotic personalities. This antipathy was reaffirmed years later, when he became aware that the hierarchical regime he had suffered at home was replicated in his country's public sphere. Peru has a long tradition of authoritarianism. Throughout its republican history, there have been numerous authoritarian governments. In fact, during the twentieth century there were almost four decades of non-democratic governments. "Military dictatorships are as common to Lima as bullfights. Peruvians of my generation have lived under them for more years than under democracy," wrote Vargas Llosa in 1983 (*The Country of a Thousand Faces* 8). The democratic governments of the last century were threatened by military coups, temporary presidencies, and populism. The result was the weakening of institutions caused by the eruption of caudillos and strongmen, whether they be farcical or subtle.

Authoritarianism has cast its long shadow on Vargas Llosa's private and public life. His father, an imperious man who ruled the home, was a version of the dictator, the prototypical despot who controlled all state institutions. In a passage from *A Fish in the Water*, Vargas Llosa establishes this connection between private and political spheres: "In October 1948, the military coup of General Odría brought down the democratic government and Uncle José Luis went into exile. My father celebrated the coup as a personal victory: the Llosas could no longer boast of having a relative who was the president of Peru" (67). In Vargas Llosa's mind, the father became associated with the figure of the dictator.

The father and the dictator are at the root of both this youthful drama and the problems of Peru. He who exercises limitless power, without restriction or mediation, corrupts both family and public institutions. Rebellion is the logical answer to this abuse of power. Vargas Llosa discovered that literature was a weapon in the struggle against oppression. First, he used it against his father, later against dictators. Alonso Cueto explains this well: "The literary vocation is not only an act of rebellion against paternal authority but even against the authority of reality itself" (12). From that moment on, Vargas Llosa realizes that nothing can annoy Ernesto J. Vargas more than his vocation for poetry. What had, until then, been a pastime becomes a vocation. Far from dissuading him, his father's anger kindles his interest in literature. As he reminisces in *A Fish in the Water*: "To write poems was another of the secret ways of resisting my father, since I knew how much it irritated him that I wrote verses, something he associated with eccentricity, bohemia and what could horrify him most: being queer" (66).

Vargas Llosa's interest in literature was the reason why his father decided to enroll him in the Leoncio Prado Military School. In Lima's *machista* society of the 1950s, military discipline was considered as the antidote to any purported character weakness. Ernesto J. Vargas believed that the military could erase from the young Vargas Llosa's mind his whim for literature and, in the process, transform him into a "real" man. The young aspiring writer saw himself immersed in a hostile environment. However, his father's action had the opposite effect. Instead of repressing his son's literary vocation, the Leoncio Prado School nourished his rebellion and his passion for literature. Furthermore, it gave him the raw material he used to write his first novel, *La ciudad y los perros* (*The Time of the Hero*, 1966).

Winner of the Seix Barral Biblioteca Breve Award in 1962 and published in 1963, *The Time of the Hero* is not only a complex literary work, but also an act of rebellion against his father, against the Leoncio Prado School, and against Lima's society. Moreover, Vargas Llosa's first novel is an act of revenge against an imperfect reality that shows all its defects and perverse mechanics. This moral X-ray of Lima's society shows what happens when, instead of teaching virtue, educational institutions reproduce the vices found in private society. From its opening lines, we know that there is no space for moral considerations within the Leoncio Prado School. Alberto Fernández, one of the novel's main characters, is discovered far from his guard post. He knows this could lead to a serious sanction, and he develops a strategy to avoid punishment. Instead of trying to escape, he approaches a lieutenant and addresses him: "I'd like to ask you for some . . . moral advice" (16). The lieutenant's answer reflects the true nature of the Leoncio Prado School: "I'm not a priest, goddamn it! Go take your moral questions to your father or mother" (17).[3] The remainder of the novel shows what happens when moral questions are banished from educational institutions.

Many of the young boys who board at the Leoncio Prado do not come there to be educated, but to have the military "shape them up" morally. Their parents have detected some suspicious moral trait, and they expect the military to correct any deviation in character from their imaginary version of masculinity. The contradiction arises in that the boys have come to an institution that, instead of being characterized by discipline and order, is governed by the law of the jungle, where the strongest determine rules and privileges. The survival of the cadets depends on their ability to violate the rule book and commit all types of infractions and outrages, from leaving the school without authorization, to smoking, drinking, and betting, to even stealing exams and engaging in bestiality with chickens. At the Leoncio Prado, lying is a way of life. While it presents itself to the outside world as an institution that inculcates discipline and honor, within its walls its students know that, in order to survive, it is necessary to either become a savage or a hypocrite.

The murder of Cadet Arana is proof of the disguised putrefaction of the Leoncio Prado School. During a military practice, the body of the young student falls to the ground with a bullet in the head. Suspicion falls on the Jaguar, the leader of a group of student thugs, but the school authorities prefer to cover up the crime in order to protect the Leoncio Prado's reputation. Lieutenant Gamboa is the only officer who attempts to find out truth, but this quest only brings him problems. He ends up reassigned to an isolated Andean post. The school thus fulfills its true function. It implicitly teaches the cadets that only through lies and cynicism can one survive in a society as decomposed as that of Lima. Alberto Fernández is a case in point. He knows very well what his father's vices are. He first attempts to resist them, but, after the experience at the Leoncio Prado, he ends up embracing them. "I'll work with my father, and I'll have a convertible and a big house with a swimming pool. I'll marry Marcela and be a Don Juan" (398–99), he concludes near the end of the novel. The youth enters the school to be taught how to be a human being, but exits transformed into a phony with the same worldly ambitions as his father.

Alberto Fernández shows a family resemblance to another of Vargas Llosa's major characters, Santiago Zavala, known as Zavalita, the protagonist of *Conversación en La Catedral* (*Conversation in The Cathedral*, 1975). The main difference between the two is that Zavalita manages to break free from the vicious circle that makes children into versions of their parents. This, however, does not mean that Zavalita has a satisfying life.

Published in 1969, *Conversation in The Cathedral* is even more complex than *The Time of the Hero* because it incorporates Peru's corrupt public and political life. Zavalita grows up in a bourgeois Lima family that enjoys all the privileges of the Latin American well-to-do: education at a private university, free time, domestic help, and the prospect of a prosperous future thanks to social and political connections. But Zavalita is a nonconformist. He knows that his father, Fermín Zavala, supported Odría's coup (the one Ernesto J. Vargas celebrated as a personal triumph). His father's wealth is the result of the favors received from Cayo Bermúdez, the sinister right-hand man of the dictator, who supervised the government's repressive and corrupt undercover operations. Zavalita had been a supporter of the deposed president Bustamante, and he does not feel comfortable enjoying privileges gained thanks to the handouts of a dictatorship. His rebellion consists of taking decisions that contradict the plans his father made for his life. He enrolls in San Marcos, the public university; joins Cahuide, a clandestine Communist group; becomes a journalist in the tabloid newspaper *La Crónica*; he even marries Ana, a lower-class, mestiza nurse.

Even though the Zavala home gives the impression of being an oasis of sophistication and elegance in the midst of the misery of Lima, this is only a mirage. Just like Alberto's father, Zavalita's is a hypocrite, who uses the splendor of his last name and the appearance of a faultless family life to hide a secret. Fermín Zavala is a homosexual, who satisfies his desire by taking advantage of his naïve and submissive chauffeur Ambrosio.

Zavalita perceives that something is rotten in his family, in his country, and in himself. "He was like Peru . . . he's fucked himself up somewhere along the line" (3), he reflects at the start of the novel. His existential drama originates in that he clearly sees that both he and Peru are "fucked up" because of the corrupt complicity of the country's bourgeois families with the abject dictatorship of General Odría. Out of this putrid marriage of convenience, only hypocrisy and abuse can be born. Economic and political power are in the same hands, and those unable to enter this small group have no access to any type of privilege. Zavalita represents this Peruvian tragedy. He does not want to be part of the problem and, therefore, rebels. He prefers personal failure to enjoying the compromised benefits of social privilege. Zavalita's moral conclusion is dramatic. In a corrupt society, where personal gain is achieved only by oppressing others, failure is more admirable than success.

*Conversation in The Cathedral* is the great novel of Latin America's failure. It shows the futility of a young man's rebellion against his father, family, and the aspirations of his social class. He achieves nothing, except to wallow in mediocrity and frustration. Zavalita searches for meaning, for something in which to believe, but he finds Communism, God, the APRA party, and even literature, wanting. The dictatorship has achieved its purpose: to disseminate apathy and submissiveness. It has ingrained the idea that nothing can be done; that no one can change individual destiny. Ambrosio, Zavalita, even Peru, have to live day to day without hope of anything ever changing. Disillusionment and a lack of personal projects are to be found in Ambrosio's statement that closes the novel: "He would work here and there, maybe after a while there'd be another outbreak of rabies and they'd call him in again, and after that here and there, and then, well, after that he would have died, wasn't that so, son?" (601).

In the fictional world of these two novels, there is no exit. Rebellion ends in failure or frustration. Alberto is corrupted, Zavalita marginalized. Those are the two possible conclusions to the moral drama faced by the characters. The despotic father and the authoritarian dictator undermine the spirit and will of the characters. Through force and oppression, they annul the spiritual qualities that permit an individual to struggle against the adversities and pressures found in their social and cultural environment. Without anything in which to believe and with a weakened will, there is no way out of the vicious circles in Peruvian and Latin American social life.

In Vargas Llosa's early novels, the individual is broken by social structures, instinctive forces, or the pressures of the environment. Characters are shaped by society. Alberto Fernández and Zavalita lack the strong convictions needed to overcome social strictures. They are adrift, lost in the midst of corrupt institutions and flawed families. It is only towards the end of the 1970s that Vargas Llosa will imagine a character able to break free from this perverse social dynamic.

In 1977, he publishes *La tía Julia y el escribidor* (*Aunt Julia and the Scriptwriter*, 1982). This novel marks the beginning of a new stage in the production of the Peruvian writer. From then on, his novels will not explore the means by which society obliterates the individual, but rather the resources with which they may be able to survive, and even thrive, against it. He now examines the dangers posed to individuals by the fanaticism of charismatic personalities, unquestioned beliefs, and dogmatic principles.

The protagonist of *Aunt Julia and the Scriptwriter* is Varguitas, an alter-ego of the author. The adventures that take place in the novel are directly inspired in Vargas Llosa's biography. Here, we see again the drama of a young man attempting to take charge of his life in the midst of hostile environment. Varguitas has two goals in life: to marry his aunt Julia, an older divorcée, and to become a professional writer. But everything is stacked against him. In the Peru of the 1950s, no one could live from literature alone. Getting married to his aunt by marriage without permission from his father is even more unlikely:

My father was a very stern man I'd always been very afraid of. I'd been brought up far away from him, with my mother and her family, and when my parents were reconciled and I went to live with him, we had never gotten along well together. He was conservative and authoritarian, given to cold rages, and if it was true they had written to him, the news would set him off like a bombshell exploding (230–31).

In this novel, we again see how authoritarian intimidation threatens individual desires. But the result is different. Varguitas has something that neither Alberto nor Zavalita possessed, and that makes it possible for him to confront authority. He believes in his vocation as a writer. He has an unquenchable desire to dedicate himself to writing regardless of the cost. This gives him the necessary courage to overcome authoritarianism and social pressure.

In *Aunt Julia and the Scriptwriter*, the son finally overcomes the father and the reality and coercion of the social environment he represents. This, however, does not mean that Vargas Llosa has finally exorcised the topics of the father and authoritarianism from his novels. In 2000, these reappear with overwhelming force in *La fiesta del Chivo* (*The Feast of the Goat*, 2001), a novel that uncovers the abject submission of a whole country to the corrupt caprice of its self-proclaimed redeemer. After a long sojourn in the United States, Urania, the protagonist of the novel, returns to the Dominican Republic to call to account her father—and through him, the country as a whole—for having submitted to the cruelest whims of Rafael Leonidas Trujillo, the dictator who ruled the Caribbean Island between 1930 and 1961. Urania needs to understand how it could be that, during those years, all the followers and associates of Trujillo, and especially her father, Egghead Cabral, had served the dictator so slavishly. She is also interested in finding out if she has been able to forgive her father for having given Trujillo the opportunity to take her virginity.

Urania's personal destiny is vilely and cowardly betrayed by her father. In order to return to the great leader's graces, Egghead Cabral offers his daughter as a sexual gift. The trauma of this first failed and brutal sexual encounter transforms Urania into a frigid woman, obsessed with work, and indifferent towards love and sex. After the incident, Urania breaks away from her family and the island. She spends her time unveiling the corruptive effects of power. Her reflections are enlightening:

> After so many years of serving the Chief, you had lost your scruples, your sensitivity, the slightest hint of rectitude. Just like your colleagues. Just like the whole country, perhaps. Was that a requirement for staying in power and not dying of disgust? To become heartless, a monster, like your Chief? (102)

Power corrupts, and in order to hold on to it, to keep enjoying its prerogatives, Egghead Cabral sacrifices all moral principles. The consequences of that moral collapse are suffered by his daughter, forever scarred by the trauma of rape.

Ten years after the publication of *The Feast of the Goat*, Vargas Llosa received the Nobel Prize in Literature. In *In Praise of Reading and Fiction*, his acceptance speech of December 7, 2010, he again mentioned his father. Through him, he "discovered loneliness, authority, adult life, and fear" (31). His salvation, he insisted in the speech, was reading and writing.

In fact, reading and writing have permitted him to lead a life full of adventure, commitment, and success. He has received all the important literary awards to which a writer can aspire, thanks to the need to gain revenge from reality through the fantasy of fiction. As essayist Enrique Krauze notes, "In a sense he has rewritten his family history and reconstructed the Eden of his childhood years in Bolivia, before the Fall that ensued with the reappearance of his father. For the son of Ernesto Vargas, scarred in his youth by parental abuse, it may be time, at last, to be happy" (402). He has struggled against his father, achieving revenge through fiction, and standing up to him symbolically whenever, in conferences or articles, he unmasks caudillos, strongmen, populist saviors, or dictators. In this manner, Vargas Llosa has become one of the most influential world intellectuals and one of the greatest novelists of the Spanish language. That childhood antipathy became the fuel for an overwhelming body of literature. Having had an authoritarian father was a virtual damnation and a formidable stimulus for his becoming the writer he is. That persistence and passion has not only earned him the Nobel Prize, it has also shown how wrong his father was and how all of his prejudices and fears had been unfounded. However, the question that one must ask oneself is: has Vargas Llosa finally been able to exorcise his paternal demon?

The answer to this question can be found in the first novel Vargas Llosa has published after having received the Nobel Prize: *El héroe discreto* (The Discreet Hero, 2013). It is, in many ways, a typical Vargas Llosa novel. In its pages, one finds topics previously explored in his works—rebellion, moral commitment, eroticism, melodrama—parallel narratives, settings in Piura and Lima, and recurring characters, such as Don Rigoberto, Lituma, Doña Lucrecia, and Fonchito. One finds all the characteristic traits of his fictional universe, except one: the authoritarian father.

This is the great surprise that awaits the readers of *El héroe discreto*. The memory of the father is present in the life of Felícito Yanaqué, the novel's protagonist, but it no longer casts the oppressive shadow it did in Vargas Llosa's earlier novels. For the first time, the image of the father is benevolent. Felícito lives in the contemporary Peru, which is experiencing political stability and economic growth. This is not only a Peru of prosperity and opportunity, but also of new evils that follow in the wake of economic development. Felícito personally experiences this dark side. Although he is not a rich man, his transportation company has grown during the last few years and this economic bonanza attracts criminals. Felícito begins to receive threats. They ask him to pay for protection. He refuses and makes it known publically that he will not pay. He thus opens the door to tragedy. What is surprising is that Felícito becomes a discreet hero—that is, a citizen that, without pomp or circumstance, stands up to corruption through ethical commitment—because of the memory he has of his father. The father is a positive example, someone to remember and emulate. "Once more, as so often in his life, Felícito remembered the words of his father at his deathbed: "never let anyone take advantage of you my son. This is the only inheritance I leave you" (13). These are the words Felícito repeats to himself when facing the hoodlums.

Rebelliousness is no longer represented by the young, but, instead by their elders, such as Ismael Carrera, the owner of the insurance company where Don Rigoberto works. Like the young Zavalita, Ismael, a man in his sixties, decides to marry a poor, mestizo woman, who works in his home as a servant. Overcoming all social taboos, Don Ismael offers his affection to the woman who has taken care of him. The ones who angrily attempt to uphold traditional social values are not the parents—as is the case in *Conversation in The Cathedral*—but Ismael Carrera's children. The Carrera twins lack any spark of rebelliousness. On the contrary, they are a pair of slackers who have survived thanks to their father and who counted on the inheritance they expected to receive at his death. The same thing occurs with Miguel, Felícito's son. Instead of experiencing the oppressive authority of the father, he is the one taking advantage of his wealth.

Fifty years have passed since the publication of *Time of the Hero*. In that stretch of time, the author has changed, as have Peru and the world. Some of the personal demons that have accompanied Vargas Llosa during those years, and that would occasionally become manifest in his novels, have stopped fueling his imagination. The demon of the father, together with the countervailing demon of rebellion, had always found expression in his literature. But now in *El héroe discreto*, the roles have been exchanged: the parents rebel against the children. Perhaps this reflects the current economic prosperity of Peru. Vargas Llosa's attempt, during the last forty years, to create political and economic consensus in his country appears to have succeeded in giving democratic stability to his country. One no longer hears the rattling of sabers. Despots rear their head, but they are defeated at the ballots. This is the reason for his enthusiasm.

A more equitable and prosperous democratic Peru is no longer the dream of a novelist. As authoritarianism fades from the political reality of Peru and Latin America, the shadow of the father also disappears. Vargas Llosa knows one should never lose vigilance and that threats against freedom always exist, but the desired changes seem to be taking root in reality. After so many books and battles, the father and reality are no longer oppressive presences against which rebellion is the only option.

## Notes

1. In this case, as in that of all works in Spanish in the Works Cited list, the translation is by the author of this essay.

2. The essay will use the titles of the translation after the first mention of a Vargas Llosa novel.

3. The English translation of this passage changes the Spanish "moral" to personal. Both quotations from *The Time of the Hero* have been thus corrected.

## Works Cited

Cueto, Alonso. "Reality and Rebellion: An Overview of Mario Vargas Llosa's Literary Themes." *The Cambridge Companion to Mario Vargas Llosa*. New York: Cambridge UP, 2012. 9–21.

Krauze, Enrique. *Redeemers: Ideas and Power in Latin America*. Trans. Hank Heifetz & Natasha Wimmer. New York: Harper, 2011.

Vargas Llosa, Mario. *A Fish in the Water: A Memoir*. Trans. Helen R. Lane. New York: Farrar, Straus & Giroux, 1994.

_____. *Aunt Julia and the Scriptwriter*. Trans. Helen R. Lane. 1982. New York: Penguin, 1995.

_____. *Conversation in The Cathedral*. 1974. Harper, 2005.

_____. "The Country with a Thousand Faces." *Making Waves: Essays*. Trans. John King. New York: Penguin, 1998. 1–15.

_____. *Historia secreta de una novela*. 1971. Barcelona: Tusquets, 2001.

_____. *The Feast of the Goat*. Trans. Edith Grossman. 2001. New York: Farrar, Straus & Giroux, 2002.

_____. *El héroe discreto*. Madrid: Alfaguara, 2013.

_____. *In Praise of Reading and Fiction: The Nobel Lecture.* Trans. Edith Grossman. New York: Farrar, Straus & Giroux, 2011.

_____. *The Time of the Hero.* Trans. Lysander Kemp. New York: Grove Press, 1966.

# Reading Mario Vargas Llosa: The Ups, Downs, and Ups of a Literary Career_____

Juan E. De Castro

Given that it is impossible to provide a detailed survey of the international reception of the writings of Mario Vargas Llosa—which include novels, short stories, plays, and essays—in such few pages, this brief study will concentrate on the response to his narrative in the Hispanic and Anglophone print media. While, with Gabriel García Márquez and Roberto Bolaño, Mario Vargas Llosa is the major Hispanophone literary figure of the last half-century, his creative longevity is unparalleled. Moreover, unlike his peers, he has become a major political voice in Latin America, Spain, and beyond. Thus the reception of his works has been influenced by his political evolution from supporter of the Cuban Revolution to defender of free market solutions to Latin America's social problems. Vargas Llosa has also participated in active politics. In 1987, he founded the Movimiento Libertad to oppose the nationalization of the banks proposed by then President of Peru, Alan García. He ran for the presidency of Peru in 1990 and was defeated by Alberto Fujimori. But as proof of this intertwining of life, politics, and literature, this defeat gave rise to one of his major works, the political and literary memoir *El pez en el agua*, 1993 (*A Fish in the Water*, 1994).[1]

While his career began with the 1959 short-story collection *Los jefes,* 1959 ("The Leaders"), first published in Spain, as would be the case with all of his work,[2] the reception of Vargas Llosa's works truly begins with *La ciudad y los perros,* 1963 (*The Time of the Hero*, 1966), his first novel and an acknowledged masterpiece. It received the Premio Biblioteca Breve given by publisher Seix Barral to an unpublished manuscript in 1962. *The Time of the Hero* also won the Premio Nacional de la Crítica, Spain's major literary award and was a finalist for the prestigious Prix Formentor. As José Donoso, another major Latin American novelist noted, "with that prize and a great deal of hoopla, his name . . . suddenly became popular in the entire Spanish-speaking world. *The Time of the Hero* caused a whole continent to talk" (61). The extent of this success is evidenced by the fact that by 1971 the Spanish edition had sold one-hundred-thirty-five thousand copies worldwide (Herrero Olaizola 18). By comparison, the usual print run of a book in Spain during the early sixties was of only three thousand copies (18).

The *Time of the Hero* set the pattern for the Hispanic reception of his next three works—*La casa verde,* 1966 (*The Green House* 1968), the novella *Los cachorros,* 1967 ("The Cubs," 1979) and *Conversación en La Catedral,* 1969 (*Conversation in The Cathedral,* 1975)—which like its predecessor were celebrated as instant classics. In addition to receiving the prestigious Premio Rómulo Gallegos, awarded to the best Spanish-language novel published within a five-year period, *The Green House* also won the Premio Nacional de la Crítica in Spain and the Peruvian Premio Nacional de la Novela in Peru.

One of the key traits of these narrations is their technical sophistication. Because Vargas Llosa is a follower of Faulkner and Flaubert, but also an innovator in his own right, these early texts exhibit a virtuoso manipulation of point of view and focalization. In particular, *Conversation in The Cathedral* exhibits the "technique of freely intermingling conversations from different situations and/or time frames in the plot line of the novel" (Bell-Villada 152). This technique, which had a timid debut in *Time of the Hero,* was developed in *The Green House,* and reached its culmination in *Conversation in The Cathedral.*

These narrative innovations help present a fictional world in which, as Efraín Kristal has noted, "social respectability is a mask for corruption, where rebelliousness is crushed by institutions that defend the established order, and where failure is a precondition to morality because success is not possible without co-optation" (*Temptation of the Word* 30). The thrilling formal experimentation of these early novels is woven with the presentation of a hopeless, debased world. Although, some saw this pessimism as ultimately incompatible with the author's socialist ideals—which are linked to the possibility of social change—"literary critics concluded in the

1960s that the novels of Mario Vargas Llosa were revolutionary" (Kristal "La política y la crítica literaria" 341).[3]

The reception of these first novels in English-language print media, while positive, was both less euphoric or political. In his *New York Times* review of *Time of the Hero*, Harry Sylvester argued that "Vargas is less concerned with society than with growth and change in the individual" (56). Leonard Kriegel, in *The Nation*, saw the novel as the "least overtly political" of those he reviewed.[4] David Gallagher, in *The Times Literary Supplement*, argued that the novel "conveys the problems of adolescence sensitively and authentically" (867). In fact, only in Susanne-Jill Levine's otherwise rave *New York Times* review of *Conversation in The Cathedral* in 1975 does politics raise its head. Levine describes Vargas Llosa as "a revolutionary, a non-conformist, using work for extra-literary functions" (250). Ironically, as Levine herself notes, he had already broken with the Cuban Revolution in 1971. But this fact had no impact on her view of the Peruvian novelist.

English-language reviewers of Vargas Llosa's novels of the 1960s were often baffled by their complex narrative structures. In the *New York Review of Books*, Bernard Bergonzi argued that *The Time of the Hero* "gets swamped in places with unnecessary attempts at literary sophistication, repeated flashbacks, multiple viewpoints, and so on" ("Anything Goes"). Kriegel patronizingly noted "Vargas Llosa has a great deal to learn, including resistance to his desire to become a technical innovator in the novel" (619). Levine, herself an eminent translator, was concerned that *Conversation in The Cathedral*'s "technique so complex . . . may scare American readers" (250), though she blamed readers who "have already forgotten their Faulkner" (250). Ironically, this mastery of narrative "technique"— for Vargas Llosa, the defining trait of the modern Latin American novel that permitted the accurate depiction of psychological and social reality—was the main complaint found in U.S. reviews of his first novel.[5]

Despite her political caveats, Levine's 1975 review of *Conversation in The Cathedral* marked a shift in the mass-media Anglophone reception of Vargas Llosa by placing him in the company of his past and (then) present peers: Henry James, Gustave Flaubert, Vladimir Nabokov, and Thomas Pynchon. However, similar opinions had been expressed in US academic circles; for instance, George McMurray, in his 1971 review of the Spanish original for *Books Abroad*, declared the novel "a tour de force that will strengthen the opinion of many critics that Vargas Llosa is one of the foremost writers of prose fiction" (84). Levine's text is proof that US academic and popular critical opinion on Vargas Llosa had begun to converge.

A second stage in the Latin American reception of Vargas Llosa originated in his break with the Cuban revolution in 1971 over the silencing and prosecution of poet Heberto Padilla. In Latin America, as Kristal has noted, "The leading role played by Vargas Llosa in the 'Padilla Affair' led to his rejection by leftist media . . . his literary ideas were condemned, then his novels" ("La política y la crítica literaria" 344). While Kristal may make the case too strongly— after all, Vargas Llosa was still considered one of the region's major writers—there was obviously a shift in the evaluation of his person and work as progressive to considering them allies of the region's retrograde movements.

Vargas Llosa's political changes overlapped with a significant literary evolution. His next two books—*Pantaleón y las visitadoras*, 1973 (*Captain Pantoja and the Special Service*, 1978) and *La tía Julia y el escribidor* 1977 (*Aunt Julia and the Scriptwriter*, 1982)— surprised critics and readers alike with what Raymond L. Williams has called "the discovery of humor" (93). Moreover, these novels replaced the challenging technique of his earlier works with a more reader-friendly, though still sophisticated, approach to narration. A direct consequence of these changes was the entrance of Vargas Llosa into the world of the best-seller. If the first Seix-Barral printings of *Time of the Hero* and *The Green House* had been of four thousand copies and that of *Conversation in The Cathedral* of ten thousand, the first run of *Captain Pantoja and the Special Service* was of one-hundred thousand (Herrero-Olaizola 39).

Bestsellerdom came with a price. According to Rita Gnutzmann, "readers and followers of Vargas Llosa felt some disappointment" with *Captain Pantoja and the Special Service*, which became "bewilderment with *Aunt Julia and the Scriptwriter*" (62). Perhaps Peruvian critic Antonio Cornejo Polar's comments about *Aunt Julia and the Scriptwriter* summarizes the opinion of the majority of Latin American critics, though obviously not the popular response, to this shift in Vargas Llosa's writing: "This minor tone, entertaining and humorous, sometimes parodical . . . represents the expansion of Vargas Llosa's creative horizon . . . but . . . does not enrich his work" (161).

However, this evolution was well-received by US and British critics and was framed by a growing recognition of Vargas Llosa as "one of the most important novelists writing in Spanish today," as Luys A. Diez stated in his review of *Captain Pantoja* for *The Nation*. He described it as "not a less good book by a very good writer, but a different book" and as his "most protean novel" (378, 379). Barbara Probst Solomon celebrated it in *The New York Times* as "the sportiest and funniest" of his novels, and as proof that "the enormously talented . . . novelist has the ability to work in many different levels" (3). In part due to the constant excellence of his novels, perhaps also due to a generational change among the critics—Levine, Diez, and Solomon, etc. are all younger than Bergonzi, Sylvester, or Kriegel—as well as the political evolution that brought him in line with mainstream U.S. opinion, Vargas Llosa was now considered a major world novelist by the US press.

Though written in a more conventional manner than his classics of the 1960s, Vargas Llosa's next novel, *La guerra del fin del mundo*, 1981 (*The War of the End of the World*, 1984)—a depiction of the anti-republican peasant rebellion of Canudos in nineteenth-century Brazil—was seen throughout the Spanish-speaking world as a return to form. Ángel Rama, perhaps the region's most influential literary theorist declared it "a masterpiece" and its author "our greatest living classic" (296). International reception was almost as enthusiastic. Robert Stone found it "powerful and haunting" (24). *The New York Times,* where Stone published his review, named it "one of the best books of 1984" (3).

---

Although most critics see the novel as a criticism of fanaticism—Rama noted that in it, "violence is procreated by fanaticism and fanaticism is procreated by idealism" (343)—*The War of the End of the World* has given rise to conflicting interpretations. Thus, for neoconservative John Podhoretz:

> This was the first of his novels to reveal Vargas Llosa's mature world view: Almost alone among Latin American intellectuals of his time, he had become a liberal in the classic sense of the word, a believer in and advocate for Western-style free speech, free markets, and free inquiry. This was the result of an ideological journey not unlike the one taken by neoconservatives in the United States" ("Contentions").

On the other hand, Slavoj Žižek provides a "leftist" reading when, after writing about "radical attempts to 'step outside' . . . to pursue the trend of self-organized collectives in zones outside the law," he notes "The greatest literary monument to such utopia comes from an unexpected source: Mario Vargas Llosa's *The War of the End of the World*" (82).

The reception of his following novels, *Historia de Mayta*, 1984 (*The Real Life of Alejandro Mayta* 1986); ¿*Quién mató a Palomino Molero?*, 1986 (*Who Killed Palomino Molero?, 1987*); *El hablador*, 1986 (*The Storyteller,* 1989); the erotic novel *Elogio de la madrastra*, 1988 (*In Praise of the Stepmother,* 1990), was framed by his growing participation in politics. They were also generally seen as a step down in quality after the widely admired *War of the End of the World.*

Despite representing a partial return to the "intermingling of conversations" characteristic of his novels from the 1960s, *The Real Life of Alejandro Mayta*, generated divergent responses throughout Spain and Latin America. A fictional investigation into the life of a homosexual Trotskyite revolutionary in the 1950s, it was seen by many as a biased attack on the Latin American left. In the *Revista de Crítica Literaria Latinoamericana,* Puerto Rican poet Iván Silen argued: "This [anti-left] hatred . . . ends up making everything vulgar . . . By responding to an ideological program, the novel . . . dies" (275). However, popular reviews, even if often written by academics, continued to praise Vargas Llosa. Miguel García-Posada, in the Spanish newspaper *ABC,* saw in it "if not the culmination of his novelistic universe, up to now, surely one of the happiest expressions of his extraordinary creative capacity" (47).

English-language reception was also divided. Some attacked Vargas Llosa for his rightwing slant: "oscillating between fury, incomprehension, and resignation, he has penned us a parable of great promise that terminates as a paltry conceit" (Dunkerley 151). Criticism was also leveled at the novel's purported homophobia. Michael Wood decried "the ugliness of Vargas Llosa's writing about the imagined Mayta's homosexuality" ("Broken Blossoms"). But there were also defenders of the novel. One was John Updike, who, in *The New Yorker*, claimed "With *The Real Life of Alejandro Mayta* Mario Vargas Llosa . . . has replaced Gabriel García Márquez as the South American novelist for gringos to catch up on" (530).

*The Storyteller*, another fictional investigation by a version of the author, this time into the life of Saúl Zuratas, a Jewish anthropology student turned indigenous Amazonian storyteller, generated a similarly divided response. Again, there were important admirers of the novel in the Hispanic press, such as Ricardo González Vigil, who declared it "one of the best works . . . of . . . Vargas Llosa" ("Vargas Llosa: El splendor del relato oral" 397) in the main Peruvian newspaper *El Comercio.*

However, other critics again tended to see the novel in terms of the author's actual politics. Cynthia Steele, whose writing in the *Revista de Crítica Latinoamericana* reflects a coming together of U.S. and Latin American academia, saw in the novel "an anti-indigenist" project and complained about its "narrative poverty" (375, 367). Reflecting the now also divided Anglophone response to Vargas Llosa's works, *The New York Times* presented two book reviews. Ursula Le Guin praised it as "Vargas Llosa's most engaging and accessible book" and, curiously, as "science fiction at its best" (7). Michiko Kakutani, on the other hand, argued that "the fusion of magical realism and domestic reality . . . never comes off" (23).

This critical polarization reached its apogee with *Lituma en los Andes*, 1993 (*Death in the Andes*, 1996). The novel was published after Vargas Llosa acquired Spanish citizenship in 1993 in response to the Fujimori regime's threat to take away his Peruvian passport. The novel's depiction of human sacrifice and cannibalism among Peru's indigenous population was strongly rejected by many in Peru and elsewhere. González Vigil, long a Vargas Llosa admirer, criticized the novel for depicting the country's indigenous population as characterized by "backwardness, ignorance, and savagery" (14). Anglo-Argentine critic Alberto Manguel wrote: "*Death in the Andes* . . .fails not because it is a racist novel (which it is) but because its racism prevents Vargas Llosa from writing well" (116). Liberal US critics also found the novel's implicit politics distressing. In *The Nation*, Patrick Markee argued that "Both Vargas Llosas—novelist and conservative ideologue appear in the novel" (30); and: "Vargas Llosa, the proud anti-Marxist of public life, becomes in this novel a sort of ahistorical spiritualist, summoning the *apus* [mountain spirits] as the culprits in the centuries of violence that have plagued the Andes" (30).

However, it also won the Premio Planeta, the most richly endowed literary award in Spanish, had a first run of three hundred thousand copies, and gathered its fair share of rave reviews. For instance, in *The Washington Post*, Marie Arana describes *Death in the Andes* as "well-knit social criticism as trenchant as any by Balzac or Flaubert . . . a novel that plumbs the heart of the Americas" (1). Ironically, the reception of this, his most polemical novel, coincided with his receiving the Premio Miguel de Cervantes, the most prestigious award given for the totality of a Spanish language writer's works, in 1994.

After publishing another work often considered minor, the comic *Los cuadernos de don Rigoberto*, 1997 (*The Notebooks of Don Rigoberto* 1998), which returned to the world and characters of his previous erotic comedy, *In Praise of the Stepmother*, Vargas Llosa produced an undisputedly major work: *La fiesta del Chivo*, 2000 (*The Feast of the Goat* 2001). Written with the full technical virtuosity of his 1960s novels, it depicts the waning days of the regime of the most brutal and megalomaniac of all Latin American dictators: Rafael Leonidas Trujillo. Noted Argentine novelist Tomás

Eloy Martínez's description of the novel as "an implacable portrait of absolute power . . . that one reads from beginning to end without taking a pause" well-represents the nearly unanimous positive response ("La resurrección del dictador"). In 2005, *The Feast of the Goat* was voted the second best Spanish-language novel published since 1980, bested only by García Márquez's *Love in the Time of Cholera* ("Las mejores 100 novelas de la lengua española"). In 2013, a poll in the influential Spanish newspaper *ABC* named it the best novel written by a citizen of the country in the twenty-first century ("Primer Plano: *La fiesta del Chivo*" 20).

The English-language reception was only slightly more muted. John Sturrock, in *The Guardian*, declared it "an ambitious novel, as sure footed as it is graphic" (n.pag.). Kakutani gave it a rave review in *The New York Times* and years later, on the occasion of the awarding of the Nobel to Vargas Llosa, declared it, together with *Aunt Julia and the Scriptwriter*, one of the two "towering achievements of his career" and "a devastating historical tragedy" (6).

Vargas Llosa's following two novels—*El paraíso en la otra esquina*, 2003 (*The Way to Paradise*, 2003 ) and *Travesuras de la niña mala*, 2006 (*The Bad Girl*, 2007)—were well-received in Spain and Latin America. However, reception in England and the US was mixed. *The Washington Post's* Jonathan Yardley's comment about *The Bad Girl* is representative: "it doesn't rank with his major novels, most notably *Aunt Julia and the Screenwriter*—but what he keeps in his second drawer is better than almost anyone else's best" ("Jonathan Yardley").

The 1990s and the new century were a period in which his supposedly minor novels began to be reassessed. In Latin America, *Aunt Julia and the Script Writer* has been cited by writers of the importance of Alberto Fuguet, Álvaro Enrigue, and Santiago Gamboa, as central to their own literary development. Earlier, Roberto Bolaño, in addition to praising established classics, like "The Cubs"—"brilliant exercise in speed and musicality" ("*The Cubs*" 321)—and *Conversation in The Cathedral*—"one of the best Spanish-language novels" (321)—singled out *The Real Life of Alejandro Mayta* for the "kindness and compassion—which others might call objectivity—that Vargas Llosa shows his own characters" ("The Prince of the Apocalypse" 324). Perhaps the most surprising rediscovery has been that of *The Storyteller* in that it hasn't been primarily writers, but mostly academics based in the U.S. and England who have made it into the second most studied of Vargas Llosa's novels.[6] It is a central text in the analysis of the relationship between literature and national identity by scholars, such as Benedict Anderson, Jonathan Culler, and Doris Sommer.

It is difficult not to feel that underlying this revaluation of Vargas Llosa's previously neglected works is the dying of the political fires that had previously affected their reception. By the 1990s, the utopian and socialist hopes of the 1960s had fully waned, as the brutality of the Southern cone dictatorships of the 1970s, and the fall of the Soviet bloc in 1989, made these seem, even if often admirable, obsolete. Moreover, a new generation of writers and critics, too young to have lived through the period and more sympathetic to the liberal and neoliberal ideas espoused by the Peruvian writer, came of age. The long justified granting of the Nobel Prize in 2010 solidified this revaluation of Vargas Llosa's works and public figure in Latin America and beyond. While in Latin America he had never stopped being perhaps the central cultural figure, in the US and England, his public reputation had "faded somewhat over the past decade," as Podhoretz stated at the time ("Contentions"). The Nobel brought him back to the very foreground of international letters.

Vargas Llosa has since published *El sueño del celta*, 2010 (*The Dream of the Celt* 2012) to mixed reviews—Colm Tóibín's comment that it "has none of the sweep and forceful rhythmic power of *The War of the End of the World*" is representative of Anglophone reception—and *El héroe discreto* (The Discreet Hero 2013). Nevertheless and regardless of his future publications or their reception, Mario Vargas Llosa's position, in Rama's words, as Latin America's "greatest living classic" is secure.

## Notes

1.  The essay will use the titles of the translation after the first mention of a Vargas Llosa book.

2.  According to Rita Gnutzmann, *Los jefes* ("The Leaders") received "brief and polite mention" in the Spanish press (57). There is no standalone English version of "The Leaders." Instead, it has been translated together with *Los cachorros* ("The Cubs") as *The Cubs and Other Stories* (1979). For convenience sake, I am providing the title of the translation followed by the original date of publication.

3.  In this case, as in all quotations from texts in Spanish in the Works Cited list, the translation is mine.

4.  The other novels reviewed by Kriegel were Tana de Gámez's *The Yoke and the Stars* and *Identity Card* by F. M. Esfandiary.

5.  Writing about earlier Latin American novelists, Vargas Llosa argued: "The failure of the primitive is to a great extent the result of the disdain which its authors demonstrated toward the strictly technical problems from the themes which they adopted, but rather from their incapacity to express these themes in a language and a structure sufficiently functional to elevate them to a universal plane" ("The Latin American Novel Today" 8).

6.  The MLA Bibliography, which tends to underrepresent Spanish-language criticism, lists eighty-eight publications on *The War of the End of the World* and eighty-one on *The Storyteller*.

## Works Cited

Arana, Marie. "Ancient Sorceries, Modern Mysteries." Rev. of *Death in the Andes. The Washington Post Book World*. 25 Feb. 1996: 1.

Bell-Villada, Gene H. "Sex, Politics, and High Art: Vargas Llosa's Long Road to *The Feast of the Goat*." *Vargas Llosa and Latin American Politics*. Eds. Juan E. De Castro & Nicholas Birns. New York: Palgrave, 2010. 139–57.

Bergonzi, Bernard. "Anything Goes." Rev. of *Time of the Hero. The New York Review of Books*. 6 Oct. 1966. Web. 11 Nov. 2013.

"Best Books of 1984." *The New York Times*. 2 Dec. 1984: A3.

Bolaño, Roberto. "*The Cubs*, Again." *Between Parentheses: Essays, Articles and Speeches, 1998–2003*. Ed. Ignacio Echevarría. Trans. Natasha Winner. New York: New Directions, 2011. 319–22.

_____. "The Prince of the Apocalypse." *Between Parentheses: Essays, Articles, and Speeches*. 322–24.

Cornejo Polar, Antonio. Review of *Aunt Julia and the Scriptwriter. Revista de Crítica Literaria Latinoamericana* 3.6 (1977): 159–62.

Diez, Luys A. "A Very Special Service." Rev. of *Captain Pantoja and the Special Service. The Nation.* 1 April 1978: 377.

Donoso, José. *The Boom in Spanish American Literature: A Personal History.* New York: Columbia UP, 1977.

Dunkerley, James. "Mario Vargas Llosa: Parables and Deceits." *Political Suicide in Latin America and Other Essays.* London: Verso, 1992. 139–52.

Gallaguer, David. "Boy's Brigade." Rev. of *Time of the Hero* and *The Cubs. The Times Literary Supplement.* 28 Sept 1967: 867.

García-Posada, Miguel. "El libro de la Semana: Mario Vargas Llosa, *Historia de Mayta.*" Rev. of *The Real Life of Alejandro Mayta. ABC-Sábado Cultural* 27 Oct. 1984: 47.

González Vigil, Ricardo. "Los Andes desde afuera." Rev. of *Death in the Andes. El Comercio* 10 Dec. 1993: 14.

_____. "Vargas Llosa: el esplendor del relato oral." Rev. of *The Storyteller. El Perú es todas las sangres: Arguedas, Alegría, Mariátegui, Martín Adán, Vargas Llosa y otros.* Lima: PUCP, 1991. 397–400.

Gnutzmann, Rita. "Mario Vargas Llosa y su obra en la prensa española." *Boom y Postboom desde el nuevo siglo: impacto y recepción.* Eds. José Manuel López de Abiada & José Morales Saravia. Madrid: Verbum, 2005. 57–76.

Herrero-Olaizola, Alejandro. "The Writer in the Barracks: Mario Vargas Llosa Facing Censorship." *The Censorship Files: Latin American Writers and Franco's Spain.* Albany: State U of New York P, 2007. 37–70.

Kakutani, Michiko. "A Storyteller Enthralled by the Power of Art." *The New York Times.* 7 Oct 2010: A6.

_____. "Vargas Llosa on the Role of Fiction and its Making." *Books of The New York Times.* 24 Oct. 1989: C-23.

Kriegel, Leonard. "Private and Public Sensibility." Rev. of *Time of the Hero. The Nation.* 5 Dec 1966: 616–20.

Kristal, Efraín. "La política y la crítica literaria: El caso Vargas Llosa." *Perspectivas* 4.2 (2001): 339–51.

---

_____. *Temptation of the Word: The Novels of Mario Vargas Llosa.* Nashville, TN: Vanderbilt UP, 1999.

"*La Fiesta del Chivo* novela del siglo." *ABC* 19 May 2013. Web. 11 Nov. 2013.

"Las mejores cien novelas de la lengua española de los últimos 25 años." *Semana.* 24 Mar. 2007. Web. 11 Nov. 2013.

Le Guin, Ursula. "Feeling the Hot Breath of Civilization." Rev. of *The Storyteller. The New York Times Book Review.* 29 Oct. 1989: 7.

Levine, Suzanne-Jill. "A Massive Novel of Peruvian Realities." Rev. of *Conversation in The Cathedral. The New York Times Book Review.* 23 Mar. 1975: 250.

Manguel, Alberto. "The Blind Photographer." *Into the Looking-Glass Wood: Essays on Words and the World.* New York: Random House, 2011. 109–20.

Markee, Patrick. "*Death in the Andes.*" Rev. of *Death in the Andes. The Nation.* 12 Feb. 1996. 28–30.

Martínez, Tomás Eloy. "La resurrección del dictador." Rev. of *The Feast of the Goat. LaNación.* 15 Apr. 2000. Web. 11 Nov. 2013.

McMurray, George R. "*Conversación en La Catedral* by Mario Vargas Llosa." Rev. of *Conversation in The Cathedral. Books Abroad* 45.1 (Winter 1971): 83–84.

Podhoretz, John. "Contentions: Mario Vargas Llosa Nobel Laureate." *Commentary 7.* Oct. 7 2010. Web. 11 Nov. 2013.

"*Primer Plano: La fiesta del Chivo.*" *Semanal ABC* 19 May 2013: 20._

Rama, Ángel. "*La guerra del fin del mundo*: una obra maestra del fanatismo artístico." *Crítica literaria y utopía en América Latina.* Ed. Carlos Sánchez Lozano. Medellin: Ed. Universidad de Antioquía, 2005. 296–343.

Silen, Ivan. "El AntiMayta." Rev. of *The Real Life of Alejandro Mayta. Revista de Crítica Literaria Latinoamericana* 11.34 (1986): 269–275.

Solomon, Barbara Probst. "Dupes of Authority." Rev. of *Captain Pantoja and the Special Service. The New York Times Book Review.* 9 Apr. 1978: 4.

Steele, Cynthia. Review of *El hablador. Revista de Crítica Literaria Latinoamericana* 15.30 (1989): 365–367.

Stone, Robert. "Revolution as Ritual." Rev. of *War of the End of the World.* *The New York Times Book Review.* 12 Aug. 1984: 1, 24.

Sturrock, John. "A Thug's Life." Rev. of *The Feast of the Goat.* *The Guardian* 5 Apr. 2002. Web. 11 Nov. 2013.

Sylvester, Harry. "The Changed Jaguar." Rev. of *Time of the Hero.* *The New York Times Book Review.* 11 Sep. 1966: 56.

Tóibín, Colm. "A Man of No Mind." Rev. of *The Dream of the Celt.* *London Review of Books* 34.17 (13 Sept 2012): 15–16.

Updike, John. "Latin Strategies." Rev. of *The Real Life of Alejandro Mayta. Odd Jobs: Essays and Criticism.* New York: Random House, 2012. 530–37.

Vargas Llosa, Mario. "The Latin American Novel Today." *Books Abroad* 44 (1970): 7, 16.

Williams, Raymond L. *Mario Vargas Llosa.* New York: Ungar, 1986.

Wood, Michael. "Broken Blossoms." Rev. of *The Real Life of Alejandro Mayta. New York Review of Books.* 27 Mar. 1986. Web. 11 Nov. 2013.

Yardley, Jonathan. "Jonathan Yardley." *The Washington Post.* 30 Nov. 2007. Web. 11 Nov. 2013.

Žižek, Slavoj. *Iraq: The Borrowed Kettle.* London: Verso, 2005.

# Natural and Built Environments: Toward an Ecocritical Reading of the Novels of Mario Vargas Llosa

Raymond Leslie Williams

Relatively little critical attention has been accorded to the natural environment in Vargas Llosa's work from an ecocritical perspective.[1] Since much of the most important critical work pre-dates the rise of eco-criticism in the 1990s, it is understandable that Vargas Llosa has not been thoroughly studied from an ecocritical perspective.[2] Nevertheless, many of Vargas Llosa's novels can be seen in a new light, when read ecocritically. The seven novels in this introductory analysis are *La ciudad y los perros*, 1963 (*The Time of the Hero*, 1966)*, La casa verde*, 1966 (*The Green House*, 1968), *Conversación en La Catedral*, 1969 (*Conversation in The Cathedral*, 1975), *La guerra del fin del mundo*, 1981 (*The War of the End of the World*, 1984), *Historia de Mayta*,1984 (*The Real Life of Alejandro Mayta*, 1986), *El hablador*, 1987 (*The Storyteller*, 1989), *La fiesta del Chivo*, 2000 (*The Feast of the Goat*, 2001) and *El sueño del celta*, 2010 (*The Dream of the Celt*, 2012).[3] This introductory overview of Vargas Llosa's work, in an ecocritical context, proposes that Vargas Llosa's early work is of ecocritical interest within the context of developing complex human relationships. His later work, however, goes beyond just complex human relationships and develops another kind of complexity related to human beings in natural and built environments.[4]

The underlying critical assumptions and main interests of ecocriticism have focused primarily on the representation of the natural environment in literature. Thinking along these lines, the editors of a special issue of *New Literary History* have defined ecocriticism as follows:

> [Ecocriticism] challenges interpretation of its own grounding in the bedrock of natural fact, in the biosphere and indeed planetary

conditions without which human life, much less humane letters, could not exist. Ecocriticism thus claims as its hermeneutic horizon nothing short of the literal horizon itself, the finite environment that a reader or writer occupies thanks not just to culturally coded determinants but also to natural determinants that antedate these, and will outlast them (Tucker 505).

This definition may be considered an acceptable main line description of the principal interests of ecocriticism from its origins in the early 1990s. In addition, however, a less developed and less predominant line of critical thought has recently begun with the provocative taking into account of built environments and, more specifically, built urban environments.[5] This line of critical thinking is particularly relevant for Vargas Llosa's primarily urban novels, such as his early *The Time of the Hero* and *Conversation in The Cathedral*.

Twentieth-century fiction published prior to Vargas Llosa's work provided ample spectrum of approaches to nature that Vargas Llosa fundamentally rejected, as did the other writers of the 1960s Boom. Vargas Llosa and Fuentes were particularly critical of the classic criollista novels, or novels of the land—*La vorágine*, 1924 (*The Vortex*, 1928) by José Eustacio Rivera; *Don Segundo Sombra*, 1926 (*Don Segundo Sombra*, 1935) by Ricardo Guiraldes; and *Doña Bárbara*, 1929 (*Doña Barbara*, 1931) by Rómulo Gallegos. In these three works, nature involves a special relationship with the land. In *The Vortex*, Arturo Cova flees from the urban environment of Bogotá to the Amazon jungle of Colombia, but the natural environment never attains the status set forth in the representation of the pampa as the very essence of Argentine identity. Similarly, *Doña Barbara* portrays the llano that serves as an essential backdrop to Gallegos' theory of his nation's need to deal with the dichotomy between *civilización* and *barbarie*. Vargas Llosa was critical of this simplistic dichotomy and rejected it in novels such as *The Green House*. At the same time, he rejected the representation of nature exclusively as a threat, i.e., the devouring the protagonist Arturo Cova at the end of *The Vortex*.

With the rise of the modern novel—the novel of human complexity—in Latin America in the 1940s and 1950s, writers found more nuanced methods for fictionalizing nature. Thus, Alejo Carpentier's *Los pasos perdidos*, 1953 (*The Lost Steps*, 1956) is a novel in which nature and time are conceived as parts of modernity, outside traditional frameworks. Nature, time, and space are uniquely reworked in Miguel Ángel Asturias' *El Señor Presidente*, 1946 (*The President*, 1963); Agustín Yañez's *Al filo del agua*, 1947 (*The Edge of the Storm*, 1963); and the later *Pedro Páramo*, 1955 (*Pedro Páramo*, 1959) by Juan Rulfo. In the case of Asturias, both this novel and his other work involve a nature that is less a mimetic representation of the natural world than a subjective account filtered through indigenous oral cultures. Among the modern predecessors, two of the most important writers for Vargas Llosa's early approach to nature were the Argentines Jorge Luis Borges and Adolfo Bioy Casares. A book that Vargas Llosa has often praised, Borges' *Ficciones*, 1944 (*Ficciones*, 1962) represented a dramatic change with respect to technology and nature in twentieth-century Latin-American fiction. In *Ficciones*, the value of nature is radically diminished from its role in previous fiction. Even in stories such as "El Sur" ("The South"), which do include a natural setting, this natural world is presented as having literary sources rather than originating from the empirical natural world: this fiction is more related to *literatura gauchesca* than the empirical southern region of Argentina.

For Vargas Llosa, another important novel of this group of the writers of the Boom was Julio Cortázar's *Rayuela*, 1963 (*Hopscotch*, 1967), a work that questions some of the basic tenets of Western Manichean thought. As a critique of very basic assumptions about "progress" as a value in itself, *Hopscotch* is an important predecessor to ecocritical thought, questioning the proposition that humans occupy a center in opposition to nature. Ecocritically conscious literature often suggests that the non-human might have value similar to the human and operates on the basis of this supposition, a phenomenon that relates *Hopscotch* to works such as *The Green House*. Along these lines, Cortázar's character Morelli sets forth elaborate and esoteric theories about "vegetable life" in one chapter, and this theory (see chapter 151 of *Hopscotch*) can also be associated with parts of *The Green House*.

For Cortázar in Rayuela, as well as for Fuentes in some of his essays, the deeper problem to be questioned was the Western Aristotelian tradition of binary thinking or the Manichean tradition of dualistic thought. In the emergent field of postcolonial environmental literary theory (or recent ecocritical studies of literature), readers have questioned the dualistic thinking that presupposes the opposition between culture and nature. As Laura Wright has pointed out, the very essence of what constitutes "nature" is an imaginary Western construction based on an Aristotelian system of binary thinking that differentiates humans from the so-called natural world. Similarly, these dualistic constructions privilege one aspect of the binary—maleness, culture, colonizer—at the expense of the other—femaleness, nature, the colonized. Coincidentally, the seminal text for many environmental movements, including ecocriticism, was the pioneer book *Silent Spring*, 1962, by Rachel Carson, a text that appeared in print exactly in the same period as the early novels of the Boom—Fuentes' *La muerte de Artemio Cruz* (1962), (*The Death of Artemio Cruz*, 1964); followed by Vargas Llosa's *The Time of the Hero* (1963); and *Hopscotch* (1963).

Vargas Llosa's fiction is engaging in the context of all these issues of postcolonial environmental theory: the blurring of the conventional boundary between natural environments and built environments, as well as the conventional Western binary opposition between male and female, and colonizer and colonized. In the early novels—*The Time of the Hero*, *The Green House*, and *Conversation in The Cathedral*—the binary opposition between maleness, culture, and colonizer versus femaleness, nature, and colonized is evident. In *The Time of the Hero*, this paradigm plays out primarily in the built environment of a military school, in which the administrative hierarchy represent and promote maleness, culture, and the colonizer, as do the dominant males among the student-cadets. In this novel, the built environment is a microcosm of Peruvian society and is the setting for dominance of group of individual human beings over others, as well as relatively complex relations among these humans. In this sense, Vargas Llosa's first novel really is more human-centered than nature-centered, and thus belongs more closely to the European and Anglo-American tradition of the urban modernist novel. Vargas Llosa employs a plethora of narrative strategies associated with the Anglo-American modernist novel written in the Faulknerian mode. The writer's first three novels do share with Faulkner this construction of a complex network of human interactions as each work's respective central focus. In *The Time of the Hero*, the novelist sets forth a moral dilemma unrelated to nature: a cadet dies of a bullet wound during a training exercise, and the reader is left to judge the moral decisions of the different human agents in the school's hierarchy.

In *The Green House*, Vargas Llosa centers a major portion of the narrative on two specific built environments in the small city of Piura in northern Peru: a brothel identified as the Green House and a working-class urban neighborhood called La Mangachería. The other major settings of the novel are the natural environments of the Amazonian jungle. With respect to the latter, nature follows two general patterns. On the one hand, nature is a fictionalized version of the Amazon centered on the city of Santa María de Nieva in Peru. Human beings who hold a non-human relationship with nature in the Amazon in this region, the aguaruna indigenous people, are dealt with as commercial objects by the power elite of the hierarchy, the military and the church. If the urban modernist novel is characterized by the complex relationships among human beings, it is noteworthy that the plot of *The Green House* can be likened to the unfolding of the fluvial web of nature with its labyrinth of rivers, tributaries, and small streams, appearing and disappearing in the undergrowth. This jungle, however, is not the wild and uncontrolled vortex (or *vorágine*) of the criollista texts, in which human beings are devoured in an irrational chaos. Rather, it is a nature that Vargas Llosa constructs in the neutral mode of scientific discourse: Santa María de Nieva is described as an irregular pyramid, whose base is formed by the rivers.

On the other hand, the other setting in nature of *The Green House* is the desert region of northern coastal Peru and the city of

Piura. Vargas Llosa questions the traditional dichotomy between "civilization" (*civilización*, among other elements, the built environments of urban space) and "barbarism" (*barbarie*, among other elements, nature) that were the premises of much fiction and critical thought of the twentieth century. Vargas Llosa employs several approaches to subvert this dichotomy and the Mannichean simplicity that it implies. The reader becomes aware that the lives and identities of certain human beings (above all, Bonifacia and Lituma) blur the boundaries of the "jungle" and "the city." In the natural environment surrounding the city, nature is not the threatening and hostile nature fictionalized in criollista novels, but a friendly element for the creation of Piura with mythic overtones. The initial descriptions create a nature that is ambiguous and mythical as the main character of *The Green House* and the town of Piura itself. In resumé, *The Green House* is an important redefinition of nature as ethereal and ambiguous.

A noteworthy work in the context of postcolonial environmental literature, *The Green House* offers, as one of its most important contexts, the biosphere of the Amazon basin. This novel can be read as Vargas Llosa's fictional representation of several environmental and ecocritical issues related to the European colonizer and the parallel Latin American oligarchy's presence in this Amazon region in the late nineteenth and early twentieth centuries. In *The Green House*, the historical context is the presence of the Peruvian rubber baron Julio César Arana and the exploitation of both natural resources and human beings in this region. In this work, unlike Vargas Llosa's later *The Dream of the Celt*, Arana is not named, and his huge rubber collection and processing empire is fundamentally a vague backdrop to those sections of the novel set in the jungle. The indigenous character identified as Jum and a Japanese character identified as Fushía are at the forefront of this story, and vaguely associated with it is the story of a young indigenous girl, Bonifacia, who is kidnapped from the jungle by the government's soldiers and sold first to nuns in the built environment of monasteries, resold to do domestic work in urban environments, and eventually sold again to work in prostitution. In this novel, Vargas Llosa portrays the violent destruction of the natural resources in the natural environment—including of human beings native to the region—at the hands of the business interests operating out of urban built environments. In this sense, *The Green House* is a valuable contribution to postcolonial environmental literary discussions.

In addition, *The Green House* leads the reader away from the standard anthro-centered vision—with human beings as the center—to an eco-centered vision, in which nature and human beings are treated equally. A revealing passage in *The Green House* appears near the end of the novel, when Aquilino watches Fushía in the natural environment of the jungle. At the beginning of this passage, Aquilino withdraws as he sees Fushía's body on a path. Then he sees puddles on the ground, and a strong smell of vegetation enters the atmosphere, with the specific smells of sap, resin, and germinating plants. As Aquilino continues withdrawing, he observes a small pile of still living and bloody flesh, still motionless in the distance. Subsequently, Aquilino turns around, runs toward some cabins, and whispers that he will be returning a year later. The narrator ends the passage by affirming that it is raining intensely. In this passage, Aquilino first begins by distancing himself from the focus of the scene and observes the water on the ground. He then looks at a personified vegetation that he senses breathing and smells plants that are germinating. (This passage recalls the vegetation chapter of *Hopscotch* mentioned earlier.) The narrator then changes the focus slightly from the natural environment to a pile of human flesh. Nevertheless, this pile appears to be part of the natural environment. The juxtaposition of the personified vegetation and human flesh in a pile creates an equivalency of sorts; this has a democratizing effect for nature and the human being are of the same order, fundamentally the same. Thus, that traditional dichotomy between nature and human being is questioned. The image of flesh behind the ferns is literarily effective with respect to this democratizing effect.

With *Conversation in The Cathedral*, in ecocritical terms, Vargas Llosa moves back to the model of *The Time of the Hero* with respect to natural and built environments. In the context of postcolonial environmental studies, this is a novel that places at the center the patriarchy of dictatorship; it is one of Vargas Llosa's most severe critiques of the patriarchal order that privileges maleness, culture, and colonizer. The vast and complex story of Vargas Llosa's most complex novel of human interaction emanates from a built environment: a bar named La Catedral in which the protagonist, Santiago Zavala, interacts with his friend Ambrosio Pardo for four hours, telling the basic story of the novel. Ambrosio works at another special kind of built environment: a dog pound. Thus, the descendants of the wolf in their natural environment are systematically caged in an urban built environment, where Ambrosio is employed. This evokes an image similar to the scenes in *The Green House*, in which indigenous peoples are captured by government soldiers in their natural environment and transported to the built environment of the monasteries. Once again, Vargas Llosa portrays the built environment as the domain of the patriarchal colonizer. The Peruvian society portrayed in *Conversation* as in *The Green House*, is a built environment that serves as an image of the nation as brothel. In the end, the brothel and the monastery of *The Green House*, as well as the bar and the dog pound in *Conversation in The Cathedral* are all an environment of exploitation controlled by the patriarchal order. The central image of these two novels—Peru as brothel—is underlined in *Conversation in The Cathedral* by the fact that the powerful Fermín (Santiago's father) is the dominant male in his homosexual relationship with Ambrosio.

*The War of the End of the World* is set in the region of Brazil with a venerable history of novels that deal with *la tierra* in Spanish or *terra* in Portuguese: land. In the Portuguese language, the term *terra* refers to the Iberian Peninsula and the Latin terra. This word *terra* is the historical backdrop to *The War of the End of the World* and many other historical discussions of the land in Latin America: the reconquering of the terra or tierra of the Americas. Carlos Fuentes' novel *Terra Nostra*, 1975 (*Terra Nostra*, 1976) is one of the most elaborate novelistic considerations of terra on both sides of the Atlantic Ocean from the *reconquista* of the Iberian Peninsula to the *conquista* of the terra and, in turn, of the destruction of the land.

The general setting of *The War of the End of the World* is the much-novelized land of northeastern Brazil, the built environment of the town of Canudos, and surrounding villages, as well as the built environment of the city of Bahia. The original Spanish edition of the novel highlighted the built environment with a full-page reproduction of a painting of Canudos: the simple portrait projects an idyllic village with three large buildings (one of which is a church), a small cemetery (with twelve crosses), and numerous small huts that are part of the built environment. When Da Cunha wrote *Os Sertões*, 1902 (*Rebellion in the Backlands*, 1944), the text Vargas Llosa rewrote, his predecessor had offered a description of considerable eco-critical interest: "Canudos, an old cattle ranch on the banks of the Vasa-Barris [river], was in 1890 a backward hamlet of around five-hundred mud-thatched wooden shanties" (143). As a cattle ranch on the banks of a river, it participates in a very basic nineteenth-century agricultural society, using the river for basic needs in this pre-industrial world. In this, as in several other of Vargas Llosa's novels (most prominently, *The Green House* and *The Real Life of Alejandro Mayta*), the author is interested in human communities not yet tainted by twentieth-century modernization and its destruction of the natural environment. In *The War of the End of the World*, as in *The Green House*, the reader sees the complex interactions involved in the modernization of the natural world.

Among the other later Vargas Llosa novels, *The Real Life of Alejandro Mayta* and *The Storyteller* are also significant contributions to a discussion of nature and fiction in the latter half of the twentieth century in Latin America. In *The Real Life of Alejandro Mayta*, Vargas Llosa contrasts two fictionalized nations with many similarities to the real nation of Peru of the early 1980s, which the novelist-figure in the novel claims to be 1983. Like *Hopscotch*, *The Time of the Hero*, and *Conversation in The Cathedral*, much of this novel is urban, in this case, taking place in Lima. The most important political context of these two periods is the presence of guerrilla groups in the novel: the earlier period is when the first armed insurrections took place in Peru; the second period, in the 1980s, is when the Sendero Luminoso (Shining Path) was operating in Peru. In Vargas Llosa's fictionalized version, an insurrection in the Andean town of Jauja took place in 1958; in real history, similar events actually occurred in 1962. In the novel, the novelist figure (in many ways similar to Mario Vargas Llosa) reads of the Jauja uprising in 1958 in *Le Monde* while in Paris; the real life Vargas Llosa did actually read of this event in *Le Monde* in 1962, while living in Paris. By 1962, Vargas Llosa had written several journalistic pieces in support of his compatriots involved in guerrilla warfare. Thus, Vargas Llosa was well aware of many of the historical facts and details of both the guerrilla warfare and the activities of the Sendero Luminoso in the 1980s. In 1987, however, Vargas Llosa fictionalizes a narrator-novelist who invents fictitious versions of Peruvian political reality in the two periods described above.

In our ecocritical reading of *The Real Life of Alejandro Mayta*, the opening and closing paragraphs of the novel are of particular interest. The opening paragraph begins with the description of an idyllic landscape, one that takes the reader to a rhapsodic level, perhaps even a transcendent state. As in novels such as *The Green House*, however, this initial gesture is soon to be negated by its darker other, for this rapture quickly becomes a scene of misery, or what Buell has identified as environmental apocalypticism.[6] Once the presence of human beings enters this ideal landscape, it becomes a scene of misery, industrial waste, and disorder. Urban life, in this first paragraph, is a portrayal of pollution and degradation. On the surface, the narrator-novelist is distant from the scene: he is a jogger who runs over the surface of the earth with a critical eye, but with no intent to reform. It might be argued that the narrator figure does not recognize his own complicity with the postcolonial order responsible for the piles of trash that threaten to choke the city, thus tacitly collaborating in its perpetuation.

Nevertheless, additional observations can be made in a more extensive ecocritical reading of *The Real Life of Alejandro Mayta* by distinguishing between the fictional entity that is the narrator-novelist in this novel and two other entities: the implied author and the real author, Vargas Llosa. Focusing exclusively on the statements of the narrator-novelist, this figure is arguably defeatist, a seemingly weak person who appears incapable of any action beyond setting forth questions, writing fictitious versions of the responses, and witnessing the environmental apocalypticism—the progressive degeneration of the world around him. He sees himself as a victim. The implied author of this work, nevertheless, offers a broader view of the scenario, and finds an order in the act of writing. He sets forth the possibility that he can make this flawed universe tolerable, and not necessarily because the environment will improve, but because the act of creation can make life bearable.

The author Mario Vargas Llosa distances himself from both Mayta (whom he portrays as a revolutionary, but an innocent one) and the defeatist novelist figure. For a comprehensive eco-critical reading, a key point is the relative power of ideology. Mayta and his cohorts are driven by ideological concepts that imbue them with total confidence that their armed insurrection will prevail, generating the revolutionary collapse of the old patriarchical order. In *The Real Life of Alejandro Mayta*, however, the power of nature prevails over ideology: altitude sickness and the cold temperatures undermine Mayta's revolutionary work, ultimately leading to his defeat. This is the worldview of the pragmatic, ex-revolutionary author Vargas Llosa, who often includes elements such as the forces of nature or sexual desire that, in the end, are more functional than politics as the catalysts of decisive human actions.

In the ecological vision of this novel, there are passages in which the misery, roughness and degradation of the external environment are contrasted with the beauty and softness of a relatively small, humanly constructed "natural" environment: the pleasant patios decorated with flowers and plants. In the space of these patios, the human figures find some brief escape from the roughness and brutality of urban life and its built environment. The fictionalized Peruvian life in *The Real Life of Alejandro Mayta* rejects the classic paradigm of *civilización* versus *barbarie*. Here, the urban space of built environments is often the *barbarie* and nature offers glimpses of the pastoral ideal, but not consistently. To the contrary, as in Fushía's death scene in *The Green House*, humans in *The Real Life of Alejandro Mayta* are portrayed as degraded as is nature. Mayta's urban world of built environment contains millions of human inhabitants living amidst urine and excrement, without water or light—essentially the same vegetative life as the plants of nature. As in Fushía's scene in the earlier novel, human beings become part of the plant biosphere in *The Real Life of Alejandro Mayta*.

As in *The Real Life of Alejandro Mayta*, with *The Storyteller* Vargas Llosa uses his *vasos comunicantes* ("communicating vessels") to alternate story lines that take place in urban built environments and rural settings, and returning to a natural setting that appears throughout much of his work: the Amazon River basin. From the 1980s, Vargas Llosa has been increasingly intrigued with the functions and forms of storytelling in different cultures, and *The Storyteller* is at the center of these matters. The juxtaposition of different kinds of chapters in this novel brings into conflict the oral and written modes of storytelling and their corresponding worldviews. Chapters Three, Five, and Seven consist of oral Machiguenga tales as they are transcribed in written form in this novel. Chapters Two, Four, and Six, as well as the first and last framing chapters, are a more conventional written narrative, as told by a narrator-novelist figure that, as in *The Real Life of Alejandro Mayta*, resembles the author Mario Vargas Llosa.

In the opening chapter of *The Storyteller*, Vargas Llosa juxtaposes an urban built environment with a natural environment, and this juxtaposition is the generator of the story. In narrating the Machiguenga's story, the storyteller, who is eventually revealed as Saúl Zuratas, tells stories of considerable ecological interest in the context of postcolonial environmental studies. The indigenous stories tell of the destruction of their people, their culture in general, and their natural environment in the context of the modernization of the Peruvian nation. In one story, the native people tell of how no one possesses the land beyond the distance that they can walk, an activity that brings them closer to the cosmic order. Their mutually dependent interaction with the natural environment, as well as their continuous movement across the land's surface without damaging it, is in opposition to modernization's dominant discourse and, at the same time, in accordance with more progressive environmental thinking. This hunter-gatherer culture of the Machiguenga, in fact, represents what is ideal for the environment.

The key issue from the beginning of *The Storyteller* is not only cultural—i.e. the acculturation of human beings—but a set of environmental issues. In the end, Saúl's decision to join Machiguenga society is, to some degree, a commitment to preserving the biosphere, for he is aware that these native people live in harmony with nature. Finally, it is noteworthy that Vargas Llosa directly ridicules the *novelas de la tierra* that aspired to enter the natural world, but actually failed to understand both oral tradition and the natural world, in which oral tradition typically flourished. With his placement of the oral storyteller in *The Storyteller*, this is Vargas Llosa's most explicity eco-friendly novel.

*The Feast of the Goat* and *The Dream of the Celt* share several of the elements noted in the *Green House, The Real Life of Alejandro Mayta* and *The Storyteller*. As in *The Real Life of Alejandro Mayta, The Feast of the Goat*, portrays an urban built environment of deteriorization (Santo Domingo) and a threatened natural environment (especially the coast and sea of the Dominican Republic). The urban and natural life of the Caribbean island seems as traumatized as the adult protagonist when she returns to the island. A thorough ecocritical reading of *The Dream of the Celt* would require more attention than is feasible here. On the one hand, Vargas Llosa continues his consideration, in this novel, of the seemingly primordial and basic need to tell stories. Vargas Llosa had already referred briefly to the Irish storyteller, the Seanchai, "the teller of ancient stories" (*The Storyteller* 107); in *The Dream of the Celt*, he also refers to the Seanchai.

In *The Dream of the Celt*, Vargas Llosa explores the international rubber industry, the exploitation of human beings and the destruction of nature with the historical detail and breadth not found in *The Green House*.[8] In the former novel, these issues are no longer the vague, mythical and mysterious operations hidden in the Amazon basin. If these operations of the Peruvian government and the rubber industry were a vaguely ugly backdrop to other more directly engaging human dramas, in *The Dream of the Celt*, a fictionalized Roger Casement carefully documents for the reader the historical record of the historical figure Julio César Arana, the rubber baron of Peruvian nationality, who founded his international, bi-national company in London. The author portrays the rubber workers in both Peru and Africa as part of a natural environment under attack by European Neo-Colonial powers. This is the ugly side of globalization in its nascent stages.[7]

In conclusion, an ecocritical reading of Vargas Llosa's novels as postcolonial environmental literature indicates that his most ecocritically engaging works, from *The Green House* to *The Dream of the Celt*, are part of an ecocritical tradition that includes *One Hundred Year of Solitude* and *Hopscotch*.[9] In general, in this Peruvian writer's fiction, natural environments are more vital life sources than the either degenerative or deteriorating built environments. The writer's postcolonial environmental interests are more explicitly articulated in the later novels, *The Feast of the Goat* and *The Dream of the Celt*, than in the earlier work. If the early period of Vargas Llosa's fiction emphasizes human complexity with the natural and built environments generally functioning as the backdrops, in the later work, the complexity of the environments themselves becomes a more important issue.

## Notes

1. Jonathan Tittler comments briefly on Vargas Llosa from an ecocritical perspective in "Ecological Criticism and Spanish American Fiction," in Adrian Kane, ed., *The Natural World in Latin American Literatures*: 11–36.

2. José Miguel Oviedo's *Mario Vargas Llosa: la invención de una realidad* is the pioneer critical work on Vargas Llosa, and it predates the rise of ecocriticism in the 1990s. Lawrence Buell's pioneer theoretical work, laying the groundwork for literary ecocriticism, appeared in the 1990s. See Buell, *The Environmental Imagination*.

3. The essay will use the titles of existing translations after the first mention of a Vargas Llosa novel or essay.

4. Laura Wright discusses "built environment" in an ecocritical context throughout her recent book, *Wilderness into Civilized Shapes: Reading the Postcolonial Environment*.

5.  Herbert Tucker, "From the Editors," *New Literary History*.

6.  See Laura Wright on built environments in *Wilderness into Civilized Shapes: Reading the Postcolonial Environment* and Adrian Taylor Kane, "Nature and the Discourse of Modernity in Spanish American Avant-Garde Fiction," in *Adrian Taylor Kane, The Natural World in Latin American Literatures*.

7.  Lawrence Buell discussed environmental apocalypticism throughout *Writing for an Endangered World: Literature, Culture and Environment in the U.S. and Beyond*.

8.  Vargas Llosa's critique of the globalized rubber industry, as well as his eco-friendly novels, justify the argument, contrary to much commentary about him, that the Peruvian writer is a progressive intellectual in many ways. For a more comprehensive discussion of his politics, see Juan E. De Castro and Nicholas Birns, eds., *Vargas Llosa and Latin American Politics*.

9.  I have discussed Gabriel García Márquez's *Cien años de soledad* (*One Hundred Years of Solitude*) and *Hopscotch* in an ecocritical context in "Nature in the Twentieth-Century Latin American Novel," in Adrian Kane, ed., *The Natural World in Latin American Literatures*: 66–88.

## Works Cited

Buell, Lawrence. *The Environmental Imagination: Thoreau, Nature Writing, and the Formation of American Culture*. Cambridge: Harvard UP, 1995.

_____. *Writing for an Endangered World: Literature, Culture and Environment in the U.S. and Beyond*. Cambridge: Harvard UP, 2001.

Da Cunha, Euclids. *Rebellion in the Backlands*. Trans. Samuel Putnam. Chicago: U of Chicago P, 1944.

De Castro, Juan E. & Nicholas Birns, eds. *Vargas Llosa and Latin American Politics*. New York: Palgrave Macmillan, 2010.

Kane, Adrian Taylor, ed. *The Natural World in Latin American Literatures*. Jefferson, NC & London: McFarland & Company, 2010.

_____. "Nature and the Discourse of Modernity in Spanish American Avant-Garde Fiction." *The Natural World in Latin American Literatures*. Ed. Adrian Taylor Kane. Jefferson, NC & London: McFarland & Company, 2010. 37–65.

Oviedo, José Miguel. *Mario Vargas Llosa: la invención de una realidad.* 1970. Barcelona: Seix Barral, 1977.

Tittler, Jonathan. "Ecological Criticism and Spanish American Fiction." *The Natural World in Latin American Literatures.* Ed. Adrian Taylor Kane. Jefferson, NC & London: McFarland & Company, 2010. 11–36.

Tucker, Herbert. "From the Editors" *New Literary History* 30.3 (1999): 505–08.

Vargas Llosa, Mario. *The Storyteller.* Trans. Helen Lane. New York: Farrar, Straus & Giroux, 1989.

Williams, Raymond L. "Nature in the Twentieth-Century Latin American Novel." *The Natural World in Latin American Literatures.* Ed. Adrian Taylor Kane. Jefferson, NC & London, 2010. 66–88.

Wright, Laura. *Wilderness into Civilized Shapes: Reading the Postcolonial Environment.* Athens & London: U of Georgia P, 2010.

# Disentangling the Knots: Vargas Llosa and José María Arguedas in *La utopía arcaica*

Sara Castro-Klarén

What was within him was a desperate nostalgia for a lost world. It was a waning world, already partly destroyed. His inner being, moving against his own convictions, against his own ideological reason, felt profoundly linked to this world.

(Mario Vargas Llosa, La utopía arcaica 273)

The Andean utopia according to [Flores Galindo], is a collective creation: The Indian masses grab hold of the mythic transformation of their past when they feel lost and disoriented due to the trauma of the conquest.... Even though I have misgivings about this collectivist and popular thesis about the origin of the archaic utopia.... there is no doubt that it embodies the atavistic 'search for an Inca' undertaken by an anonymous mass.

(Mario Vargas Llosa, La utopia arcaica 292-3)[1]

*La utopía arcaica. José María Arguedas y las ficciones del indigenismo*, 1996, (The Archaic Utopia: José María Arguedas and the Fictions of Indigenism) is a book dedicated to a polemical examination of at least two objects of interest (Arguedas and *indigenismo*) conflated into a single, conflicted, whole. On the one hand, it includes a series of rewritten book reviews that look at the life and works of the great Peruvian writer José María Arguedas (1911–1969). On the other hand, *La utopía arcaica* collects a number of essays written over the span of the last forty years of the twentieth century on important Peruvian intellectuals who, in the first half of the same century, took up the difficult, unsettled, and divisive question of Peru's modernity and ethnic identity. For better or for worse, the intellectuals and artists who looked at Peru's ancient indigenous past in conjunction with the present oppressive conditions and abject poverty of the Indian majorities were lumped together as *indigenistas* by their contemporaries. Arguedas is generally considered foremost among these.

*Indigenismo*, in contrast with the earlier idealizing Indianism, makes the vindication of the Indian peoples of the continent as a whole its principal objective. As Jorge Coronado writes, "Indigenismo takes a critical position with respect to the dominant society and accuses it of exploiting and debasing indigenous peoples and their cultures" (5). "Indigenismo" as a literary, cultural, and political movement has received ample attention by literary scholars from its inception to the present day.[2] Indigenismo posits that:

1. Peru has an ancient and invaluable pre-conquest culture that is still alive in the *ayllus* (collective agrarian communities).
2. This ancient culture was forged independently of any other by very intelligent people whose descendents are today's *Indios*.[3]
3. This culture is misunderstood and denigrated by colonialism. The coastal cities of Peru, as well as other urban centers in the country, harbor strong cultural colonial attitudes towards its own citizens of clear Indian descent.
4. As Peru must enter modernity, its political leaders and enfranchised and disenfranchised masses should understand that the Indios, with their cultural traditions, compose its majority population, and thus its future.
5. The colonized and marginalized Indios should be vindicated, in order for them to participate in Peru's proper entry into modernity.

Indigenismo migrated into several leftist platforms, with which the *cholos*, or common (mixed ethnicity) people, attempted to wrest political power from the established elites. Vargas Llosa's essays, dispersed over time, but constant and consistent in perspective, attempt to critically draw the intellectual panorama of Indigenismo, in order to show how Arguedas, at one or another moment and in different degrees, represented its key tenets in his fiction.

In attempting to transform a collection of essays written over a span of forty years into an organic book, Vargas Llosa deploys his well-known alternating or double-stranded disposition of chapters. The double-stranded or double-helix structure is not new to Vargas

Llosa, who first used it to great effect in the composition of his first and highly acclaimed novel, *La ciudad y los perros,* 1962 (*The Time of the Hero,* 1966).[4] The disposition of chapters in *La utopía arcaica* is a back and forth between Arguedas and indigenismo, one acquiring aspects of the other until they come to resemble each other in a sort of embracing metonymy.

However, the mutually reflecting relation between Arguedas and indigenismo, although continuous, is not static. As the volume moves forward, the Arguedas/indigenismo construct gives way to a third matter of concern: the constitution of Peru's future national subject and the nature of the subjects that represent and act on behalf of the nation, its governance, and thus the type of inevitable entrance into the West's (second) modernity.[5] The reason for thinking about a writer and a literary corpus, which, he acknowledges, he finds of little interest, is that both Arguedas and Indigenismo espouse an ideology that Vargas Llosa considers dangerous. For him, Indigenismo is founded on a questionable, contradictory, perhaps even false, but curiously persuasive, set of ideas.

For example, Vargas Llosa analyzes *Todas las sangres,* 1964 (*All Bloods*), Arguedas' most openly political novel. The novel narrates the social and economic convulsion generated by the coming of U.S. (mining) capital into an Andes, in which colonial socio-ethnic and political hierarchies are being undermined by both the rise of local entrepreneurs and the growing social conscience and unrest of the indigenous population and the ayllus. Vargas Llosa establishes that, the novel aims to examine allegorically the possible shape of an acceptable form of capitalist development for Peru. It then calls for an evaluation that attends to its double condition as fiction and social document. He writes: "A novel that presents such an ideological scheme must be approached, inevitably, as both a social and political proposal for Peru and also as a work of fiction" (261). However, in his analysis of the novel as a proposal for the future economic, social, and ethical organization of Peru, Vargas Llosa skirts the proposal itself made in the novel—a nationalist capitalism—(260). In this scheme, Arguedas would seem to be proposing capitalism with a difference. The difference would, of course, be provided by the Indian labor leaders, who in equal footing with capital, would participate in the creation of system fair to Indian labor interest and ayllu traditions. Natural "resources" would somehow remain in "Peruvian" hands.

But in his essay, Vargas Llosa does not appear to see Arguedas' specific proposal. Instead, he goes on to quote the critique of the novel leveled by two leftwing sociologists: the Peruvian Aníbal Quijano and the Frenchman Henri Favre. They state that, in their fieldwork, they never met an Indio like Rendón Willka, the indigenous "labor" leader protagonist of *Todas las sangres*. These scholars note that they had studied impoverished *campesinos* (peasants), a category that, by definition, does not correspond to ayllu heads and that, therefore, belongs in a totally different order of knowledge from the kind of ayllu member and leader portrayed in the person of Willka, the martyred would-be revolutionary (261). With the erasure of the ayllu Indian under the sociologists' term "campesino," strong criticism was leveled against the novel at a round table held in Lima on June 23, 1965, barely a year after its publication. Indians, even at the scholars' round tables were once again totalized by the junction of power and knowledge, and Arguedas' lived experience seemed suddenly stripped of authority. Vargas Llosa characterizes the event not only as proof that Arguedas' indigenista theses are wrong, but as the total debunking of the writer's personal and non-"scientific" ideas and testimony on Indians. This knowledge acquired "personally," not "scientifically," echoed Rendon Willka's ungrammatical, but certain question—"Why have you killed me?" This is precisely the kind of knowledge that Arguedas claimed as the province of those who like him had grown up with Indians and always identified as such. Clearly for Arguedas, the Indian condition is not a question of skin color, but rather a situational status experienced under colonialism.

However, in order to bolster his assessment of Arguedas' de-authorization, Vargas Llosa also quotes the sociologist Jorge Bravo Bresani (a Lima-born and based scholar) expressing his disagreement with Arguedas' view of the Indian: "I don't believe it strictly corresponds to reality; nor do I believe it to be a useful or operative myth for the transformation of Peru" (262). In this round table, "reality" has been claimed by the sociologists, and Arguedas, in a way, gets shoved off the table, where "reality" as very much a discursive construct gets created and certified. The round table was, of course, devastating to Arguedas. Vargas Llosa corroborates Arguedas intellectual and emotional assessment of this debacle, let us say defeat, with a quotation from the distraught indigenista author's private notes: "Today, it has been almost completely proven by two great sociologists and one economist that my book *Todas las sangres* is detrimental to Peru. I have nothing more to do in this world. My energies have declined irremediably" (*La utopía arcaica* 203). Clearly Arguedas, too, believed that the object of his fiction and ethno-political reflection was the same as, or similar to, the object of discourse constructed by the social sciences in Peru at the time.

The moment when Arguedas makes this entry in his diary constitutes the prelude to his 1966 suicide attempt, and it is to be read as such in *La utopía arcaica*. Thus the book begins, tellingly, with an essay on Arguedas' funeral procession—"Los funerales de Arguedas" (13–16)—that describes the massive funeral with which the university students and the public at large honored the memory of the great Peruvian writer in 1969. However, more to the point, regarding his polemic with Indigenismo, we need to take into consideration the two key points made by Vargas Llosa in his reading of *Todas las sangres*. The first is that Arguedas' indigenista vision of Peru and the Indians is, if not downright wrong, certainly disputed by the "scientific" knowledge of the sociologists and economists, who, in this instance, happen to be people from the left. The second point has to do with the dangers of Indigenismo in as much as, although seductive, it lacks any basis in reality. In fact, it is so dangerous that it can even lead astray a person like Arguedas, whose foundational knowledge is predicated on his filiations and intimate experience with Indians to the point of "being" one himself.

However, the novel's implausibility as a sociological study is not the only evidence of Arguedas' "pathetic life," as Vargas Llosa terms it (9). The novel, the social and symbolic capital, on which Arguedas' fame is based, is a failure as fiction also.

The description of Peruvian society comes over as profoundly false and unpersuasive. That is not so much due to the lack of fit with the factual reality. Rather it is because it is missing that force that springs forth from the hidden layers, the mesentery, the entrails of fiction itself. When that is achieved [the novel] manages to convince the reader of the verisimilitude of what is being narrated, even when it does not coincide with the reader's own experience of reality (263–64).

In support of this assessment of the novel's failure, Vargas Llosa advances his often repeated understanding about the play between "lies and truths" in fictional texts. *"Todas las sangres* fails as fiction, "because the truth or lies of a novel—concepts that in literature are synonymous with either artistic excellence or poverty—are not measured by confronting it with objective reality. The truth and the lies of a given fiction are fundamentally determined by their internal power of persuasion, its capacity to convince the reader of what it is narrated" (263). This is not the place to examine in depth Vargas Llosa's use of the dichotomy "truth/lies" as a tool of literary analysis. It is, however, important to look at the question of persuasion as it is deployed in this assessment of the failure of Arguedas' novel and the "fiction"—understood as absence of truth—of indigenismo.

Vargas Llosa makes here a complicated and perhaps misleading argument regarding persuasion and its relation to reality, a term that is never questioned. Rather it is assumed that all communities of interpreters agree on what "reality" is always, everywhere. Of course, this assumption constitutes grounds for many misunderstandings; the polemic between indigenistas and *hispanistas* chronicled by Vargas Llosa in this book, being just one such struggle for overriding meaning. On the one hand, the reference to the "power of persuasion" of a novel evokes Aristotle's notion of verisimilitude and his defense of fiction from Plato's charges regarding its capacity to lie. For Aristotle, and it would seem also for Vargas Llosa, fiction tells stories that *could* be true, that is to say, that are verisimilar. But persuasion, which is examined in Aristotle's *Rhetoric*, differing from fiction's verisimilitude, aims to convince the audience of a certain argument to be considered as a preamble to political action. For Aristotle, persuasion does not belong to the order of mythos. Persuasion in discourse moves on the basis of enthymemes and not syllogisms, as in dialectics. An enthymeme is "a syllogism with one premise left out" (Sachs 134).[6] Therefore, persuasion always already relies on an existing consensus between the orator and his/her public and, therefore, is subject to the dimensions of the imagination of the interpretative community (highland Indians, coastal Peruvians, academics, ethnographers, etc.). The sociologists that criticized the novel did not talk about persuasion, but rather about the lack of coincidence between their understanding ("reality") of their object of discourse—campesinos—with Arguedas' novelistic character taken as an object of social science discourse—Rendon Willka an ayllu Indian turned into revolutionary leader. The latter—a revolutionary ayllu Indian—they had never observed.

Persuasion and verisimilitude are clearly not interchangeable terms of analysis, for one applies to the logic of reasoning based on shared views of "reality" and the other to the art of storytelling or mythos. Like the relation between Arguedas and Indigenismo, there is also a metonymy at work in the conflating of these two sets of interpretative expectations. For many other readers, *Todas las sangres* succeeds in showing a portrait of what *could indeed be* if Indians like Rendon Willka were to participate in the leadership of the country. But *could be* does not fall within the parameters of "reality," as understood by neither the sociologists nor Vargas Llosa.

If, for Vargas Llosa, *Todas las sangres* is a failure, it is because the novel does not fulfill either one of the objectives it has set out to achieve—to make us believe in the possible reality of the world it narrates and to persuades us of the 'truth" of its social analysis. But as it turns out, analytically both objectives depend as much on the author' skills as they do on the capacity of reception and the world view of the interpretative community, a fact that the *Rhetoric* highlights over and over again, and which is the missing enthymeme in this argument. The fact of never having met anyone like Rendon Willka; not having heard his Andean rhetoric; not understanding his ambitions; not having deliberated over his ethical preoccupations, led the sociologists, when doing fieldwork, to overlook someone like him as yet another poor campesino. This is why the sociologists do not hesitate to declare his existence as not coincidental with reality, that is to say, in that which they can believe given their life experience. Thus, given that the novel does not depart from the discursive demands of sociology, nor yet actually tries to fulfill them, it fails as such. Furthermore, given that the novel attempts to narrate a world that is not only alien to readers like Vargas Llosa, but about whose economic, social, ethical, and imaginative structures they have doubts, it fails to present a persuasive argument for the main tenets of Indigenismo, which these readers have already put in question. Under these reception conditions, the novel fails to properly fictionalize (verisimilitude) its mythos.

Beyond a receptive grid based on a dichotomy that divides the novel into a political proposal to be evaluated by sociologists and a fiction capable of passing the test of verisimilitude before all audiences, there is the third possibility of reading *Todas las sangres* as a poetic totality. This third way attempts to read the novel within an Andean cosmological grid that inquires about the question of justice. The presentation of an overarching dimension of an ethical discourse that could account for the novel's fictional and discursive dimensions has been successfully attempted by Fernando Rivera in his *Dar la palabra. Etica, política y poética de la escritura en Arguedas*, 2011 (Having a Say: Ethics, Politics, and Poetics in Arguedas). Rivera argues that this novel is not unlike other works by Arguedas in that it posits the question of responsibility and reciprocity, as understood in Andean polities, such as the ayllu, as the basic human arrangement running up and down and across all forms of the continuum of being, which include man, but does not privilege his existence above what the we call nature. Individual desires, projects, property, and ambition occupy a lesser position in this arrangement. Drawing on the political philosophy of Georgio Agamben, especially on his *Sovereignty and Life*, 2007, Irina Feldman analyzes *Todas las sangres* as a space where the legitimacy of the state is placed into question with arguments that stem from the ethical indictment voiced from the site of the experience of bare life that is Rendon Willka, the very character that seems to be neither verisimilar nor persuasive in Vargas Llosa estimation of the novel.[7]

Indigenismo and Arguedas fail doubly in their lack of persuasiveness and verisimilitude. For Vargas Llosa, whose argument implies Aristotles' inescapable presence of an audience in tune with the orator for persuasion to work, this deficient condition is the more dangerous given the fact that, at the end of his life, Arguedas was writing letters to the Trotskyite agrarian leader Hugo Blanco, praising him for his "plan for a revolution made by Indians" (15). The implication is that, despite his failed analysis, Arguedas remained hopeful that the demonstrably unpersuasive and fictive thesis of Indigenismo would somehow become a living reality. A decade after Arguedas' death, the Shining Path terrorist guerrilla movement was to emerge and wreck Peru's society. But this occurred after the oppressed and impoverished highland Indians in the ayllus, haciendas, and villages invaded the coastal cities in search of work, thereby transforming Peru in ways unexpected and unimagined by almost all observers, Arguedas and the sociologists included. This massive migration to the coast constituted a devastating and unarmed attack on the historically established structures of Peruvian life. In the wake of the collapse of the Peruvian state, a surprising number of epoch-making cultural and political actors came to the fore. In addition to the leaders and cadres—many of them women— of the Shining Path, there appeared a previously unknown son of Japanese immigrants as candidate to the presidency of the country, as well as, of course, the famous writer Mario Vargas Llosa, as the presidential candidate from the Right, who was sure to defeat Alberto Fujimori in the elections of 1990. It is for another occasion to ascertain to what extent *La utopía arcaica* should be read in the context of this crucial moment in the political vicissitudes of Peru, but the country has since seen two presidents—Alejandro Toledo and Ollanta Humala—self identify as Indios.

In understanding the genealogy of this polemical book and its place among Vargas Llosa's essays, it is also important to underscore that he did not intend to publish this collection of essays, that is, *La utopía arcaica*, as a book until his friend, the Peruvian poet, Blanca

Varela suggested the idea. She encouraged him to "bring together in an organic book the myriad of ideas and contradictory emotions that mark my long years of contact with the work of Jose Maria Arguedas and the land that touched us both" (12). Although Vargas Llosa's focus is on the ideas of Arguedas and other indigenistas, it is clear that not only the tone, but the specific choice of terms and metaphors anchor the series of essays in a tornado of emotions. These range from a sort of compassion for Arguedas mixed with the dismissal of him as a person and writer, to a respectful attitude for empirically oriented ethnographers like Luis Millones Santagadea, to a clear rage towards the historian Luis. E. Valcárcel (1891–1987), one of the early and most vocal architects of indigenismo.

Vargas Llosa is not impressed with Arguedas as a writer, although he credits him with having written some beautiful pages. Arguedas is at best a "good writer," who wrote one unforgettably "beautiful novel" (9). Although he believes Arguedas to be an admirable moral being (265–275), he finds his novels preachy and argues that they suffer from a simplistic construction based on the organization and classification of characters and events into a dichotomy of good versus evil. For Vargas Llosa, the best example of reliance on this dichotomy is *Todas las sangres* (265). Nevertheless, the reason why Arguedas is of interest is because of his "pathetic" and "sad life full of childhood traumas that he never managed to overcome" (9).

Although Vargas Llosa feels sorry for Arguedas, he chastises him for having accepted, in his novel about life in a notorious prison in Lima, *El Sexto* (1964), Valcárcel's belief in the cultural and moral superiority of the culturally indigenous Andean highlands over the deeply colonial Coast. (Vargas Llosa dedicates a whole chapter to *El Sexto* [212–322]). There, he takes issue with Arguedas' fictional mouth-piece, the prisoner Gabriel. It is of interest to note that, despite his overall negative opinion about Arguedas as a writer, Vargas Llosa took the time to write the prologue to the Spanish edition of *El Sexto* in 1974.

Vargas Llosa attempts to demonstrate that, although "The racist, regionalist and anti-Lima prejudices—against whites, mestizos, the Coast and Lima—were in themselves an answer to the anti-Andean, anti-highland and anti-provincial prejudices that had dominated Peruvian life from Colonial times" (73), these came to constitute the core of Indigenismo. What is more, they appear in Arguedas' "literary work elaborated into a subtle tissue of fiction mixed in with personal stories." (73). Indigenismo and Arguedas are faulted for these prejudices, that is, for exercising judgments based not on reason or knowledge, but rather on emotions. This portrayal de-authorizes the thinking of these intellectuals and of everyone else who holds similar views in the country. Given the fact that Peruvian life brings people from all geo-political national locations and all ethnicities into daily contact and friction, for Vargas Llosa, retaining such views speaks of an inability to learn from one's own experience and participate in an ongoing generalized blindness.

Vargas Llosa finds an exception to these indigenista prejudices in José Uriel García's (1884–1965) *El Nuevo Indio*, 1930 (The New Indian). According to Vargas Llosa, the books were written in response to Valcárcel's indigenismo and Jose Carlos Mariátegui's (1894–1930) Marxist interpretation of history (74). Given the terms of the polemic about the Indian as possible revolutionary agent posited by Mariátegui (Coronado 25–52), it is important for Vargas Llosa's argument to show that, for García, Indianness was not a question of "ethnicity", "blood," or geography, but rather "a moral entity" (75). Unlike most indigenista texts, *El Nuevo Indio* did not "idealize the Inca empire" (75) and most importantly looked forward to a "spiritual mestizaje" (78). In fact, in this polemic, the Indians—or are they now mestizos?—envisioned by Uriel García are termed to be "models" (79). Moreover, García is commended for the choice of his intellectual sources: Miguel de Unamuno, Nietzsche, Thomas Carlyle, Freud, José de Vasconcelos and the Bolivian Alcides Arguedas (76). The absence of Marx, widely read at the time and put into heated circulation by Mariátegui, is notable in this list. The other major absence in García's sources is the most obvious one: the Inca Garcilaso, who coined the term *mestizo* as a self-descriptor and also as a model for harmonious post-conquest colonial interactions. This absence can be linked to the fact that the Inca's discourse is later exposed by Vargas Llosa as the origin of the *utopía arcaica* that he believes is pernicious, due to its questionable existence.

On the other hand, Vargas Llosa shows impatience and derision for historian Valcárcel's daring appropriation of Oswald Spengler's thesis of the decline of the West (68). Vargas Llosa seems irked by the unlikely or "odd" combination of—what he calls—a "provincial" person and the use of the work of a European philosopher of history. This irritation is not only directed at the daring appropriation by a local intellectual of a universalizing theory of the rise and fall of civilizations. It is also aimed at the fact that, by appropriating Spengler, Valcárcel, originally from the province of Moquegua and resident of Cuzco, had questioned the unchallenged superiority of the West. Spengler's thesis on the rise and decline of all civilizations, including that of the West, eroded the hierarchical difference maintained by Europe between itself and its other. Thus Valcárcel could even make the case for the coevalness of the Inca's "good" government and Europe's conflicted and, for some terrifying, modernity.[8] Could the provincial man credibly challenge Europe's unique claim to civilization, not from without as a lone and distant voice of protest, but, rather, based on a discourse developed at the very entrails of Western civilization itself? If so, what kind of unholy alliance could this be?

The very idea that the West might be in decline and that such claims might not only be persuasive to people in Peru, but to audiences at the center (as, for instance, in the case of Samuel P. Huntington's *Clash of Civiliizations and the Remaking of World Order*, 1996) causes an annoyed response from Vargas Llosa. He seems caught between derisive laughter and complaint: "His ideological mentors are made of strange panoply where Oswald Spengler, Frederick Nietzsche rub elbows with anarchists like González Prada" (68). What is more, empowered by the idea of the decline of the West, Valcárcel, an ardent admirer of Inca collectivism (70–71) and the Inca Garcilaso's rendition of Inca government, waves the flag of socialism in the face of liberal capitalism as the correct route for Peru's entrance into modernity.

Valcárcel, living and teaching in Cuzco, felt confident (at least in theory, for he was married to landed wealth [Coronado 152]), that Peru could build upon on its own ancient, effective, and still alive "collectivist" tradition. Vargas Llosa's polemic with indigenistas, who, like Valcárcel, engage not just the past but specifically the nation's future, leaves little doubt that the discussion is not so much about Indians or indigeneity, as it is about the shape of modernity for Peru. That is why the polemic is so rich, complex, contradictory, and enduring. The Shining Path would be only one more, albeit violent, expression of this profound disagreement on the meaning of Peru's ancient past and its future.

As previously mentioned, the origin of *La utopía arcaica* has little to do with any interest in Indigenismo itself. As its author tells the story, its writing has its remote inception in the need to prepare for the courses he taught as visiting faculty, first at Cambridge University (1977–1778) in England, later at Georgetown University (1994) in Washington D.C., and at other elite universities. Thus, while much of the book comprises book reviews written for immediate publication in Spanish-language newspapers and magazines and is, therefore, destined for an audience with an interest in Arguedas or indigenista topics, the origin of his meditation on Indigenismo has much to do with an English-speaking public for whom the problem of Indigensimo and Arguedas' fiction play in a very different field of ideological interests and resonances. There seems to be a sort of chasm in this genealogy, where two different publics, oriented in criss-crossed directions intersect at the site of reflection and address.

In this genealogy of *La utopia arcaica*, we find a young and aspiring writer uninterested in the intellectual or literary tradition of his own country. He leaves for Europe in search of new horizons, in part due to his disgust at the surveillance on university students and the jailing of intellectuals by the Dictator Manuel Odría in the 1950s. He quickly finds fame abroad with the publication of a novel celebrated as the brilliant answer to the stagnation of the corpus that has been meaningful to him, that is to say, the European novelistic tradition. However, when, as a celebrated figure in Paris, New York, London, and Madrid, he is invited to teach at a university in England, he is presumed to be an expert in something distinctly Peruvian, and by this, the English mean something "Inca" or "Indian." Surely, the irony of the situation was not lost on Vargas Llosa, just as it is not lost on the reader of *La utopía arcaica*. But in case readers are unaware, they are informed at the outset of the author's complete lack of interest in Peruvian writers and thus of the purely coincidental genesis of this volume. In the opening paragraph of *La utopía arcaica*, Vargas Llosa states "Even though I have dedicated a good part of what I have written to Peru, as far as I can tell, Peruvian Literature has had a very scant influence in my vocation" (9). Closing the door to any possible mistake on the matter, he adds that not even the great Peruvian writers, like César Vallejo or the Inca Garcilaso, ever became part of his "spiritual family"(9). In fact, Vargas Llosa states that he never registered a level of spiritual connection with any Peruvian writer, and this stands in clear contrast with his filiations and debts to Gustave Flaubert, Jean-Paul Sartre, Albert Camus, and later with William Faulkner, Jorge Luis Borges, Isaiah Berlin, and Karl Popper, to name a few European and Euro-American writers with whose work Vargas Llosa dialogues.

While it is clear that Vargas Llosa is perfectly comfortable acknowledging his debt to Flaubert as mentor in the art of writing fiction, writing a whole book about it, *La orgía perpetua. Flaubert y Madame Bovary*, 1975 (*The Perpetual Orgy: Flaubert and Madame Bovary*, 1986), his intertextual relations with Latin American writers belong to a different order altogether. Whereas there is no question that *García Márquez: Historia de un deicidio*, 1973 (García Márquez: History of a Deicide) is written in praise of *One Hundred Years of Solitude*, 1967, his debt to those Latin American writers with whom he differs aesthetically or politically, such as Rómulo Gallegos, Arguedas, or Euclides da Cunha, is quite problematic. Their work inspires a sort of rejection, which, at the same time, convokes a meditation on the very problems they tackle—the jungle, the nation, the "Indian", the earth's damned. These ungraspable figures and topics never cease to challenge disciplinary knowledge or the social and aesthetic imagination that attempts to represent them in literature. They are intellectual and emotional black holes and, as such, create anxiety that spills over from the representation onto the creator of such figures.

In closing this short essay, it is fair to say that these intertextual relations exist under the sign of the anxiety of influence. Vargas Llosa's meditation on these texts and issues in *La utopía arcaica* makes one return to a zone of discomfort in Latin America's history. The world that Arguedas embraces with fervor and pain, as well as the rural and remote Brazil that Euclides da Cunha (1866–1909) scorchingly represents in *Os Sertoes*, 1902 (*Rebellion in the Backlands*, 1944), live like traumatic wounds that never go away, no matter how many veils of forgetting are cast over them. So, in this sense, we can say that, while Vargas Llosa sees the open wounds in Arguedas and his traumas from childhood—one must note that the author of *La utopía* has written courageously of his own childhood traumas in both essays and his novels—when writing on Arguedas and Indigenismo, he draws a distance, he opens a gap, that enables him to keep his own traumas away. It is because of this tension between the desire to forget and the temptation to know the defiant and returning unknowable—the sierra, the *indio*, the 'archaic' peasant—that the author engages in a repetitive meditation. *La utopía arcaica* posits the figure of Arguedas as a sort of an archaism itself and Indigenismo as the misguided discourse that provides an opening for its (undesirable) pouring into modernity.

These two haunting figures or phantasms disturb modernity's path forward, a path which includes leaving behind such wounds. It would seem that the dichotomous casting of the tensions and contradictions in Peru's historical formations leave no room for the contemplation of an alternative modernity, or for a poetics of non-dialectical heterogeneities.[9] And thus, the rich paradox of an archaic utopia swings back and forth interminably, caught in a time of its own, suspended in the doubled-stranded helix, where it makes its discursive, jeweled appearance.

## Notes

1. In this case, as in that of all works in Spanish in the Works Cited list, the translation is by the author of this essay.

2. Coronado's *The Andes Imagined* is but the most recent book on the subject. Comprehensive books on the image of the Indian in Peru and the history of indigenismo begin to appear in the second half of the twentieth century, so that information on the topic is abundant. The names of writers, artists, and political thinkers involved in the movement far exceeds the number of intellectuals chosen by Vargas Llosa. Salient among other studies are Luis Enrique Tord, *El Indio en los ensayistas peruanos 1848–1940*, 1976 (*The Indian in the Peruvian Essay 1848–1940*). Tord includes important poets, of which the stellar figure of Gamaniel Churata is said to rival Arguedas in *El Pez de Oro*, 1957 (*The Gold Fish*). Dora Mayer, herself considered an indigenista, authored a retrospective on the movement: *El Indigenisno*, 1950 (*Indigenism*). Indispensable for a proper contextualization of Vargas Llosa's portrayal of Indigenismo are the following: Fernando Fuenzalida's edited volume *El Indio y el poder el Peru*, 1970 (*The Indian and Power in Peru*); Antonio Cornejo Polar's *La novela indigenista*, 1980 (*The Indigenist Novel*); and Efraín Kristal's *The Andes Viewed from the City: Literary and Political Discourses on the Indian in Peru, 1848–1930*, 1987.

3. "Indios," a word that for the first time made its appearance in Columbus' text as a descriptive and identificatory term for the heterogeneous peoples and civilization that he encountered in this hemisphere, has been a misnomer and has thus given rise to many polemics since 1492. It has been the harbinger of much confusion, erroneous assumption and knowledge and of course oppression. Indigenismo has been one of the discourses of protest that contributed to the present de-stabiliaztion of the term.

4. See Castro-Klarén, "Fragmentation and Alienation in *La casa verde*."

5. In developing the concept of the "coloniality of power" accepted in most contemporary circles of discussions regarding the historical formation of modernity, Aníbal Quijano shows that Europe's first modernity occurs only after and when Europe conquers the Americas and is able to incorporate its wealth and its peoples (cultures and labor) into its domain. The Enlightenment's modernity, intertwined with a second European colonial expansión, is what I refer to as the "second" modernity. See "Coloniality of Power, Ethnno-centricism, and Latin America" in *Nepantla* 1.3 (2000): 553–580. For further discussion on the coloniality of power, see Mabel Moraña et al.

6. In his "Introduction" to his translation and edition of Plato's *Gorgias* and Aristotle's *Rhetoric*, Joe Sachs argues that, for Aristotle, all persuasive speaking is the art of showing "something as factual or true, or at least worthy of belief" (16). Sachs goes on to state that "rhetoric has rational content but cannot have proof, and this, according to Aristotle, is what defines it by analogy to and in contrast with dialectic" (17). In this contrast, we see that dialectic uses syllogisms and induction, based on necessary and contingent premises, while rhetoric uses enthymemes and examples, based on likelihoods and signs" (17). In the *Rhetoric*, Aristotle writes that "rhetoric reasons from things that people already have been accustomed to deliberate about... and we deliberate about things that appear to admit of being two different ways" (140).

7. See Irina Feldman, "Moments of Revolutionary Transformations in the Novels of José María Arguedas" and *Rethinking Community from Peru*. On the Andean cosmology that holds the idea and practice as a continuum of being, see Castro-Klarén, "'Como chancho cuando piensa.' El afecto cognitivo en Arguedas y el con-vertir animal." For an in-depth comparison of Arguedas and Vargas Llosa see Moraña's *Arguedas/Vargas Llosa*.

8. For more on the concept of "coevalness," see anthropologist Johannes Fabian's book *Time and the Other: How Anthropology Makes its Object*. New York: Columbia UP, 1983. 25–35. In the book, Fabian argues that Europe invents the notion of "primitive cultures" and "advanced cultures" in order to deny coevalness of time to the cultures and peoples it colonized.

9. With respect to alternative modernity, see Walter Mignolo. The concept and phrase "a non-dialectic heterogeneity" belongs to Antonio Cornejo Polar and seem a most fitting description of Peru's variegated geo-political and cultural formations; see Cornejo Polar, *Writing in the Air*.

## Works Cited

Aristotle. *Plato* Gorgias *and Aristotle* Rhetoric. Trans. & Ed. Joe Sachs. Bemidji, MN: Focus Publishing, 2009. 1–28.

Castro-Klarén, Sara. "'Como chancho cuando piensa.' El afecto cognitivo en Arguedas y el con-vertir animal." *Revista Canadiense de Estudios Hispanico* 26.1–2 (2001, 2002): 25–39.

_____. "Fragmentation and Alienation in *La casa verde.*" *MLN* 87.2 (March 1972): 286–99.

Cornejo Polar, Antonio. *La novela indigenista*. Lima: Lasontay, 1988.

_____. *Writing in the Air: Heterogeneity and the Persistence of Oral Tradition in Andean Literatures*. Durham, NC: Duke UP, 2013.

Coronado, Jorge. *The Andes Imagined: Indigenismo, Society, and Modernity*. Pittsburgh: U of Pittsburgh P, 2009.

Feldman, Irina. "Moments of Revolutionary Transformations in the Novels of José María Arguedas." *MLN* 27.2 (2012): 302–317.

_____. *Rethinking Community from Peru: The Political Philosophy of José María Arguedas*. Pittsburgh: U of Pittsburgh P, 2014.

Fuenzalida, Fernando. *El Indio y el poder el Peru*. Lima: Instituto de Estudios Peruanos, 1970.

Kristal, Efraín. *The Andes Viewed from the City: Literary and Political Discourse on the Indian in Peru, 1848–1930*. New York: Peter Lang, 1987.

Mayer, Dora. *El indigenismo*. Callao: Imprenta del Colegio Militar Leoncio Prado, 1950.

Mignolo, Walter. *The Darker Side of Western Modernity: Global Futures, Decolonial Options*. Durham, NC: Duke UP, 2011.

Moraña, Mabel. *Arguedas/Vargas Llosa. Dilemas y ensamblajes*. Madrid: Iberoamericana/Vervuert, 2013.

Moraña, Mabel, et. al., eds. *Coloniality at Large: Latin America and the Postcolonial debate*. Durham, NC: Duke UP, 2008.

Quijano, Aníbal. "Coloniality of Power, Ethnno-centricism, and Latin America." *Nepantla* 1.3 (2000): 553–580.

Sachs, Joe. "Introduction." *Plato* Gorgias and *Aristotle* Rhetoric. Trans. & Ed. Joe Sachs. Bemidji, MN: Focus Publishing, 2009. 1–28.

Tord, Luis Enrique. *El Indio en los ensayistas peruanos 1848–1940*. Lima: Editoriales Unidas, 1976.

Vargas Llosa, Mario. *La utopía arcaica: José María Arguedas y las ficciones del indigenismo*. Mexico: Fondo de Cultura, Económica, 1996.

# CRITICAL
# READINGS

# Charisma and the Structures of Power: Vargas Llosa's Early Short Stories_____

Nicholas Birns

## Vargas Llosa as Short Story Writer

Mario Vargas Llosa's short stories were all written early in his career, in the decades of his twenties and early thirties, between 1953 and 1967. This essay provides a general overview of the stories before proceeding to close analysis of each story, one by one.

In his introduction to the English translation of his short stories, *The Cubs and Other Stories*, 1979, Vargas Llosa speaks of the stories as being the product of a frenetic youth, in which Vargas Llosa took on adult responsibilities at an early age—he married at age nineteen—but also read widely and deeply in European literature. Thus, his stories are not just responses to the experiences around him but to his reading, which in turn called out possibilities as to how his own experience could be figured in fiction. Although the short story form in Peru had a long history behind it, indeed being the more favored literary form over the novel, Vargas Llosa calls far more on the international tradition of the short story, particularly in English and French. This is notwithstanding the Peruvian tradition stemming from the anecdotal *tradiciones (traditions)* of Ricardo Palma, the *cuentos criollos* (Creole tales) of Abraham Valdelomar, the fantastic fables of Clemente Palma, or the austere social realism of José Díez Canseco and Vargas Llosa's older contemporary, Enrique Congrains. Nor do they have anything in common with the most famous short story writer in Latin America, the metaphysically inclined Jorge Luis Borges. Enrique López Albujar's stories and short novels, set in non-metropolitan and rural Peru, might be possible precursors to such tales of Vargas Llosa's as "El hermano menor" ("Younger Brother") and "Un visitante" ("A Visitor,") originally included in *Los jefes*, 1959 (The Leaders).[1]

Yet this is not to say they are merely Peruvian adaptations of global formulae. Vargas Llosa is already putting his individual imprint on what he has learned and read, infusing his literary vision with his sense of the individual in situations where they are deprived of power, and the interaction of desire and will in seeking personal freedom. Moreover, nearly all of them are set in places and educational institutions, which figured in his own life. As opposed to his novels, which are equally divided between potentially autobiographical subjects, places, and milieus that did not figure in the author's direct life experience, the stories are all recognizable reflections of contexts which affected Vargas Llosa's youth and growing-up. However, the author has denied they are directly autobiographical, and although the stories share some family remembrances with the semi-autographical novel, *La tía Julia y el escribidor*, 1977 (*Aunt Julia and the Scriptwriter,* 1982) and the avowedly autobiographical *El pez en el agua*, 1993 (*A Fish In The Water*, 1994) they are more case studies in the behavior of children and adolescents, set in places the author knew, than evocations of his own past based on particular memories. Vargas Llosa speaks of these stories as being set in the *barrio*, a word used in a slightly different sense than in the US Latino usage of "ghetto" or "specific neighborhood for Latinos;" it refers to a sense of locality and living in community with one's peers, who share certain specific assumptions. In other words, even if these stories have individual protagonists, they are set in communities.

The stories have one dominant theme: power. This, theme extends from the personal to the national level. From the time Vargas Llosa was twelve to when he was twenty, the dictatorial president Manuel Odría ruled Peru. Moreover, the country and its institutions were dominated by authoritarian, hierarchical models, as seen in the military, the Catholic Church, and structures whose values stemmed from them. The sense of pervasive social control in these stories is chafed against by their young male protagonists' desires for freedom and self-definition, which solicits another one of Vargas Llosa's major themes throughout his career: personal liberty.

The stories are largely told from the viewpoint of young and adolescent boys, and the world they take place in is a virtually all-male world, with girls present only as an absent or evanescent ideal. Whereas so many of Vargas Llosa's mature novels dwell in the world of Eros, these stories are early exploration of another world adjacent to, and sometimes permeable with, that world: the world of power, a world which young boys growing up know well before they have first thought of kissing a girl's lips.

## Los jefes/The Leaders

"The Leaders" bears the title "los jefes" in Spanish, which could also be translated as "the bosses;" another possible title might be "the ringleaders," as Javier and his friends play that role in arousing resistance by asking the principal of the school, Ferrufino, to post an exam schedule. Somewhat like the subjects of the New Zealand singer Lorde's 2013 hit "Royals," the students are disempowered in one role, as students in an institution run by adults, but on another level, they are the ideologues and organizers, who give voice to dissenting elements within their population. The story is also reminiscent of Philip Roth's contemporaneously written "The Conversion of the Jews," in which a precocious boy strives to get the adult power structure to respond to his dissent. The issues here, though, are less between children and adults than between children and each other. After Javier, the chief ringleader, mobilizes the students to leave the school and go down to the river until an exam schedule is posted, it turns out all the students do not end up joining in the protest. This leaves one student, Lou, who had taken an early position by the river, exposed to the other (non-participating) students, who beat him up. Javier's charisma has failed to motivate all the students to resist the principal. His charisma, however palpable, was only temporary and yielded to the surrounding instructional reality: that the children were more afraid of bureaucratic authority than swayed by Javier's personal magnetism. Javier acted as if a matter of justice motivated his rebellion, when, in fact, it had been an excuse to promote his own power. The hand Javier extends to the narrator at the end of the story, after the rebellion has been foiled, suggests, though, that the two boys will have a new relationship: person-to-person, not leader to led. In a sense, Javier realizes that his earlier rebellion has simply mimicked the power structure animated by the arbitrariness of Ferrufino. It is only now, after the revolt has ended, that a true

---

friendship based on personal freedom and individual choice can ensue. Importantly, the actions at the end of the story occur so rapidly and are related in so clipped a fashion that the reader has to do a fair amount of work to ascertain the meaning. Influenced both by modernist opacity and the fast pace of adolescent life, Vargas Llosa shows circumstances in which meaning-altering changes can happen rapidly and be absorbed on the level of emotional understanding before they are intellectually formulated.

## El hermano menor/The Younger Brother

In "Younger Brother" two brothers, Juan and David, are in the Andean wilderness looking for an Amerindian man, whom their sister Leonor says tried to rape her. David is the older and, in their quest for revenge, looks out for his younger brother; for instance, he shines a flashlight to show where Juan should step as they descend a mountain slope. They are championing their sister, but also engaging in an exercise of machismo and male bonding. In a scenario somewhat reminiscent of E. M. Forster's *A Passage to India*, when the boys cannot find the culprit, Leonor seems relieved and confesses that the man had not really tried to hurt her. Juan, the younger brother, becomes furious and takes Leonor's temperamental roan horse, riding it so furiously that the horse buckles, knocking Juan around in the saddle. Juan and David then have a consolatory drink as Leonor, in a resumption of traditional gender roles (disrupted by her accusation of rape) tends to Juan's knees, injured while riding. Even though Leonor and David have played as pivotal a role in the events of the story, the tale is called "Younger Brother" because it is Juan who is changed the most by what transpires. In this story, the young Vargas Llosa departs from his usual urban setting towards the Andean milieu favored by writers who concentrated on the indigenous people, such as José Maria Arguedas. The wilderness background of "Younger brother" allows Vargas Llosa to bring in the Native American population and themes of racial difference, which he would later explore in works such as *El hablador*, 1987 (*The Storyteller*, 1989), *Historia de Mayta*, 1984 (*The Real Life of Alejandro Mayta*, 1986) and *Lituma en los Andes*, 1993 (*Death in the Andes*, 1996).

## El abuelo/The Grandfather

In "The Grandfather" Don Eulogio, the story's eponymous grandfather, finds a skull on the road and makes up a dummy that, when set alight, will scare his grandson. He does it to provide a thrill of delight to the grandson, who had been punished for a week. It is a story of an affectionate and ingenious old man, still fully committed to living life to the maximum extent. Yet even as the grandfather engagingly schemes to give his grandson a thrill, there is a slight element of sadism in scaring him so thoroughly that may be a final capstone to the punishment rather than an amelioration of it. Finally, the presence of the skull suggests the old man's awareness of his age and impending death, adding an undertone of morbidity to what is, on the surface, a tale of an affectionate and attentive grandfather. The story is about family relationships and the many ways love can manifest itself within families. But it also evokes the sinister side of the spiritual realm in a way more reminiscent of writers associated with magic realism, such as Carlos Fuentes and Alejo Carpentier, than the usually rationalistic Vargas Llosa.

## El desafío/The Challenge

In "The Challenge"—one of Vargas Llosa's earliest stories—Julián and León are two teenage boys who are told by an old man, Leonidas, that their friend, Justo, is fighting a fearsome man nicknamed "the Gimp" at a damaged tree nicknamed "the raft." Justo fights valiantly, but the Gimp prevails. Leon tells Leonidas not to cry, that Justo had fought bravely against long odds, but the old man is inconsolable. It is thus revealed that Justo is Leonidas' son. It becomes clear that Justo's antagonism towards the Gimp is in some way motivated by having to prove himself to his father. The position of the point of view character, Julian, is interesting narratively, providing a slightly askance perspective in the story's brutal events. The story, like others in this group, is about how constellations of power and disparities of charisma persist, in spite of attempts to equalize them, and how the gap between aspiration and reality often disillusions and ensnares characters, such as Julian. But the narrative perspective of Julian, somewhat of an authorial stand in, gives some hope that the rules of the game are not eternally ordained.

## Un visitante/A Visitor

"A Visitor" concerns a Jamaican man, who has agreed with the police to cooperate with them to help arrest a man named Numa, gaining his freedom in return. He waits in an inn with its proprietor Doña Merceditas, anticipating the arrest of Numa and his permanent freedom. When the police come, they arrest Numa, but kick the Jamaican away when he tries to join them; he can have freedom, but they will not help him return to civilization. Dona Merceditas, paramour of Numa, pledges to visit him in prison every Sunday. Even after his arrest, Numa remains the local big man, his charisma unimpaired, whereas the hapless Jamaican remains cast out even in freedom. Essential psychological and racial hierarchies remain; the deep structures of power prove invulnerable even to one ingenious attempt to overturn them. The anecdotal aspects of the story and its undercurrents of violence and idolatry are reminiscent of the work of Ernest Hemingway, an avowed influence on the younger Vargas Llosa. Inspector Lituma, a character in this story, will later appear in the novels *La casa verde*, 1966 (*The Green House*, 1968), *La tía Julia y el escribidor*, 1977 (*Aunt Julia and the Scriptwriter*, 1982), *¿Quién mató a Palomino Molero?*, 1986 (*Who Killed Palomino Molero*, 1987), *Lituma en los Andes*, 1993 (*Death in The Andes*, 1996) and *El héroe discreto* (The Discreet Hero), and the play *La Chunga*, 1986, and will become a recurring character in Vargas Llosa's work.

## Día Domingo/On Sunday

"On Sunday" is Vargas Llosa's most serene short story. Miguel is in love with Flora, an adolescent girl still keeping herself slightly aloof from the world of dating. His chief rival is the more charismatic Rubén, who seems better than Miguel at everything; for instance, Rubén handily defeats Miguel in a beer-drinking contest. Miguel and Rubén, though, are also friends, part of the same neighborhood group of teenage male friends in the picturesque Miraflores district of

Lima. The climax of the story occurs when Miguel and Ruben engage in a surfing competition. While swimming, Rubén gets a stomach cramp and Miguel has to rescue them. Even as Miguel delights in winning the competition and, thereby, potentially impressing Flora, he agrees to Rubén's plea to cover up for his unimpressive showing and pretends he won by just a bit. Miguel manages to both impress Flora and adhere to the male solidarity of his friends in the *barrio*. As opposed to the other, more pessimistic stories of this era, "On Sunday" has an idyllic glow to it, as it depicts a moment where individual fulfillment and loyalty to a larger community can exist at the same moment.

### Los cachorros/The Cubs

If Vargas Llosa can be, at times, a panoramic chronicler, revelling in the possibilities of the "total novel", in "The Cubs," he is what Roberto Bolaño would call a "visceral realist," feeling the characters situations, as it were, from the gut. Not surprisingly, in his collection *Between Parenthesis*, Bolaño singles out this story for particular praise and gives a very convincing analysis of it.

"The Cubs" reminds one of *La ciudad y los perros*, 1963 (*The Time of the Hero*, 1966) the earlier novel about a harsh military school (based on the one Vargas Llosa attended, the Academia Leoncio Prado) and the goon-like treatment meted out to the Vargas Llosa analogue. As opposed to that harrowing school novel, this is a lighter, albeit at times wistful and poignant, look at adolescence, although Cuellar's abnormality makes it ultimately subtly tragic. The reader gets third-person, where first person "we did this, we said that" might have been expected. The story is told in the collective consciousness of the boys, but it is put in the third person 'they,' only occasionally switching to the first person plural 'we,' which in itself is an atypical form of relation for a narrative of any extended length. This provides a sense of distance, a way for the story to not become too sentimental or nostalgic about boyhood. Even though Cuellar is the most distinct character, we are not totally inside his point-of-view; the 'they' kind of hovers around all four boys, not quite omniscient, more of an objective version of an internal collective voice. It reminds us that one of the real platforms provided to a writer by the short form is the opportunity to experiment with technique and not have the material (as most likely occurs in a longer book) overshadow it.

The key turn of the story occurs very early on, with the accidental castration of Cuellar after playing soccer. This foreshadows the way Cuellar is always slightly separate from the rest. Again, the third-person collective narration makes this not an instrument of self-pity or excessive subjectivism, but there is a tension between the group of four boys as a collective, and the one who does not quite fit in, who seems unlucky—from his being injured at sports to later on, when the other boys all are going steady with girlfriends, while he is not. The story is told at such a fast pace and in the colloquial collective memory of the boys that narrative bells and whistles do not signal this drastic change, but the effect is palpable. Because the adults pity Cuellar, he is passed in all the subjects with minimum work and drifts more towards sports, even though that is where he was injured. Although he keeps up with the other boys in the most obvious register, he ends up falling behind them ultimately as their lives become more differentiated and adult. Vargas Llosa seems to make the point that the ultimate sign of castration, real and symbolic, may not be effeminacy but machismo, as keeping up the external signifiers of masculinity is compensation for feeling one is not man enough physically. Machismo is seen as a pathology, as what keeps this sort of man, whether literally 'castrated' or not, from accepting the discipline of nine-to-five jobs, committed relationships, and general personal responsibility. Thus Cuellar's story is not just a chronicling of a poignant or pathetic "case" but of a symptomatic example. Cuellar's castration is metaphorically symptomatic as well as literal and on the surface. Machismo is precisely the side effect of not being fully masculine, or fully adult.

Cuellar's castration occurs very near the beginning of the story—the result of being attacked by the maddened dog, symbolically named Judas, whose canine ferocity is so great it is actually phonetically represented in the text with *grrr* sounds. From the beginning, Cuellar is marked out by his accident. At first, when he returns, not that much seems to have changed; the teachers make a fuss over him, and he resumes his normal activities of soccer and friendship with the other boys. Of course, the accident has happened when he is pre-pubescent, only eight or nine years old, and he cannot physically, affectively, or intellectually understand the full force of his disability. The poignancy of the story comes from this: that things have irreversibly changed for Cuellar and that he has no control, or feels he has no control, over this change. Cuellar is tagged with the sarcastic nickname P. P. His difference from the other boys is sealed. The course of a life is determined, all by what happens in boyhood. Of course, given the terms of the story—the accident—a lot of this is inevitable given the medical techniques available at the time (today they might have been able to reattach the mutilated body parts) but Vargas Llosa is also commenting about a society that knows no way to have Cuellar adjust to his changed conditions and cannot find a path other than oscillating between pity and the expectations of apparent normality to give the benighted Cuellar succor and encouragement.

This story of truncation—literally—and failure is different from the classic European *Bildungsroman* (novel of growing up, novel of cultural formation) where young male protagonists often have horrible boyhoods filled with sadism, persecution, poverty, and deprivation, but survive to flourish and become more or less normal. Some have speculated that Cuellar's failure to grow up is a kind of allegory of the Peruvian situation: that Peru nominally had all the apparatus of statehood—a parliament, an army, a constitution—but little of the sense of actually being a nation that, say, France or Britain has. In turn, even though books, like Dickens' *David Copperfield* or Flaubert's *Sentimental Education*, have little to do with politics or the nation-state, one could argue that the models of more or less successful maturation they provide are contingent on or mirror such realization on the national level. Not just Cuellar's castration—and one can read all sorts of things into that, even going so far as talking about Peru's loss to Chile in the War of the Pacific of the late 1870s, which still rankles Peruvians (and even more so Bolivians, who lost their 'outlet to the sea,' a phrase which could also serve as a euphemism for Cuellar's situation)—but his abnormality is the key. There is a dissatisfaction, a lack of integration, and this is arguably reduplicated even in the form of the story, whose brevity, as opposed to the massive length of the European books, is itself another kind of truncation.

Champagnat Academy is a Catholic school and the boys' rebelliousness and macho camaraderie are prompted and magnified by the authoritarianism and discipline of the school. The school knows only one way to adulthood and one mode of culture and presumes 'normal' development, and even there tension exists, i.e., the key role sex plays in 'normal development' generates inevitable conflict with the tight sexual regulation of the church and the paradox of clerical celibacy. It may just appear to be the five cubs as characters in this story, but the adults who train, supervise, and monitor them influence their conduct. In this context, Cuellar is not a total object of pity. He is not shown as financially disadvantaged— he comes from the exclusive neighborhood of Miraflores—but he is the new kid in school, as opposed to Choto, Chingooo, Manny, and Lalo, (Vargas Llosa, an admirer of Flaubert, surely remembered the beginning of *Madame Bovary* where the similarly hapless Charles Bovary is introduced as the new kid in school). The other boys do not at all ostracize or reject Cuellar after the accident; indeed, he is so seamlessly re-included in their collective life that the reader is apt to miss the profound and life-altering significance of the accident. What Bolaño calls the "speed" and "musicality" (319) of the story are crucial to the success of the narrative. Other writers would be languorous and mournful about the accident and give extended buildups and postmortems with respect to it. Here, the intensity of the story goes on, not missing a beat, much like a soccer game where even after a key player is seriously injured the game has to go on, and people still try to win. The divisions are subtler, being revealed when the other boys go onto things Cuellar either physically or psychologically cannot do. At age twenty-two, when the girls are asking why Cuellar does not have a girlfriend, the boys are speculating whether they know about his condition or not. What they do not realize is that they may be subtly giving away cues or clues to the girls even if nothing is directly said, indicating, in so many words, that he is off the map, sexually speaking. Cuellar intuits this and becomes hostile to the girls when he should be ingratiating himself to them and trying to impress. Cuellar tries then to act normally towards the girls, only to do so in a kind of overstated manner, and lapses back to his old "outsider" hijinks by playing up being an outsider precisely because he feels he can never be an insider. But the point is that Cuellar is never overtly excluded; it is all covert, between the lines.

Cuellar's exclusion is also double-sided. If he remains a perpetual boy, never growing up, he is also free from the compromises his now-married *barrio*-mates have had to make: taking jobs only for money, letting their wives boss them around. If Cuellar is literally castrated, the fate of the other boys is in a sense a symbolic castration, as their dynamism and drive are channeled into an annealing domesticity and a futile corporate conformism.

In a sense, the children are too democratic to exclude Cuellar entirely; not yet conscious of adult hierarchies, they feel he is their friend before and their friend after, and, of course, not having attained puberty, they do not themselves totally understand the full significance of Cuellar's mutilation, how profoundly it makes his sense of being human different from theirs. In another sense, though, children are apt to be more conformist, to not dare to directly challenge authority; thus the four other cubs, despite still liking, caring about, and keeping in full contact with Cuellar, cannot but signal their sense of his difference; it would take a conscious act of overcoming it, far more the propensity of adults than children, to alter this situation.

There is something else going on. Bolaño points to this when he says "…what terrifies the narrators is that P. P. Cuellar is one of them and never stops trying to be one of them" (321). It would be so much easier if he were decisively desegregated, but his continuing similarity is enough to make the entire relationship uncanny, make them wonder how close to being castrated they are, and how different in fact they are. The other issue is that, for all the pathos of Cuellar's inability to be an adult, adulthood is not painted positively in the book: the state of being mature and settled men with wives, cars, homes is limned as being perilously close to death, as if with all the instabilities of boyhood eliminated, there is nothing left to live for. In terms of the title, for most of the book, there were the five cubs, but now all the rest have grown up, leaving only one residual cub: Cuellar. The other four are pitying of this, but are also in a sense envious, as Cuellar still has the interesting, less predictable life; he is still, in an odd way, the star, or at least the exception.

Vargas Llosa himself is not against boyishness. One of his favorite writers growing up was Alexandre Dumas, famous for his swashbuckling historical novels, such as *The Three Musketeers* and the "all for one, one for all" ethos of this book pervades the camaraderie of the five cubs' friendship. Vargas Llosa himself still seems very boyish for a man of his age, now in his late seventies— he is not simply the gray literary eminence. Vargas Llosa himself is not Cuellar—this is shown in how thoroughly Cuellar is separated from the narrative function in this story, where the storytellers are a group of five boys, who, at different times, may or may not include P. P. Cuellar. But he is not totally *not* him either, and in more than the sense in which Flaubert famously said, "Madame Bovary, *c'est moi*." Sometimes, Vargas Llosa seems to argue that pathologies or flaws are what make life interesting, and people who fit in and conform in a conventional sense are not very interesting subjects for fiction.

Bolaño is very apt in describing this story as "a horror tale mixed with social realism" (320)—indeed, this description might apply to quite a few of Vargas Llosa's texts—"The Grandfather," for instance, more appositely than the magic realism label usually stuck to Latin American narrative. Vargas Llosa is indeed uncanny in his ability to register realities of power without committing himself to naturalistic social representation. Like his elder contemporary, the French theorist Michel Foucault (1926–1984), Vargas Llosa writes about the way human freedom is contained within structures of power that prove both adamant and malleable when they need to be, either excluding outsiders directly or seeming to bend only to have their existing contours reaffirmed. Though Vargas Llosa believes far more fervently in the intrinsic value of individual freedom than did Foucault, his early stories resound with a fundamental pessimism— palliated only by "On Sunday" and to an extent "The Grandfather"— about the capacity for change and improvement. Though Vargas Llosa's Peruvians are resilient, the Peru depicted in these stories is a place dotted with continuing obstacles in the path of resilience.

Interestingly, Vargas Llosa's first book of stories is dedicated to the memory of Sebastián Salazar Bondy, a great Peruvian intellectual, suggesting that, in some way, the title story is not just about its manifest subject but is more invisibly about "the Peruvian condition." The story resonates as a universal narrative of childhood and how children deal with maturation and differences; but its Peruvian setting is hardly accidental. The stories are suffused with specific Lima references, and even though outsiders are excluded from a full sense of the connotations, the sense of being soaked in a felt locality, much like Joyce's *Dubliners*, is a substantial part of these stories' success. For instance, the Ricardo Palma movie house referenced in the story is named after the previously mentioned author of *tradiciones*. Vargas Llosa repeatedly mentions this theater in his nonfiction autobiographical writings. Even when he was just starting out as a writer, Vargas Llosa had international aspirations and absorbed global influences, but he also was a faithful observer and monitor of the Peru of his youth and conveys this to the reader with honesty, pertinacity, and flair.

## Note

1.  While the stories that comprise *Los jefes*, 1959 (The Leaders)—"Los jefes" ("The Leaders"), "El desafio" ("The Challenge"), "El hermano menor" ("The Younger Brother"), "Día Domingo" ("On Sunday"), "Un visitante" ("A Visitor"), and "El abuelo" ("The Grandfather")— and the novella *Los cachorros*, 1967 (The Cubs) circulate in Spanish in independent editions, in English translation they are all included in the volume *The Cubs and Other Stories*, 1979. For convenience sake, the stories, after their first mention of their original title in Spanish, are referred by their English language title.

## Works Cited

Bolaño, Roberto. *Between Parentheses*. Ed. Ignacio Echevarria. Trans. Natasha Wimmer. New York: New Directions, 2011.

Vargas Llosa, Mario. *The Cubs and Other Stories*. 1979. New York: Farrar, Straus & Giroux, 1989.

# The Time of the Hero: The Moral Itinerary

## Versions of Innocence

*La ciudad y los perros*, 1963 (*The Time of the Hero*, 1966) begins
with a ritual whose effects will unfold throughout the first section
of the novel.[1] The dice have been cast and the book's first phrase
is a judgment: "Four, the Jaguar said" (7). From then on, the novel
continues its unmodifiable course. The three and the one can be
clearly, indisputably, seen in the humid air. The syllable that makes
up the Jaguar's guilty verdict is framed by the silence of the other
cadets. When the Jaguar insists on knowing who has been chosen,
Cava admits to having the number four. He must steal the chemistry
exam. There is no time to complain or request modification of this
judgment. In that moment, the Jaguar is a god who delivers fate's
decision. Nevertheless, the result does not seem accidental. The
presence of the Jaguar, Cava's fear, the obscure humidity of the
enclosure, are as impossible to appeal as the numbers on the two
dice. The narration tells us that Cava starts to tremble. It is cold
at that time in the barracks of the Leoncio Prado Military School,
but we know that Cava, who comes from the Andes, is used to the
cold. He is trembling out of fear. The decision has been taken, and
there only remains to go over the circumstances in which it must
be fulfilled. The Jaguar gives a new order that reminds him of their
previous pact: "You know which one, the second on the left" (7).

This initial sentence determines the shape of the novel. The fact
he has been chosen makes Cava nervous. This leads to his breaking
the window, which, in turn, will lead to the detention of the other
cadets in his class. This detention will have, as its consequence, that
the Slave cannot see Teresa and thus will lead to his informing on
the Circle (Jaguar's closest collaborators). This delation also leads
to his death, to the later accusation of murder against the Jaguar
by the poet Alberto, and to the Jaguar's marginalization by his

---

classmates. Until the conclusion of the novel, the facts continue their progression, as if they were stages in a predetermined fate. Each member of the system, the military institution, and the city of Lima are overwhelmed and condemned by the forward march of these episodes. The narrative machine has been set in motion by a throw of the dice and, especially, by the voice of a strange and savage god, the Jaguar.

*The Time of the Hero* begins in a moment that manifests power and submission. This is the basic premise of the novel and the world it represents. Although Cava is condemned, he exhibits no hint of rebellion or protest. This is an oppressive reality, whose rules cannot be rebutted. Slowly, Cava begins to stumble to the location where he must steal the exam. But we already have all the information we need.

The Jaguar is the nucleus of the system, the author of the fate of others and himself. The heavy, pestilential air, the somber enclosure, seem a fit background to his orders. This connection between actions and the background in which they take place is essential to the point of view of the novel. The Jaguar's violence is nothing but an answer to the violence of the place and its system. The humid, somber, pestilential school and city are the ideal locations for the actions narrated.

In the following sections of the novel, the focus shifts onto the Slave and Alberto. Unlike the Jaguar, the Slave appears as a character conditioned by his mother's affection, kisses, and pampering. During his trip to Lima, the Slave feels an exhaustion that dampens his senses. He is a deadened, passive, and tragic character. The Slave is at the mercy of his surroundings, his family, the humid weather, and the exhaustion that overwhelms him. Within the structure of power and control depicted in the novel, the Slave is at the other extreme from the Jaguar. While the Jaguar controls and defines the unfolding of reality, the Slave is overwhelmed by his environment. Nevertheless, we soon find out that, like the Slave, the Jaguar is a victim of the system within which he lives.

In the following passage, the third protagonist of the novel, the poet Alberto, is introduced. Protected from the cold by his overcoat, "he was so used to the weight of the rifle that he hardly felt it" (11). Unlike the Slave, Alberto has adapted to reality. He is one with his rifle, which is the emblematic object of the school and of the reality he has been given. At the beginning of the novel, Alberto simulates belonging to the system, in order to take advantage of it. If the Slave lives in the past, the poet Alberto exists in the present. He makes plans to get money in order to visit the brothel the following Saturday. One of his schemes is to write love letters and porno novellas for the cadets in exchange for money. When he goes to the Lieutenant to confess his problems, we do not know if his words are sincere or a means to gain influence. This ambiguity is essential to the book. Many of the actions that take place in the novel have no clear or explicit reason. Actions do not respond to specific motivations. A good example of this is Alberto's delation to Gamboa of the Jaguar. We do not know if it originates in his feeling of guilt over having betrayed the Slave by dating Teresa, in a sincere search for justice, or in a desire for vengeance. Actions never have one single dimension in the works of Vargas Llosa.

Unlike the Slave, Alberto has adapted to the system. He can survive in it because a writer can defend herself with words. He sells his love letters and "novels" to the other cadets. But as we will see below, his rebellion is conceived through words. Words define his being.

Already in the passage previously quoted, Alberto seems to have a place in the structure of power; somewhere between the Jaguar and the Slave. He can manipulate his environment, but does not control it. He offers letters and novels for sale, but is not a member of the Circle. He is basically a loner, a writer without a group supporting him. Throughout his life, Vargas Llosa has always defended this model of the writer as a free, independent being, without ties or compromises, who always tells the truth.

### A Mediator

There are several narrators in *The Time of the Hero*. One of them is an omniscient narrator who narrates events, such as the death of the Slave. There is also a narrator for the interior monologues of, for instance, the Boa (another member of the Circle) and the Jaguar. There is also a third person narrator who identifies with a specific character, for instance in the passage where Alberto telephones Lieutenant Gamboa to inform on the Circle. With his location at the center of the network of students, Alberto is a useful character for this narrator. By occupying a space midway between the powerful Jaguar and the passive Slave and by having personal relations with both, the poet Alberto becomes the central conscience of the novel, an agent of the story. He is the character with whom the reader can identify. He is at the center of the action and helps guide the story's moral journey.

The novel's moral evolution goes from Alberto's affection and compassion towards the Slave to his growing admiration for the Jaguar. In both cases, the moral impulse is essential to the story's unfolding. Alberto pities the Slave out of solidarity with a protagonist who suffers. Nevertheless, Alberto later admires the Jaguar, appreciating his integrity and nobility in not betraying him to the other cadets. If, at the start of the novel, the Jaguar is a cruel and violent character, towards its conclusion, he is shown to have acquired unexpected nobility. The narrative begins with the suggestion that the Slave is the hero of the story. Then this function is passed on to Alberto. By the ending, we discover that the true hero is the one who seemed less plausible: the Jaguar.

Alberto is a loner with a private moral code. He lives at the margins of the two systems that place pressure on him: the first is centered on the school authorities, the second, on the Circle. He has not given up on justice. Nevertheless, his conduct is not governed by a strict moral code, such as the Military School's manual of conduct, but, instead, by instinctive passion. In the writings of Vargas Llosa, morality is never disassociated from emotion or instinct. There is an emotional obligation that compels Alberto: the feeling of loyalty towards a friend. It is this emotion that leads him to defend the Slave. The Slave suffers the unjust abuses meted out by a reality determined by the law of the jungle. In the second part, however, it is the Jaguar who singly resists the attacks and accusations of the other cadets. It is then that his true personality is revealed. The novel is an exploration and unveiling of the Jaguar's hidden identity. The Jaguar's mystery is insinuated at the start of the novel. Early on, Alberto asks if anyone has seen the Jaguar:

"Have you seen the Jaguar?"

"He hasn't been here" (21).

This is a premonition. No one knows who the Jaguar is. He is one of the mysteries of the novel. He is someone who seems to be the key to understanding the society of violence that has developed in the school and beyond. No one really knows him. Only at the end do we see him as he really is, when we discover that he was the young boy who had suffered mistreatment and had later been corrupted by Skinny Higueras.

The Jaguar is so strong a character that, near the beginning of the book, when Alberto finds that the Jaguar is not around, he tries to imitate him, even to replace him: "'I don't play poker with peasants,' Alberto said. He put his hand to his penis and aimed at the players. 'I just mow them down'" (21). If the Poet tries to imitate the Jaguar, it is because of the influence his personality exerts from the beginning of the story. Efraín Kristal has explored, with great insight, the similarities, as victims of the system, that exist between the Jaguar and Joe Christmas, the character from Faulkner's *Light in August*. As is the case with Christmas, the Jaguar ends up becoming an obscure, unfathomable, victim of violence.[2]

The moral itinerary of the story has three major stages. In the first, by assuming the defense of the Slave, Alberto becomes a rebel against the power exercised by the other cadets. Defending the Slave from the abuses of the other cadets is Alberto's first goal. During the second stage of this evolution, after the Slave dies, Alberto decides to inform on the Circle and its actions. In the third and definitive stage, he stands up to the Jaguar. It is then that the fundamental revelation of the book takes place. By facing the Jaguar, the novel takes a fundamental turn: Alberto ends up forgetting the Slave and begins to admire the Jaguar's moral solidity.

*The Time of the Hero* acquires a new dimension thanks to this masterful twist. When it seemed it was only going to present a Manichean disquisition between a supposed hero (the Slave or the Poet) and an aggressor (the Jaguar), the book begins to relativize the latter's evil. If, at the end, the Jaguar is a hero, it is because the novel finally affirms that all are heroes within a system that devours them. At the end of the sixth chapter of the second part, as he confronts the Jaguar, Alberto says to him:

> "Do you know what your life's going to be like? You'll just be a cheap crook, and sooner or later you'll land in prison."

> "That's what my mother told me." Alberto was surprised, he had not expected a confidence. But he understood that the Jaguar was talking to himself: his voice was a dull mutter" (347).

This is a moment of enormous importance because it takes place during the confrontation between Alberto and Jaguar. When he expects a violent answer, the Jaguar's face becomes somber, and he answers with that premonition that seems to indicate a destiny. It is an individual destiny, but it is also a social fate: that of the marginalized. In that instant, Alberto begins to feel empathy towards the Jaguar, who thus displaces the Slave. The murderer he had denounced has become a strange and somber young man, who remembers his mother's premonitions.

The surfacing of the Jaguar's humanity, his unexpected nobility, coincides with his loss of power. After the death of the Slave and the rebellion of the cadets who blame the Jaguar for informing on their drinking, smoking, and other vices, he loses his position as leader. Only then has he humanized himself. In the works of Vargas Llosa, power has a moral connotation. It is the source of evil.

## Reading and Writing

The characters of *The Time of the Hero* use words as instruments to either exercise or resist power. The Jaguar gives the Slave his name. However, he avoids providing his own real name. We know the real names of the poet (Alberto Fernández) and the Slave (Ricardo

Arana), but the name of the Jaguar is never given. It is the Jaguar who names the world. He calls Alberto a squealer. He insults the cadets who rebel against him. He is a creator of words.

The acts of writing and narrating—debased by Alberto when he sells his letters and novellas—is vindicated when he denounces the Circle. In the fourth chapter of the second section, Alberto tells Captain Garrido everything that has been happening in the barracks. "His voice grew stronger, steadier, even aggressive at times" (307). He adds: "I'm telling you so you'll believe me, Sir" (307). Alberto tries his best as a narrator before the captain, in order to be believed.

Narrating is, for Vargas Llosa, as well as for Alberto, a moral act. Alberto tells Lieutenant Gamboa about what happens in the barracks and uncovers the immorality and abuses of the Circle. Nevertheless, when he tries to do the same before the Colonel, he is not successful. Authority suffocates his story. It questions it. It brings to light his pornographic novellas. By doing so, the Colonel diminishes Alberto's role as a writer. But for Alberto, as for Vargas Llosa, writings is an act of denunciation, of revealing reality. Narrating is uncovering the injustices hidden by the system. The Jaguar does the same thing when, at the end of the novel, he attempts to save Gamboa by declaring himself guilty of the Slave's death. This confession is an act of writing. "Why have you written this note?," Gamboa asks him (386).

Finally, Sergeant Gamboa is accused of being a reader. "'Nonsense,' the major said angrily. You must like to read novels, Gamboa. We're going to clean up this mess right now and stop wasting time" (328).

Reading and writing become pure acts that are punished by the system. Storytelling, writing, using words is, for Vargas Llosa, a moral act. The writer fulfills an essential role in this world: he is an objector to the system.

## The Ritual of Power

None of these three characters can be understood on his own because the game that has been established among them is that of power. This game changes when Alberto faces the Jaguar: "I am not afraid of you" (348). It is then when, by facing him as an equal, Alberto gets to know him. And with him, so do the readers.

These power relations create instinctive links central to the identity of the characters. The Jaguar exerts his power over the Slave. Alberto rebels against the Jaguar, in order to end up admiring him. But these identities fluctuate throughout the book. The three appear as victims of a superior power.

The three characters share an interest in Teresa, who functions as a distant and agglutinating character. She arouses the Slave's desire and Alberto's guilt. Finally, in an unexpected and ironic development that closes the circle of relations among the cadets, the Jaguar marries her. This is a singular event because Teresa, who is frequently considered to be a passive character, is actually an active agent in the story. She represents an ideal of innocence in the midst of a violent reality that links the three protagonists. She constitutes the moral center towards which they gravitate, in order to free themselves from the evil of the Military School.

One cannot understand any of these three characters without Lieutenant Gamboa. Although a good intentioned paternal figure, Gamboa is distant from the reality of the cadets. However, the Jaguar admires his purity and confesses having killed the Slave. According to Efraín Kristal, "from the point of view of the Jaguar, Gamboa is the only faculty of the school who has been faithful to its codes of behavior, in the same manner he has been loyal to his code of loyalty and revenge" ("Refundiciones biográficas y literarias en *La ciudad y los perros*" 551).[3] Javier Cercas states:

> The Jaguar is a strange and perverse descendant of the protagonists of novels of chivalry, read often by Vargas Llosa during the years he was writing the novel. He is a knight errant who makes no concessions to his moral code, made up of inflexible rules of honor, courage, vengeance, loyalty, betrayals, and punishments, that resembles that of the medieval knights. . . . From this comes the ambiguity of the character and our vertigo. Towards the end of *The Time of the Hero* we cannot avoid acknowledging a certain kind of greatness to the Jaguar . . . there is a purity that interpellates and disturbs us (494).

Cercas' opinion coincides with that of Kristal who states: "The realism of *The Time of the Hero* . . . goes from cruelty to disillusion and from disillusion to submission to a world that knows how to coopt its rebels in order to reproduce a corrupt social order" ("Refundiciones literarias y biográficas en *La ciudad y los perros*" 545).

One can even dare to propose that the Slave, Alberto, and the Jaguar all express alternative identities that converge in the writings of Mario Vargas Llosa. Within the system portrayed in the novel, the Slave is the marginal and the Jaguar is the rebel against it. Alberto is the mediator, the writer, he who tells, a predecessor of the myopic journalist in *La guerra del fin del mundo*, 1981 (*The War of the End of the World*, 1984). Alberto alternatively rebels and submits. The moral impulse and the ritual of power are two key traits of Vargas Llosa's characters. The power game becomes a clash of moral codes. Each character has his own moral code, according to his particular perception of the world. The Jaguar holds a morality of violence as a strategy of survival. The Poet defends a morality based on helping his friend, the Slave, against the Circle. Gamboa believes in the army's morality of discipline. The only character who has lost—or never had—his moral energy is the Slave, who informs on the Circle only because of his desire to see Teresa. Based on moral considerations, it is curious that, at the end, the Jaguar, the murderer of the first part of the novel, acquires a higher moral stature than the other cadets, including his supposed victim, the Slave, and Alberto.

The two characters who hold on to an unchanged moral code throughout the novel are the Jaguar and Gamboa. That is why the encounter between these two dissimilar characters is a significant moment in the novel.

When the Jaguar is accused of being a "squealer" by the other cadets, he becomes a "damned" character in Vargas Llosa's imaginary world. Being a "squealer" implies violating the code of the rebel, that is, the transgressor. The lack of solidarity, of belonging and being committed to a group, is morally sanctioned in Vargas Llosa's fictional universe.

Towards the end of *The Time of the Hero*, the Jaguar writes a confession to the murder of the Slave. Gamboa knows he could avoid being reassigned to a remote Andean outpost if he takes the Jaguar to the authorities. "Take me to the colonel," the Jaguar asks him (387), but the lieutenant does not do so. There is a combination of nobility and skepticism in his decision, even if hidden under a military explanation: "Don't you know what useless objectives are?" (387). The Jaguar is eloquent when explaining his confession: "I didn't know what it was like to have everybody against you" (387). The Jaguar's confession is a sign he has become human. Nevertheless, he does not convince Gamboa. Gamboa does not accept his own salvation. He decides to be condemned because he has discovered that the army, in which he had such faith, is a farce. During that encounter, the moral drama that defines Gamboa's future life, his loss of faith in the military that had given meaning to his life, even his probable abandonment of the army, is played out. In reality, the Jaguar and Lieutenant Gamboa are incorruptible characters, who feel respect and admiration for each other. The exit of Gamboa from the novel "down Palmeras Avenue in the direction of Bellavista" as "the waves broke on the shore and died almost instantaneously" is one of the culminating moments of the novel (387, 388).

From the letters and documents found in the archive at Princeton University, we know that in earlier drafts of the novel, the Slave and the Poet were one character. Both characters incorporate traits and events from Vargas Llosa's life. Like the author, both come from families with tyrannical fathers. One must keep in mind that in the novel the Slave, who thought his father was dead, is told he is alive. The same thing happened to Vargas Llosa. The Poet represents Vargas Llosa's activity as writer in school. And, though not linked to specific biographical events, the Jaguar reflects the opposition of the author against the power of the military institution.

The three cadets, who have such different personalities and identities, progressively converge in Vargas Llosa's imaginary world. The three are heroes because they represent aspects of the author's life. Despite being so different, the three are both victims and victimizers. All are ultimately crushed by an impersonal system. Individuality only exists in opposition to the system.

Despite its violence and sordid settings, *The Time of the Hero* is an optimistic novel. In a certain sense, its characters become heroes who manage in some way to delineate their desire to be moral in a corrupt world. All, however, end up as victims of a faceless system. In *The Time of the Hero*, the individual is, by definition, an innocent being dehumanized by the social system into which he has been born. The Romantic inheritance of this notion is evident. Rousseau and his view of society as corrupting individuals is one of the sources of *The Time of the Hero*. The novel is an homage to the individual's eternal capacity for rebellion. *Conversación en La Catedral*, 1969 (*Conversation in The Cathedral*, 1975) and *La casa verde*, 1966 (*The Green House*, 1968) will present a similar point of view. Although the system crushes individuals, they will still keep rebelling, even if they know they are defeated beforehand. The works of Vargas Llosa are a paean to humanity's endless capacity for rebellion and for the most important form it may take: the art of telling stories.

## Notes

1. The essay will use the titles of the translation after the first mention of a Vargas Llosa novel.

2. On the similarities between the Jaguar and Joe Christmas, see Kristal, *Temptation of the Word* (34–37).

3. In this case, as in that of all works in Spanish in the Works Cited list, the translation is by the author of this essay.

## Works Cited

Cercas, Javier. "La pregunta de Vargas Llosa." *La ciudad y los perros: edición conmemorativa del cincuentenario*. Mario Vargas Llosa. Madrid: Real Academia Española yAsociación de Academias de la Lengua Española, 2012. 478–98.

Kristal, Efraín. "Refundiciones literarias y biográficas en *La ciudad y los perros*." *La ciudad y los perros. Edición conmemorativa del cincuentenario*. Mario Vargas Llosa. Madrid: Real Academia Española y Asociación de Academias de la Lengu Española, 2012. 539–58.

_____. *Temptation of the Word: The Novels of Mario Vargas Llosa.* Nashville, TN: Vanderbilt UP, 1999.

Vargas Llosa, Mario. *The Time of the Hero.* 1966. Trans. Lysander Kemp. New York: Farrar, Straus & Giroux, 1986.

# From *Conversation* to *Feast*: Vargas Llosa's Bookend Novels of Dictatorship_____

Gene H. Bell-Villada

In memoriam Audrey Dobek-Bell, 1945–2013, who passed away
during the writing of this essay.

*Conversación en La Catedral*, 1969 (*Conversation in The Cathedral*,
1975) and *La fiesta del Chivo*, 2000 (*The Feast of the Goat*, 2001)
both stand out as Vargas Llosa's high instances of the narrative of
dictatorship.[1] The former evokes, in close detail, the daily life under
the shabby military regime (1948–56) of Peruvian General Manuel
Odría, and its anticlimactic aftermath. The latter vividly hones in
on the brutal, megalomaniacal, thirty-one-year despotism (1930–
61) of Dominican Generalissimo Rafael Trujillo and its sad, sordid
aftermath.

The dictatorship genre in Latin America, of course, has a long
literary pedigree, stretching at least as far back as the Argentine
activist Domingo Sarmiento's hybrid classic *Facundo* (1845). And
in the 1970s, at the height of the legendary "Boom," there suddenly
sprung forth a series of such novels by Alejo Carpentier (*Reasons
of State*), Augusto Roa Bastos (*I, the Supreme*), and Gabriel García
Márquez (*The Autumn of the Patriarch*), all of them now canonical
of their kind. As it happens, Vargas Llosa can lay claim to double
membership in that august company via these two thick bookends:
one published when he was just thirty-two years old, the other issued
when, at sixty-four, he was a seasoned master with a long list of two
dozen volumes of fiction, drama, and essays to his credit.

Those twin pillars, moreover, occupy a special place in that
they are arguably among the Peruvian's two greatest and most
widely admired works. As early as 1970, Arturo Oliart wrote, in the
respected Iberian monthly *Cuadernos Hispoanoamericanos*, that
*Conversation in The Cathedral* had struck him as "a great novel... a

masterful novel" (210), one that, "with all its structural complexity and its audacious technique, follows in and is the descendant of the great nineteenth-century novelist tradition" (212).[2] Likewise, much more recently, in 2012, Efraín Kristal states simply that "*Conversation* is one of the greatest literary creations in the Spanish language" ("The Total Novel and the Novella" 46).

*The Feast of the Goat*, in turn, took things further as its publication grew into a kind of popular happening. Besides its coming out to massive critical acclaim in the general press, there were such dizzying public facts as the immediate sale of its entire print run of ten thousand copies in *a single day*, the author's presentation of the novel before an audience of one thousand in the very same Santo Domingo hotel where fictive female protagonist Urania stays, the Peruvian's extensive book tours and public readings up and down the Americas, the polemics sparked by the *The Feast of the Goat* in the Dominican Republic among surviving Trujillistas, and the thousands upon thousands of readers who were devouring the book and discussing it amongst themselves (Bell-Villada 139–140).

In retrospect, the two novels show inevitable similarities in both content and form. A key resemblance: in each of them, its dictatorship is largely perceived, experienced, and gradually understood (and this knowledge conveyed to us readers) via the afflicted eyes of the damaged, disaffected, adult offspring of an élite-level ally of the régime—specifically, Santiago in *Conversation in The Cathedral*, the estranged son of corrupt crony capitalist Don Fermín Zavala, and Urania in *The Feast of the Goat*, the long-traumatized daughter of a gracious, cultivated, refined, yet spineless and pitifully corrupt Senator Agustín Cabral.

The dissimilarities, however, are many. One obvious difference is that the *The Feast of the Goat* features Trujillo as a leading character who, from chapter two on, shares center stage with his eventual victim Urania. In *Conversation in The Cathedral*, by contrast, General Odría is seen exactly once, from afar, in chapter one of book two, where he appears on the balcony of the Presidential Palace, flanked by civilian dignitaries and army men, and where, at a staged, Potemkin-style rally, he reportedly delivers an (unquoted) speech about his so-called "Revolution." For the actual face of the dictatorship, the narrative spotlight falls mainly on a fictional Cayo Bermúdez, the regime's director of security, loosely based on Alejandro Esparza Zañartu, who was the real-life Odría's right-hand man in charge of intelligence, censorship, political arrests, and periodic police assaults on leftist groups and on followers of the APRA (Alianza Popular Revolucionaria Americana). Of the flesh-and-blood Esparza, the author observes in an interview that he was "an insignificant man, who could hardly express himself, who gave the impression of great mediocrity" (Setti 70).

In *Conversation in The Cathedral*, his stand-in character, Bermúdez, is originally an obscure businessman from Chincha—a small town with a strong Afro-Peruvian and *mestizo* demographic, located about one-hundred fifty miles south of Lima. A provincial nobody, Cayo will rise to prominence thanks to a long-standing childhood friendship with the regime's Colonel Espina (himself modeled after Gen. Zenón Noriega), who recruits him for the position. Once in power, Bermúdez shows an immense capacity for work, spending fifteen hours a day on the job and also conniving against his own buddy-patron. Lacking in any military experience, he's basically a deskman, who leads a monkish existence (his brothel escapades aside), living at first in hotels and eschewing luxury or ostentation. Never having learned to drive, he depends initially on taxis for getting about the city. Essentially apolitical, with no interest in ideologies, principles, ceremonies, public works, or the details of governance, Cayo lives solely for the Machiavellian tasks of surveillance, intrigue, intimidation, press control, and all-around repression. Henchman Bermúdez, moreover, is in close cahoots with Santiago's father Don Fermín; yet the dour bureaucrat also resents the flamboyant entrepreneur's wealth and privilege, and will eventually lead a prosperous Fermín Zavala to economic near-ruin.

Physically and personally, Cayo cuts an unimpressive, mildly grotesque figure. Gross and unmannerly, he casually boasts about being no gentleman. (Ditto for the company he keeps: there are scattered references to his ugly wife back in Chincha.) A sloppy dresser with chronically dirty fingernails, he seldom bothers to greet people or say good-bye. Carlota, a sex worker at the bordello, is quoted as describing Bermúdez thus: "Don Cayo was very small, his face was leathery, his hair yellowish like shredded tobacco, sunken eyes that look coldly and from a distance, wrinkles on his neck, an almost lipless mouth, and teeth stained from smoking... He was so skinny that the front part of his suit almost touched the back" (198–199). Villainous Cayo's slight stature can be seen as literally embodying his moral smallness of character, his littleness as a human being.

Cayo, again, is fictional, while *The Feast of the Goat*, on the other hand, focuses directly on Trujillo—who, like the former, is a disciplined, power-hungry, and diminutive sort, albeit meticulous and maniacal about his dress habits and physical appearance. In Johnny Abbes, however, Trujillo's infamous director of military intelligence, we have the real-life equivalent to Bermúdez. Johnny resembles the Peruvian top cop in having no previous army experience (which earns him the contempt of the dictator's officer corps) and in being burdened with an unattractive spouse, though he himself is flaccid and lumpy to Cayo's short and skinny. Early on in the novel, Abbes is described thus: "that flabby figure, stuffed into a colonel's uniform, the personified negation of [military] bearing . . . that fat-cheeked, funeral face with the little mustache trimmed in the style of.... Mexican actors, [with] a capon's dewlap hanging down over his short neck" (37), and with "no muscles" (57). And even more so than Cayo, Johnny revels in intrigue, evil, and sheer physical cruelty. Already as a child, he derived pleasure from sticking pins into the eyeballs of baby chicks; and when facing the apprehended, wounded conspirator Pedro Livio Cedeño in hospital, Abbes casually presses a burning cigarette next to the hapless patient's left eye.

The relationship with Abbes' boss—who actually characterizes their bond as "a marriage" (60)—is closely drawn; Johnny even states that he lives for Trujillo (71). Both Cayo and Johnny serve as the behind-the-scenes "bad cop," doing the dirty work of the dictatorship even as the actual tyrant, with his florid rhetoric and beribboned uniforms, lends the regime an air of dignity as its chief of state. As Bermúdez admits at one point to cabinet member

Arbeláez, "Everything positive done in the ministry is done by you, doctor... I take care of the negative side... I'm doing you a great service, relieving you of everything that has to do with the everyday police work" (*Conversation in The Cathedral* 282).[3] Each of these two hatchet men come to an ignominious end: a mass uprising in Arequipa leads to Cayo's downfall, with his flight to Brazil and exile abroad; Johnny, in turn, is sent off by Trujillo's wily successor Balaguer to a consular post in Japan and later winds up in Haiti, where strongman Duvalier has Abbes and his entire family brutally murdered.

*The Feast of the Goat* indeed stands out for its near-unbearable scenes of torture and emotional-sexual abuse—all true to the sadistic history of the regime. Surprisingly, physical violence plays but an incidental role in *Conversation in The Cathedral*. There are police raids on leftists and attacks on mass rallies (where Trinidad, the first lover of the servant Amalia, dies); and there is the indirectly reported murder of prostitute Hortensia, "La Musa," under possible orders of Don Fermín. Yet close-ups of killing and torture are largely absent. What we see much more of is the generalized corruption, the intricate ties of people from all walks of life—rich and poor, small-town and big-city, respectable and disreputable, businessmen and brothel dwellers, journalists and chauffeurs, senators and thugs—with the regime. As Vargas Llosa himself noted in an interview with Luis Díez, "the mediocre dictatorship of Manuel Odría ... ruled ... not by outright violence ... but by hypocritical corruption" (Díez 170). Or as critic Oviedo points out, the politics were marked more by "*ruindad*" (meanness, shabbiness, baseness) than by cruelty (Oviedo 247). Trujillo in *The Feast of the Goat* does, for his part, resort to corruption, buying off disaffected elements with contracts and economic concessions; yet these episodes seem almost incidental to the horrific atmosphere of brutality that pervades the book.

In both novels, the actual, formal dictatorship comes to its end at precisely the midway point—in *Conversation in The Cathedral*, with Cayo's fall from grace and with Odría stepping down and allowing elections between books two and three (out of four); in *The Feast of the Goat*, with the assassination of Trujillo at the end of chapter twelve (out of twenty-four). And yet in both instances, the system goes on, if in somewhat modified form—*continuismo*, as they call it in Mexico. Dr. Balaguer brings a more cultured, civilized veneer to the sociopolitical order, even as Ramfis Trujillo tortures and kills conspirators, their allies, and close kin by the hundreds. And in *Conversation in The Cathedral*, under the successor administration (1956–1962) of President Manuel Prado, the corruption remains fully in place. President Prado in fact owns the scandal sheet where Santiago and his disillusioned, scribbling peers earn their keep. As Don Fermín observes, "Under Prado, the government has become a terrible Mafia" that has now left him high and dry (365), as a loser confronted by the new faces in the musical-chairs game.

In keeping with their subject matter, *Conversation in The Cathedral* and *The Feast of the Goat* are both marked by a strong sexual component. By contrast, with Europe's harsh fascist and dreary communist dictatorships at the time, a certain crass erotic laxness has been (for the men) as much a part of Latin America's military regimes as were their guns and soldiers, parades, and *pronunciamientos*. (Batista's Cuba, for instance, had a reputation as "the brothel of the Caribbean.") Both in real life and in his novel, Trujillo qualifies as a pathological lecher, who slept with the wives of his associates and then bragged about it in his speeches and who, every week, would deflower a few young girls of his choosing. Novelist Vargas Llosa masterfully creates, in playboy Manuel Alfonso, a composite character for the diverse hired hands who had pimped for the Antillean Lothario. And the horrific last chapter of the *Goat* depicts—in a spine-chilling scene—Trujillo's unsuccessful bedding-down of Urania that serves as the book's original sin and narrative pretext.

Sex also permeates *Conversation in The Cathedral*, if at a different sort of level. Approximately one-fourth of the action takes place in a high-class brothel (managed by Frenchwoman Ivonne) that, we happen to find out, is owned by Bermúdez, and where many of the women provide service to assorted governmental figures. (Don Cayo, for his part, always sleeps with two girls, and gets his kicks from watching lesbian sex.) Several of the bordello females are fully developed secondary characters in their own right, with narratively rich and detailed subplots and dialogues of their own. As protagonist Santiago remarks to Ambrosio at the ironically named bar La Catedral, "you're closer to reality in a whorehouse than in a convent" (143). Further worth noting is the clandestine homosexual affair that Ambrosio, out of loyalty, carries on with his patron Don Fermín.

*Conversation in The Cathedral* is, in fact, remarkable in the extent to which it depicts society from the perspective of its lower depths—not just the eroticized night life, but also through such humble folk as the innocent mestiza servant Amalia and her first boyfriend Trinidad, as well as by means of Ambrosio, the Afro-Peruvian who, in the course of the book, will converse with Santiago for four hours straight and reveal his adventures as a driver to both Cayo and Don Fermín, but also as an occasional hired thug (which his father Trifulcio had also been). There is the entire band of professional goons—Ludovico, Lozano, Hilario—whose chief goal in life, their very dream, is to attain the ranks of full-time, salaried staffers. And there is the quasi-netherworld of cheap, sensationalistic, yellow journalism, as sordid in its own way as are the physical goings-on. Last but not least, through casual, passing references, Vargas Llosa captures the life of simple, ordinary Peruvians—soccer and boxing fans, lottery-ticket sellers, textile workers, coffin-makers, bus drivers, house servants, and more.

The book thus serves as a prime instance of the "total novel" that a younger Vargas Llosa, in frank emulation of the nineteenth-century masters, had set out to fashion from his early twenties on. In this regard, *Conversation in The Cathedral*'s epigraph from a novel by Balzac—himself the very epitome of such a literary project, and famous for his nocturnal roamings about the streets of Paris as his means of pursuing "research"—is perfectly à propos. (The epigraph reads "One needs to have rummaged through the entirety of social life in order to be a true novelist, given that the novel is the private history of nations.") The vast, all-inclusive social purview of *Conversation in The Cathedral* is thus among its signal strengths as a work of art. *The Feast of the Goat*, by contrast, concentrates solely on the Dominican elites—army officers, senators, government ministers, and Trujillo's willing minions along with their next of kin. That more precise, narrowed focus, on the other hand, is what gives the later novel its greater crispness and its compelling lucidity.

Both these books are supremely bleak in their outlook. In *Conversation in The Cathedral*, however, there are actually some positive elements. The student leftist group that a youthful Santiago gets temporarily involved with provides the one extended saving moment in the novel, a glimpse of an alternative. The author, at the time of the writing, was frankly a Marxist, and he had once belonged to a cell bearing the exact name—Cahuide—as does his fictional one. Not surprisingly, then, the activists are portrayed in highly admiring terms: intelligent, articulate, idealistic, clear in their thinking, courageous in their opposition, and in the end the undoubted victims of Cayo's opportunistic repression. In addition, maid servant Amalia shows the basic humane virtues of dedication and is incapable of evil. Ambrosio (who does love Amalia) is loyal to a fault, even possibly murdering prostitute Hortensia to protect his boss Fermín (who, in turn, clearly loves his wayward son). Santiago's eventual marriage to Ana, a sweet, provincial nurse of modest mestizo origin is actually a redemptive step for him and a touch of genuine, unpretentious romance in what is a bleak, affectless world.

*The Feast of the Goat*, on the other hand, has but a handful of positive moments, all toward the end: the Italian couple named Cavaglieri ("gentlemen") who, in chapter twenty-three, give refuge to conspirator-on-the-lam Antonio Imbert (the husband, in turn, being protected by his post with the Italian embassy); the nuns who spirit Trujillo's young rape victim Urania off to safety in Michigan; and the hints of a possible reconciliation between Urania and her once-estranged relatives. (The concluding line reads, "'If Marianita writes to me, I'll answer her letters,' she decides" [405]) That, however, is literally all.

In form and structure, the two works may seem superficially different. *Conversation in The Cathedral*, with its girth, teeming plot, and up to one hundred characters, qualifies (in Henry James' oft-quoted dictum about Tolstoy's novels) as a "loose and baggy monster." *The Feast of the Goat*, by contrast, impresses one with its rigorous architecture; its opening and closing with Urania; its strict organization, in the opening half, in groups of three chapters that focus respectively on Urania, Trujillo, and the conspirators; its division into two exactly equal halves marked by Trujillo's death; and its eventual "scrambling" of the narrative system as the Trujillista order comes undone. (See Bell-Villada 143–146.)

As one looks deeper, though, more similarities come into view. Both novels start out with the main character moving about their home city: Santiago strolling through Lima, returnee Urania going jogging in Santo Domingo. The two of them work with words— Urania as a lawyer, Santiago as a reporter and editorialist—while seeing their occupations as just a job; their true vocation consists in finding out about and rejecting their troubling backgrounds. Each protagonist will experience a momentous encounter that leads to "conversations"—Santiago with the house chauffeur and with colleague Carlitos, Urania with successive members of her alienated family—dealing with a painful past that will unfold before our eyes.

And, speaking of conversations, both books make broad use of Vargas Llosa's signature technique, a device that he picked up in seminal form from the livestock fair scene in Flaubert's *Madame Bovary* and then made into his own: namely, the use of dialogue montage, the systematic gathering and fusing of spoken material from numerous past episodes (from as many as eighteen different scenes in his more elaborate passages). Indeed, the plot, as recounted in book three of *Conversation in The Cathedral* (i.e. the beginning of the novel's second half), is conveyed almost entirely via this technique, either with an extensive string of dialogues, or imbedded in lengthy paragraphs with no indentations, dashes, or quotation marks (as happens in its chapter three). Conversational montage is also deployed in evoking the past histories of Urania, her father, and the conspirators throughout *The Feast of the Goat*.

Underlying the structures of both these books is the modernist legacy of Joyce, Faulkner, and Dos Passos, with their narrative innovations that have since become standard items in the novel-writing workshop. First of these is Faulkner's representation of time, whereby the story moves effortlessly between past, present, and future, and whereby chronology is flattened out into what Joseph Frank dubbed "spatial form." Equally important is the Joycean-Faulknerian resource of splitting the narrative point of view among diverse characters, giving us not a singular, seemingly authoritative story line but rather a grand collage, a plurality of versions, in which the various tellings matter as much as what is being told. Although in these novels, Vargas Llosa sticks with third-person accounts that are focused on one character each (what is sometimes called "free indirect discourse"), both these organizing devices are at the heart of *Conversation in The Cathedral* and *The Feast of the Goat*, placing the Peruvian among the inheritors of the Irishman's and the Mississippian's high fictive art.

In this regard, both Mary Davis and Efraín Kristal make a direct link between *Conversation in The Cathedral* and Faulkner's greatest book, *Absalom, Absalom!*, a novel built around a series of conversations narrating the rise and fall of a local, slaveholding oligarch in Mississippi, all of it prompted by Shreve McCanon, the Canadian roommate of Quentin Compson at Harvard College, who casually asks the brooding, displaced Southerner, "Tell about the South" (Davis 42; Kristal *Temptation of the Word* 59). Similarly, Santiago and Ambrosio will "tell about Peru" to each other in a scruffy bar in Lima; and in the same fashion, Urania Cabral will "tell about Trujillo" to her proper, upright, formerly deluded, and now shocked and dismayed relatives in her belated return home.

An additional feature characterizes book two of *Conversation in The Cathedral*. That portion is dominated in its entirety by the technique first launched by Dos Passos in *Manhattan Transfer* (1925): the use of short narrative fragments, each ranging from one to three pages maximum. Vargas Llosa adopts the device at that point presumably for the sake of a change of pace, to achieve a somewhat lighter and more transparent texture from the rest of the book and its thick, at times relentless dialogue montage (something along the lines of what Faulkner does in *The Sound and the Fury*, with its own four varieties of prose fabric). In *The Feast of the Goat*, on the other hand, such changes in method are less pronounced, and have to do mostly with the altering of the sequence of the three-part bundles in the second half, and the emergence of Dr. Balaguer and his flowery and ornate style of delivery in chapters fourteen and twenty-two (Bell-Villada 144–146).

Save for Urania and a few secondary characters, all of the actors in *The Feast of the Goat* are true-life, historical figures. The novelist thus had little opportunity to establish any sort of system with names. In *Conversation in The Cathedral*, by contrast, a certain amount of name patterning is discernible. Alphabetically, the first letter of the names of the participants runs the gamut from "A," as in Ambrosio, to "Z," as in the Zavala family—and indeed Santiago is often addressed and referred to as "Zavalita." Taking things further, it is probably not accidental that the three positive figures who happen to be female—the leftist activist Aída, the loyal Amalia, and Santiago's caring wife Ana—have names beginning with the letter "A." Conversely, the one unabashedly *negative* female character, Santiago's snobbish, racially prejudiced mother, is called Zoila, with a "Z." ("Zoila" could even be seen as a pun with "*Soy la...*," "I am the...".)

Continuing with the pattern, *A*mbrosio, as we have observed, has worthy attributes of his own. The names of his father Trifulcio and of Amalia's earlier lover, Trinidad, share in the initial syllable "Tri," and both men die violently, albeit in differing circumstances. Among other supernumeraries, one sees parallels worth considering in the lumpen thugs *L*udovico and *L*ozano, the bodyguard hooligan *H*ipólito and the star prostitute *H*ortensia, and the two high government figures *A*révalo and *A*rbeláez. Even evil *C*ayo and cynical reporter *C*arlitos are worth passing mention in this regard. Significantly, both Santiago and Don Fermín are alphabetically unique: no other characters have in common their initial phoneme. The total system, I grant, is not completely consistent nor rigorous across the board, yet the very fact of these repetitions is worth noting.

Vargas Llosa, in his novels, shows himself to be not only a master technician but a consummate architect. The rigorous two-part design and three-chapter bundles of *The Feast of the Goat* constitute that work's outstanding formal feature. The larger picture of *Conversation in The Cathedral* is, on first inspection, somewhat diffuse: the four "Books" have differing numbers of chapters. Several critics, however, have discerned a series of interlocking triangular arrangements among the novel's characters. Dirk Gerdes notes, for instance, "the following sequence: Amalia-Cayo Bermúdez-Santiago ... in part 2, and Santiago-Queta-Ambrosio in part 4" (102). Sara Castro-Klarén singles out no fewer than six such triangles of characters "that struggle over possession of a secret" and lists "La Musa-Queta-Cayo" and "Jacobo-Aída-Santiago" among her half-dozen (100–101). José Miguel Oviedo, in his foundational study (whose chapter on *Conversation in The Cathedral* bears the subtitle "*Pirámide de voces*" [Pyramid of Voices]), remarks that "the work ends up being a kind of pyramid of dialogues that expand their concentric waves through time and space" (Oviedo 253). Oviedo further supplements his exhaustive analysis with an elaborate graphic pyramid. Raymond Leslie Williams, for his part, notes three main conversations in a bar or brothel and offers a series of concentric apexes of his own (76–77).

Space does not allow for an in-depth look at such patterns, but each of the above scholars demonstrates, to some degree or other, the role and presence of tripartite structures throughout *Conversation in The Cathedral*—in ways that anticipate the more visible, rigorous threefold clusters in *Feast of the Goat*. Few novelists, of course, have proven as conscious of matters of design as is Vargas Llosa, and the elaborate constructs in many of his works naturally invite graphic representations and diagrams thereof. The above critics (as well as others not cited here) thus ably and fruitfully bring out the hidden, formal features of *Conversation* in ways that further illuminate the Peruvian's virtuosity as literary artificer.

If, for any reason, Vargas Llosa had ceased to write novels after *Conversation in The Cathedral*, he would still be considered a major fictioneer, a writer indeed canonical. Previous to this work, he had in *La ciudad y los perros*, 1963 (*The Time of the Hero*, 1966), an unforgettable first novel about military boarding school, his Peruvian equivalent to Austrian author Robert Musil's *Young Törless*, to which it inevitably invites comparison. And *La casa verde*, 1966 (*The Green House*, 1968), Vargas Llosa's second novel, captures the interconnected worlds of South American jungle, desert, and river travel as few dedicated regionalists have succeeded in doing.

Still, after *Conversation in The Cathedral*, Vargas Llosa continued to evolve, producing, among many other works, an ambitious, if somewhat flawed, portrait of fanaticism (*La guerra del fin del mundo*, 1981 [*The War of the End of the World*, 1984]); some fine comic novels (*Pantaleón y las visitadoras*, 1973 [*Captain Pantoja and the Special Service*, 1978]; *La tía Julia y el escribidor*, 1977 [*Aunt Julia and the Scriptwriter*, 1982]; the later *Travesuras de la niña mala*, 2000 [*The Bad Girl*, 2007]); a novelized look at the lives of Paul Gauguin and Flora Tristán, the Franco-Peruvian socialist-feminist who was the painter's grandmother (*El paraíso en la otra esquina*, 2003 [*The Way to Paradise*, 2003]); and a fascinating, horrific depiction of rubber-based colonialism in Congo and Peru, intermingled with a fictionalized account of the life-path of Irish activist Roger Casement (the recent *El sueño del celta,* 2010 [*The Dream of the Celt*, 2012] a work easily likened to Joseph Conrad's *Heart of Darkness*).

In *The Feast of the Goat*, however, Vargas Llosa demonstrated a special capacity for flexibility and growth, an ability to take on the forbidding subject of tyranny in a real country far from his own, all done with formal and narrative mastery when he was in his sixties. Both *Conversation* and *Feast*, in sum, exist as two great novels of dictatorship, while also—their subject matter aside—enduring as two superb fictions in themselves.

## Notes

1. The essay will use the titles of the translation after the first mention of a Vargas Llosa novel.
2. All quotations from text in Spanish in the Works Cited are by the author of the essay.
3. In the Spanish original, "police work" is "*baja policía*," literally "lower police" (*Conversación en La Catedral* 317).

# Works Cited

Bell-Villada, Gene H. "Sex, Politics, and High Art: Vargas Llosa's Long Road to *The Feast of the Goat.*" *Vargas Llosa and Latin American Politics.* Eds. Juan E. De Castro & Nicholas Birns. New York: Palgrave Macmillan, 2010. 139–157

Castro-Klarén, Sara. *Understanding Vargas Llosa.* Columbia: U of South Carolina P, 1990.

Davis, Mary. "La elección del fracaso: Vargas Llosa y William Faulkner." *José Miguel Oviedo.* Ed. Mario Vargas Llosa. Madrid: Taurus, 1981. 35–46.

Díez, Luis. "*Conversación en La Catedral*: Saga de corrupción y mediocridad." *Asedios a Vargas Llosa.* Santiago de Chile: Editorial Universitaria, 1972. 168–192.

Frank, Joseph. "Spatial Form in Modern Literature." *The Widening Gyre: Crisis and Mastery in Modern Literature.* New Brunswick: Rutgers UP, 1963. 3–62.

Gerdes, Dirk. *Mario Vargas Llosa.* Boston: Twayne Publishers, 1985.

Kristal, Efraín. *The Temptation of the Word: The Novels of Mario Vargas Llosa.* Nashville, TN: Vanderbilt UP, 1998.

_____. "The Total Novel and the Novella: *Conversation in The Cathedral* and *The Cubs. The Cambridge Companion to Mario Vargas Llosa.* Eds. Efraín Kristal & John King. New York: Cambridge UP, 2012. 37–48.

Oliart, Alberto. "La tercera novela de Vargas Llosa." *Mario Vargas Llosa.* José Miguel Oviedo. Madrid: Taurus, 1981. 201–213.

Oviedo, José Miguel. *Mario Vargas Llosa: La invención de una realidad.* Barcelona: Seix Barral, 1982.

Setti, Ricardo A. *Diálogo con Vargas Llosa.* Mexico City: Kosmos, 1985

Vargas Llosa, Mario. *Conversación en La Catedral.* Barcelona: Seix Barral, 1969.

_____. *Conversation in The Cathedral.* Trans. Gregory Rabassa. New York: Harper & Row, 1974

_____. *The Feast of the Goat.* Trans. Edith Grossman. New York: Farrar, Straus & Giroux, 2001.

Williams, Raymond Leslie. *Mario Vargas Llosa.* New York: Frederick Ungar, 1986.

# From Parable to Pedagogy: Mario Vargas Llosa's War on Fanaticism_____

Jeff Browitt

Mario Vargas Llosa's novelistic production after *Conversación en La Catedral*, 1969, (*Conversation in The Cathedral*, 1975) increasingly became over-determined by the context of the Cold War and moved from parables of moral corruption to thinly disguised pedagogical instruction on ideology and fanaticism, marked by an authorial anxiety over reader reception. Two novels in particular represent this trend in his oeuvre: *La guerra del fin del mundo,* 1981, (*The War of the End of the World*, 1984) and *Historia de Mayta,* 1984 (*The Real Life of Alejandro Mayta,* 1986).[1] The kind of historical perspective brought to bear on Latin American history in these novels' creation, allied to the concern with fanaticism and violence, would play out in different formats in many subsequent novels. How one reads *The War of the End of the World, The Real Life of Alejandro Mayta*, and many of Vargas Llosa's other novels, then, is in large part a function of how one reacts to the aesthetic presentation of history generated from his liberal-individualist perspective; that is, whether one is persuaded by the fictional employment of Latin American civil strife and not just entertained. It becomes a question of verisimilitude—the ability to construct a persuasive likeness. This would seem important, since Vargas Llosa has been so forthcoming about wanting a novel like *The War of the End of the World*, for example, to be read as an allegory in a political-philosophical register:

> The tragedy of Latin America is that in different moments of our history we have been divided in civil wars, in repressions, and massacres often worse than Canudos because of similar, reciprocal blindness (...) it's a general phenomenon: fanaticism, basically, the intolerance that weighs on our history. On some occasions the rebellions were messianic; on others utopian or socialist; yet others were fights between conservatives and liberals (Setti 67–8).[2]

*The War of the End of the World* is largely a novelistic re-writing of *Os Sertões* (*Rebellion in the Backlands*), Euclides da Cunha's famous account of the Canudos War, a major traumatic military-political event in Brazilian national history at the end of the nineteenth century. A large community of mostly poor rural folk, led by the charismatic, millenarian preacher Antônio Conselheiro, had sought to establish an autonomous territory, a religious commune, in the north-eastern Brazilian backlands of Bahia. It was an attempt to withdraw from what the community regarded as an increasingly overbearing federal government and the economic hardships wrought in the countryside by agricultural modernization and a prolonged period of drought. Gerald Michael Greenfield highlights the effects of the Great Drought of 1877 to 1879 on the Northeast of Brazil and the unwillingness of urban coastal elites to understand the hardships of rural life and the forced migration of *retirantes* (drought-stricken rural peasants):

> Instead, elite discourse created a landscape filled with lazy *sertanejos*, indolent and arrogant *fazendeiros* wedded to their *rotina* [traditional agricultural practices], and ineffective government policy. The *sertão* could flourish—as could all Brazil—if only the masses were uplifted, the stranglehold of the *rotina* abolished, and rational, modern techniques encouraged by a progressive state (400).

This attitude to rural backlanders became a self-perpetuating myth as the cycle of droughts continued into the last decade of the century. Alarmed by the image of an autonomous territory within the new republic, the national army was sent in to disperse the community, but the first three military campaigns ended in defeat and humiliation. A final, ferocious assault destroyed the settlement.

The Canudos Massacre, as it is also referred to, occurred at a unique juncture in Brazilian history: the struggle between the forces of republicanism and monarchism, the coastal elites and the landed oligarchy, during the tumultuous decade of the 1890s. The event became the most potent symbol of the newly-formed republic's search for a sense of national identity and unity in the face of an uncertain future. Vargas Llosa claims that *The War of the End of the World* had its gestation ten years earlier in the context of the jailing of the dissident Cuban poet Herberto Padilla in 1971 for allegedly counter-revolutionary writings. It was during these "years of ideological crisis" ("El arte nuevo" 12) that he became aware of the story of the Canudos massacre ("El arte nuevo" 12). He believed he had found the outline of a recognizable template, in which "one could see in a palpable, flagrant way, the deformations which you can arrive at if you impose an ideological vision on real experience"; "[it] imposed itself on me as a topic to write about" (12).

Raymond Souza regards the struggle between Conselheiro and ill-fated General Moreira César as the principal ideological battle in *The War of the End of the World* (80). This may well have been so in the historical event, but in the novel, the more interesting ideological struggles involve the three intellectuals: Galileo Gall (a roving anarchist revolutionary), the Baron of Cañabrava (a monarchist landowner), and the near-sighted journalist (unnamed in the novel), who all filter events through their own political-philosophical viewpoint. The sheer novelistic space ceded to the intellectual figures makes it clear that Gall, the Baron, and the journalist establish the ideological grid through which Vargas Llosa's literary construct will critique the struggle between modernization and rural traditionalism, the past and the present. Each, in their own way, is prisoner to ideological blindness, though Gall and the Baron are also prisoners to sexual repression, which influences their ideological perspectives and serves to "explain" their deviant actions. It follows that revolutionary activity and other forms of "fanaticism" and dogmatism are related to a denial of sexual and bodily pleasure. No less than three of the main characters—Conselheiro, Gall, and the Baron—practice sexual abstinence for years and pay the price through an unbalanced sense of judgment (Conselheiro and Gall also pay with their lives). This kind of heavy-handed Freudianism is one of the least satisfying aspects of *The War of the End of the World*.[3]

The question of morality has always been Vargas Llosa's major preoccupation in both his literary and non-literary considerations of politics and history. He juxtaposes morality to what he regards as the "idolatry of history," taking his cue from Franco-Algerian novelist Albert Camus. In his early essays first collected under the title *Entre Sartre y Camus*, 1981 (Between Sartre and Camus) he was eager to associate himself with Camus' Hellenistic moralism, since it speaks for values in balance with human needs, aspirations, and possibilities. In one of these essays, "Albert Camus y la moral de los límites" ("Albert Camus or the Morality of Limits") he writes of "the cult of artistic beauty and the dialogue with nature; restraint, tolerance and social diversity; the balance between the individual and society; a democratic arrangement of both rational and the irrational factors in life and a rigorous respect for freedom... [a] relative utopia" (112). To achieve such a relative utopian balance of forces and desires, Vargas Llosa refers us to Camus' appeal to moral behavior. We must "reject fanaticism, recognize our own ignorance, the limits of the world and man (...) admit that an adversary might be right, let him express himself and agree to reflect on his arguments" ("Albert Camus o la moral de los límites" 94).[4] It is difficult to disagree with such intentions, though Vargas Llosa does not always adhere to his own rules. The problem, however, is how to arbitrate in situations where groups or individuals *are* aware of each other's position and reasoning and still cannot agree. If dialogue, argument, and understanding fail to throw off the yoke of an oppressor, then recourse to arms might remain the only avenue for transformative action, as in Cuba before the revolution.

But violence begets violence and has a way of spiraling out of control beyond the original parameters of a conflict. This is what concerned Camus during the Algerian War (1954–62): both the violence done to the *pied noir* by nationalist, Arab radicals and that done to Arab nationalists by the French military, both in Algeria and in France. He thus became a pacifist over Algeria. The difference surely lies in his inability to break free of affective ties to the *pied noir* community; in short, to "historicize" his own perspective.[5] Whatever might be wrong with Sartre's philosophy (which Vargas Llosa came to reject), he seems right to have supported Algerian independence. But while Vargas Llosa champions Camus' supposed pacifism, he seems to have had no issue with Camus' active participation in the French Resistance to German fascist occupation of France in WWII. In other words, armed resistance in a case of oppression does not have the same legitimacy if it is carried out by the Left or by traditional, pre-modern societies. Vargas Llosa thus follows Camus into a metaphysical explanation for events that often have more pragmatic and historically understandable causes.

The Baron of Cañabrava in *The War of the End of the World* encapsulates much of the Camusian philosophy adopted by Vargas Llosa and many of the Baron's pronouncements read as if loosely paraphrasing Camus himself in *L'homme révolté*: "a strange breed, idealists" (244); "that stupid, incomprehensible history, of blind and stubborn peoples, of opposing fanaticisms" (533). But the Baron is an unconvincing character: Vargas Llosa spreads the righteous moral center between the journalist and the Baron, and even though the Baron is undone by the plot towards the end (the rape scene), he is nevertheless portrayed as politically coherent and "reasonable." But his past is hidden from analysis, even though such estate owners often figure in Brazilian history as monarchist fanatics and notorious exploiters, as Ángel Rama has pointed out.[6] The idealists in *The War of the End of the World*, principally Moreira César, Gall, and Conselheiro, are each rigid in their commitment to political ideals and their intention to make them a concrete reality. The Baron sees the same dogmatism in Pajeú, one of Conselheiro's feared lieutenants, who has channeled his formerly violent life as a bandit into an equally resolute subservience to the dictates of his charismatic leader. He has come to the Baron's hacienda for the express purpose of burning it down: "The Baron recognized that tone of voice; it was that of the Capuchin Fathers of the Sacred Missions, that of the sanctimonious wandering sects who made pilgrimages to Monte Santo, that of Moreira César, that of Galileo Gall. The tone of absolute certainty, he thought, the tone of those who are never assailed by doubts" (245). The Baron tries to reason with Pajeú, but to no avail: "it was as if the world had taken leave of its reason and blind, irrational beliefs had taken over" (246). Characters in *The War of the End of the World* are thus often set up to deconstruct themselves (most noticeably the revolutionary Gall), either through espousing farcical beliefs or through immoral and corrupt actions. If not hoisted by their own words and actions, an intrusive narrator (as with the interpretation of Pajéu) draws the conclusions for the reader in didactic asides about dogma, fanaticism, and bankrupt foreign ideologies, counterpointed to the simple virtues of love, childhood, and friendship.[7] While we cannot demand that literary discourse mimic the known historical record in some kind of dour reflectionism, we can debate the general contours of the real historical period and the ideological matrix through which they are portrayed, especially in an avowedly historical novel of a major catastrophic event. The fictional Canudos War is presented as a tragic "misunderstanding," due to lack of communication (the Camusian theme Vargas Llosa reiterates to explain historical struggles). The implication is that if the contending sides had understood each other's concerns and motives, the conflict would have been avoided. But there is no good reason to accept this proposition. Conselheiro and his community chose to withdraw from coastal progressivism; for its part, the republic chose not to let them do so. This is not to say that the violence could not have been ameliorated in some way by dialogue. But to imagine a congenial conversation resolving the issue is simplistic. Robert M. Levine's revisionist history, *Vale of Tears: Revisiting the Canudos Massacre in North-eastern Brazil, 1893–1897*, convincingly shows that both groups were, in many respects, quite aware of each other's point of view. Nor were the residents all religious zealots.[8] Nonetheless, they had diametrically opposed projects: autonomy versus republican consolidation of the national territory. Yet Vargas Llosa readily accepts and narrativizes the popular and conventional historical version propagated by da Cunha about crazed religious fanatics. But the perpetuation of this myth, even if in forgivable ignorance (to be fair, Vargas Llosa did not have access to revisionist histories like those of Levine), fits neatly with Vargas Llosa's own view that traditional societies are destined to die out or be incorporated—acculturated—into the modern nation and that the popular classes are ignorant and easily led.[9] The latter clearly animates his invective against scurrilous ideologues who take advantage of ignorance to enact utopian, collectivist fantasies.

---

One does not have to practice esoteric literary criticism, then, to unearth a hidden ideology in Vargas Llosa's writing: he would readily admit to core political values of individual liberty and laissez-faire capitalism. One finds these political-philosophical in his novels (at least since *Conversation in The Cathedral*) and in his extra-literary political writings. They bear the impress of not only Vargas Llosa's personal experience, but also the political views of Camus and the liberal political philosophers he cites as political influences, namely, Isaiah Berlin, Friedrich von Hayek, and Karl Popper.[10] Their opposition to what they regard as totalitarian tendencies in any Leftist political philosophy orients the intentional moral-political center implied in *The War of the End of the World* and elsewhere in his narrative (epistemologically skeptical, classically liberal), readily discernible in key dialogues between major characters and in narrative commentary. The novel is, among other things then, a fictional *mise en scène* of this personal ideology. Unfortunately, Vargas Llosa's championing of skepticism doesn't go all the way: he ends up in performative contradiction by declaring his own unbending commitment to a particular political ideology (libertarianism in the U.S. conservative sense of the word; see Bell-Villada 149), while excoriating others for doing the same, which is precisely the thing that skepticism is supposed to guard against, in order to avert fanaticism and tyranny. For this reason, therefore, Vargas Llosa does not often argue well politically either inside or out of his fiction, which often draws the scorn of the Left. For William Rowe: "the style of his discourse is polemics, a style that includes an invitation of *ad hominem* argument in order to advance its claim to superior moral capital" (45).

In his fictional Canudos, Vargas Llosa tries to steer a path between the two alternatives: on the one side, supposedly atavistic and retrograde collectivism; on the other, the constructivist rationalism of the coastal positivists. And by parodying the socialist and anarchist ideals embodied in the revolutionary character Galileo Gall, the only path left open (the only one not criticized) becomes the type of social order Hayek champions, which unifies the novelistic construct at the level of values. For all the litany of complaints about constructivist rationalism, however, both Vargas Llosa and Hayek themselves resort to rational argument when deciding between courses of actions and principles to be followed. But which deployment of reason will be considered acceptable and which unacceptable? Increasingly, unacceptable uses of reason simply become the preserve of one's ideological opponents and criticisms are based on moral grounds: the immorality of collectivist engineering of society versus the immorality of capitalist, possessive individualism. These are rival readings of reality that cannot accept each other's existence. It is also pretty much the same tension that lay between the Canudos community and the Brazilian government. This in no way is meant to imply that Vargas Llosa is necessarily wrong or right in his political views (that is an argument for comparative politics), but rather that he changes the philosophical rules to suit the moment.

Vargas Llosa's narrative trajectory after *The War of the End of the World* remained firmly fixed on Peru for many years. His next major work, *The Real Life of Alejandro Mayta* (1984), tells the story of an ex-leftist revolutionary, Alejandro Mayta, painted with similar satirical strokes to those used to portray Galileo Gall in *The War of the End of the World*, and continues to mine its author's preoccupations with fanaticism. The narrator's personal history—a period at San Marcos University alongside Mayta and fame as an internationally-recognized novelist—runs parallel to that of the author. The narrator sets out to investigate Mayta's life and relate his trajectory from revolutionary idealism through failure to indifference. Each chapter is dedicated to an interview with one of the people who have known Mayta, portraying him variously as naïve young student, fanatical revolutionary, CIA stooge, and homosexual, until the last chapter, which recounts a meeting between the narrator and Mayta himself. Progressively expelled from one group after another, Mayta eventually becomes involved with an equally bizarre fellow revolutionary, Lieutenant Vallejos. The portrait that emerges is of Mayta as a pathetic and confused figure and no doubt a stand-in for all Leftists. Vargas Llosa returns to the familiar theme of the contrast between literature and ideology and to the question of fiction:

literature's fictive representations of the real world are morally defensible because writing entails the free rein of invention and is thus a valuable source for the construction and replenishment of the social and cultural imaginary; ideology, on the other hand, posits the fiction of an objective, scientific knowledge of society and history, thereby creating a false appreciation of reality, which often leads to violence and destruction. The novel is peppered with discussions of left-wing thought and revolutionary strategy, some of which has an authentic ring and which promises an ambiguous and open dénouement to the main narrative. Nevertheless, such dissenting political viewpoints are firmly subordinated to narrative control and interpretation and the primacy of individualism and the liberal nation-state as the cure for Peru's social and economic discontent.

Like *The War of the End of the World*, the novel is loosely based around a real historical event, the attack on Jauja prison in 1958 by a Trotskyist revolutionary group composed mainly of high school students. The uprising ended in failure and the death of its two main leaders. In the novel, however, Mayta survives and is jailed. After his release from prison, he is accused of taking part in a bank robbery and, later, a kidnapping. By the time the narrator meets him face to face at the end of the novel, Mayta has been out of jail for only one month. In the last chapter, Vargas Llosa springs a few narrative surprises: Mayta is not dead after all and, like the myopic journalist in *The War of the End of the World*, has become a chastened individual distanced from Peruvian politics. It also turns out he was never a homosexual at all. The meeting with the narrator provides the occasion for Mayta to deconstruct himself, so to speak, via a vacillating account of the past (not dissimilar to the ramblings in free indirect discourse of the revolutionary in *The War of the End of the World*), running in counter-point to the narrator's leading questions and to his role as center of moral propriety in the novel. Sara Castro-Klarén sees an obvious problem in this scenario:

> Mayta is unconvincing because his revolutionary project is never unfolded for the reader's consideration. It is a secret, a vague hope, a senseless crisscrossing of activities that seem unjustifiable. Mayta, in

fact, never had a chance in real life, nor does he get a chance in this fictional pseudobiography of the historical referent (196).

As with *The War* and the anarchist Gall, the individual (the focus of Vargas Llosa's politics and morality) dissolves into tendentious caricature. Vargas Llosa thus seems to display an anxiety about reader reception, a worry that the reader might not draw the appropriate conclusion about irrationality and fanaticism. More surprising and inappropriate in the closing pages is the ploy by which the narrator reveals that all this has been invention:

> Of course I've changed dates, places, characters, I've created complications, added and even taken away thousands of things. Besides, I've invented an apocalyptic Peru, devastated by war, terrorism, and foreign intervention (...) I've pretended as well that we were schoolmates, that we were the same age, and lifelong friends (288).

Vargas Llosa here draws attention to the artifice at the heart of fiction—the pact of suspension of belief between writer and reader—and then proceeds to destroy it. This is surely a deliberate attempt to persuade us of the novelist's "narrative honesty," but it transgresses the most fundamental narrative conventions of the novel genre, in effect unraveling not only the carefully and painstakingly constructed biography produced by the narrator, but also the very sincerity of the narrator as character. These seemingly capricious revelations about "lying" lack structural coherence: whimsical imagination undermines the moral lesson Vargas Llosa appears to wants to impart. But you can't have your referent and eat it, too. The irony should not be lost that this is a writer who very much wants his representations of Latin American civil strife to be taken seriously. Consider one example of this performative contradiction. Mayta's biographer/narrator defines his task as to write a fiction that is closer to the truth than the real events:

> It won't be the real story, but, just as you say, a novel (...) A faint, remote, and, if you like, false version.

—Then why work so hard at it? (...) Why not just lie and make the whole thing up from top to bottom?

—Because I'm a realist, in my novels I always try to lie knowing why I do it ...That's how I work. And I think the only way to write stories is to start with History (66–7).

*The Real Life of Alejandro Mayta*, as with *The War of the End of the World*, is thus ambivalently poised as a literary discourse that wishes to retain its constitutive being—its fictiveness—but also wishes to present itself as exemplary allegory, as having a readable referential function. But allegory, by definition, reduces polysemy. If there is a "truth" to literature (if we wish to make such a claim), it is merely that it knows it is fiction. When it forgets this and masquerades as didactic parable, it collapses into a kind of political propaganda and takes on a transcendental force. Of course, this depends on whether one agrees with the idea that literature is the perpetual denial of its own referentiality, or whether one believes that literary realism is really "real." The combined effect on Vargas Llosa's narrative is an elaborate defense of a method, which cedes all rights of invention to the literary writer, but recognizes no responsibilities other than to be persuasive; in short, the ideal vehicle with which to attack one's opponents, whilst securely quarantining one's own views within appeals to artistic autonomy.

The international reception of Vargas Llosa's novels is often predicated on ignorance of the historical realities to which they do, in fact, refer. Consider the extract from the review in *New Society*, which is quoted on the back cover of the 1987 edition of the English translation of *The Real Life of Alejandro Mayta*: "brave, superbly written work which strips bare self-indulgent insurrection and shows its descent into squalid criminality." This pat thesis—Mayta's turn to crime after the failure of his misguided idealism—seems to construct for the metropolitan reader the stereotypical image of Latin America many seek to re-confirm.

In the 1993 *El Pez en el Agua* (*A Fish in the Water*, 1994), Vargas Llosa reviews his Calvary—his failed presidential political campaign—punctuated by the story of his first departure for and stay in Paris. It provides the opportunity for literary revenge against both his enemies and many of those who were his campaign allies and friends. The impression of the author is characteristically one of self-righteousness and embitterment, admitting no mistakes, save that of naïveté vis-à-vis the realities of electoral politics:

> It was ingenuous on my part to believe that Peruvians would vote for ideas. They voted the way people do in an underdeveloped democracy, and sometimes in the mature ones as well—on the basis of images, myths, heartthrobs, or on account of obscure feelings and resentments with no particular connection to processes of reason (81).

For more than two decades after the Padilla Affair, then, Vargas Llosa's narrative imagination was subordinated to an increasingly familiar and shrill denunciation of irrationalism, fanaticism, and Leftist ideology. It would not be until the 2000 *La fiesta del chivo* (*The Feast of the Goat*, 2001) that he would make a triumphant return to his best work: the anti-statist, neoliberal politics had not changed, but the art had begun to reassert its power over easy moralizing.

## Notes

1. The essay will use the titles of the translation after the first mention of a Vargas Llosa novel.

2. In this case, as in that of all works in Spanish in the Works Cited list, the translation is by the author of this essay.

3. Vargas Llosa frequently associated sexual orientation with corruption in his novels up to the 1980s. Besides three of the main characters in *The War of the End of the World* displaying bad moral judgment due to lack of control of their sexual desires, Zavala's corrupt father in *Conversation in The Cathedral* is exposed as Lima's most renowned homosexual and Mayta is first portrayed as a homosexual only to be "redeemed" by the narrator at the end, once he has shed his ideological delusions.

4. This passage has been omitted from the English translation of "Albert Camus y la moral de los límites."

5. For a fascinating discussion of Camus' politics and his relation with Sartre, see Peter Royle's *The Sartre-Camus Controversy*.

6.  "He is the only political, economic and social force that accepts, without a struggle, his defeat, which makes the republican campaign against him unreal and unintelligible (...) In order to paint his character in *claroscuro*, it would have been enough to reflect on the operations that provided his wealth" (Rama 633).

7.  A similar opposition is established between Vargas Llosa's non-fictional political writings and his Leftist opponents: liberal individualism versus socialism. Both of these propose different versions of modernity, but modernity nonetheless. For all his parodying of da Cunha, Vargas Llosa thus holds a remarkably similar view on at least one major issue: collectivist communities are archaic throwbacks and their prolongation into Western modernity is irrational.

8.  According to Levine, Canudos was not a rebellion *per se*, as da Cunha chose to describe it, but merely a rejection of the state and withdrawal from its influence. In no way did the Canudos settlement represent a violent threat; rather violence was done to it: "What outsiders chose to see as a rebellion was, in fact, a collective statement by a unified community demanding the right to live in a place they considered a haven from an unfriendly world" (228).

9.  Writing ten years after the appearance of *The War of the End of the World*, Vargas Llosa would still declare: "The price they [the Indians] must pay for integration is high—renunciation of their culture, their language, their beliefs, their traditions and customs, and the adoption of the culture of their ancient masters [...] Perhaps there is no realistic way to integrate our societies other than by asking the Indians to pay that price" ("Questions" 52–3). Interestingly, only four years later, and after having left Peru to take up Spanish citizenship after his failed presidential bid, Vargas Llosa seemed to have a change of heart. In "Nations, Fictions" (originally published in *Desafíos a la libertad*, 1994) he adopts a skeptical stance towards all nation-states and their modernizing projects: "No nation has arisen naturally (...) we find [in nations] pitilessly destroyed those 'contradictions and differences'—creeds, races, customs and languages, which are not always minority—which the nation (...) needs to destroy in order to feel safe, to guard against the risk of fragmentation" (301).

10. Hayek, in particular, seems to have been very influential in Vargas Llosa's political thinking. Hayek's key indicator of totalitarian tendencies is the restriction of the free market and the attempt

to substitute for it collective, centralized control. Fascism and communism are seen as having grown out of socialist tendencies increasingly manifest from the end of the nineteenth century. These, in turn, are seen as arising out of rationalist constructivism, which dates back to Descartes and Rousseau and initiates a line of thought that aimed at the constitution of a utopia. In contrast, Hayek proposes the capitalist market as a spontaneous and historically evolved system, nothing more than free individuals producing and choosing according to their individual needs (See Hayek, esp. 73–91, 215–31).

## Works Cited

Bell-Villada, Gene H. "Sex, Politics, and High Art: Vargas Llosa's Long Road to *The Feast of the Goat.*" *Vargas Llosa and Latin American Politics*. Eds. Juan E. De Castro & Nicholas Birns. New York: Palgrave, 2010. 139–57.

Camus, Albert. *L'homme révolté*. Paris: Les Éditions Gallimard, 1951.

Castro-Klarén, Sara. *Understanding Mario Vargas Llosa*. Columbia: U of South Carolina P, 1990.

Greenfield, Gerald Michael. "The Great Drought and Elite Discourse in Imperial Brazil." *Hispanic American Historical Review* 72 (1992): 375–400.

Hayek, Friedrich von. *The Constitution of Liberty: The Definitive Edition*. Ed. Ronald Hamovy. London: Routledge, 2013.

Rowe, William. "Liberalism and Authority: The Case of Mario Vargas Llosa." *On Edge: The Crisis of Contemporary Latin American Culture*. Eds. G. Yúdice, J. Flores, & J. Franco. Minneapolis: U of Minnesota P, 1992. 45–64.

Royle, Peter. *The Sartre-Camus Controversy: A Literary and Philosophical Critique*. Ottawa: U of Ottawa P, 1982.

Setti, Ricardo A. *Diálogo con Vargas Llosa*. México: Editorial Kosmos, 1988.

Souza, Raymond. *La historia en la novela hispanoamericana moderna*. Bogotá: Tercer Mundo, 1988.

Vargas Llosa, Mario. "Albert Camus and the Morality of Limits." *Making Waves: Essays*. Trans. John King. New York: Penguin, 1998. 107–16.

_____. "Albert Camus o la moral de los límites." *Entre Sartre y Camus*. San Juan: Ediciones el Huracán, 1981. 79–108.

_____. *The War of the End of the World*. Trans. Helen R. Lane. New York: Farrar, Strauss & Giroux, 1984.

_____. *The Real Life of Alejandro Mayta*. London: Faber & Faber, 1987.

_____. "El arte nuevo de escribir novelas clásicas." Interview with Ana María Moix. *Quimera* 14 (December 1981): 10–13.

_____. "Questions of conquest: What Columbus wrought, and what he did not." *Harper's Magazine* 281.1687 (December 1990): 45–51.

_____. *A Fish in the Water*. Trans. Helen R. Lane. London: Faber & Faber, 1994.

_____. "Nations, Fictions." *Making Waves*. London: Faber & Faber, 1996.

# The Real Life of Alejandro Mayta and The Storyteller: Success at Last for Mario Vargas Llosa's Professional Narrators

Jean O'Bryan-Knight

Beginning with Alberto, the adolescent pornographer of his first novel, and continuing through Mascarita, the Amazonian bard of his ninth, storyteller characters appear repeatedly throughout the first half of Mario Vargas Llosa's career. Their study permits us to identify clear trends that, in turn, help us see where the Peruvian novelist stood in the 1980s, at the midpoint of his own development as a professional narrator.

This essay will start out with an overview of storyteller characters from Vargas Llosa's novels published before 1984 that serves as introduction to a more sustained study of the two novels in which this figure is central: *Historia de Mayta*, 1984 (*The Real Life of Alejandro Mayta*, 1986) and *El hablador*, 1987 (*The Storyteller* 1989).[1] Before proceeding, however, a clarification of terms is in order. The focus here will be on professional narrators, that is, those characters that identify themselves as writers or storytellers and are identified as such by their communities, which compensate them in some way for their efforts. Alberto of *La ciudad y los perros*, 1963 (*The Time of the Hero* 1966) is a good example. After he composes ten notebook pages of erotic fantasy, he credits himself with having begun his career as novelist. Impressed with their classmate's talent, his fellow cadets dub him "the poet" and begin to treat him with a respect he had not previously enjoyed in the military academy, and they even pay him for his racy pages.

Other memorable professional narrators from Vargas Llosa's novels include Zavalita, the mediocre journalist of *Conversación en La Catedral*, 1969 (*Conversation in The Cathedral*, 1975);[2] the Sinchi, the sensationalist radio journalist who controls the airwaves in *Pantaleón y las visitadoras*, 1973 (*Captain Pantoja and the Special Service* 1979); Pedro Camacho, the scriptwriter of radio soap operas, and Marito, the teenage apprentice writer in *La tía Julia y el escribidor*, 1977 (*Aunt Julia and the Scriptwriter* 1982); the myopic journalist, the dwarf bard, and the freak scribe, of *La guerra del fin del mundo*, 1981 (*The War of the End of the World,* 1984); the unnamed novelists who narrate in *The Real Life of Alejandro Mayta* and *The Storyteller*; and Saúl Zuratas, the Machiguenga *hablador* who also appears in *The Storyteller*.

Besides sharing a common profession as narrators, perhaps the only characteristics that unify this group are that all of the above are male, and nearly all are Peruvian. Beyond this, the group is hard to classify. They appear as both protagonists and secondary characters. Some tell stories orally, others in print; and their stories span a number of fiction and non-fiction genres. How do we make sense of this variety? If we evaluate these figures according to their overall levels of self-fulfillment, measured in terms of professional accomplishment and personal integrity, some tendencies emerge.

In *The Time of the Hero*, Alberto initially appears to be a strong individual when he befriends the outcast known as the Slave and subsequently attempts to bring another student, Jaguar, to justice for his friend's murder. However, when the colonel threatens to expose Alberto as a deviant, should he persist in his assertion that Jaguar shot the Slave, he is quick to recant and thereby reveals himself to be a morally weak, social conformist, whose sense of right and wrong is subordinated to his sense of self-preservation. Unlike Alberto, Santiago Zavala, the protagonist of *Conversation in The Cathedral*, rejects his privileged class and its values. Although he has an inclination for poetry, Zavalita's decision to become a reporter demonstrates a deliberate attempt to break away from the corrupt and exploitative world of Lima's elite. However, avoiding corruption is not the same as overcoming it. At the newspaper, Zavalita barely ekes out a living writing inconsequential editorials. Although morally superior to Alberto, this writer is certainly no success, and his unrealized potential echoes that of his country. Unlike Zavalita, the Sinchi, an influential secondary character in *Captain Pantoja and the Special Service,* engages in sensationalist journalism. He claims to broadcast in the name of truth and justice, but his program is comprised of cliches, commercials, and scandalous details obtained through unprofessional practices. His fervent nationalism, the sycophantic flattery he heaps upon his listeners, and his constant appeals to morality are merely a smokescreen for self-promotion. As the Sinchi demonstrates, journalistic power, when obtained immorally and exercised irresponsibly, only adds to Peru's problems.

The narrator characters we have examined thus far have been thwarted or deficient individuals, and their situations as storytellers have been secondary concerns of the works in which they appear. *Aunt Julia and the Scriptwriter*, therefore, marks a turning point in Vargas Llosa's narrative because, here, the predicament of the professional narrator is the focal point of the work. The two main characters, Marito and Pedro Camacho, are writers whose careers diverge radically as the novel progresses. Marito, who is based on the real author's experiences as an adolescent, wants desperately to grow up and become a successful fiction writer. In the meantime, he practices by plagiarizing news wires for radio broadcasts and composing short stories that inevitably wind up in the trash. After a protracted, often hilarious struggle, Marito demonstrates his emotional maturity by marrying the older woman he loves, and the couple goes abroad to pursue the young man's literary dreams. In the last chapter, which serves as an epilogue, we catch up with mature Mario decades later. The marriage did not work out, but the writing did. He has remarried and, more importantly, is a published author who has produced a number of novels, including the one we hold in our hands. Mario's personal and professional achievements make him Vargas Llosa's first fully successful professional narrator, and the story of his ascent stands in marked contrast to that of his mentor's decline.

Bolivian radio scriptwriter Pedro Camacho is introduced in the first chapter of *Aunt Julia and the Scriptwriter* at the apex of his career. He is wildly popular among Lima's radio listeners, who crave his melodramatic stories of family intrigue laced with sex and violence. For the young apprentice, the remarkably productive scriptwriter is a model of dedication to his craft. Camacho is the only real writer Marito has ever known, and the teenager finds much to admire in him, including his work ethic and his single-minded dedication to his craft. As the novel progresses, however, it becomes clear that Camacho is self-destructing. His inability to keep various story lines straight is the first symptom of a breakdown that eventually lands him in an asylum. His failure, both personal and professional, is absolute. In the epilogue, mature Mario finds Camacho reduced to the lowly position of messenger boy at a lurid tabloid, where his coworkers ridicule him for being a cuckold. Mario's triumph in Europe, when considered in light of Camacho's decline and fall in Lima, seems to suggest that sustained success as a writer is possible only if one first quits Peru.

Because the narrator's own formation as a young novelist is the focal point of his story, and because he so closely resembles the real author, *Aunt Julia and the Scriptwriter* presents us with a narrative situation that is without precedent in the works of Vargas Llosa. Prior to 1977, Vargas Llosa entirely avoided the use of personal or dramatized narrators in favor of impersonal or "invisible narrators."[3] That is, he favored disembodied voices that relate the events of the story from the perspective of objective observer. He even asserted that it was incumbent upon the novelist to disguise the autobiographical content of his creations. Given these beliefs, why then did Vargas Llosa take up the project of representing himself in his fiction, and why did he choose an autobiographical narrator to do it? Perhaps he wanted to entice a wider readership by offering a glimpse of a literary celebrity's piquant personal life. Or perhaps the decision was made in response to the need to find a realistic story to counterbalance the unrealistic soap opera chapters of the novel, as the author himself has suggested (*A Writer's Reality* 110–11). Whatever the reason, Vargas Llosa must have been pleased with the result because he returned to further develop this new narrative situation not once but twice, first in *The Real Life of Alejandro Mayta* and again in *The Storyteller.* However, before considering these novels in detail, we should not overlook the next novel in which storytellers appear, *The War of the End of the World.*

*The War of the End of the World* presents us with three professional narrators, all physically limited men who gain social acceptance thanks to their storytelling talents. The Lion of Natuba is a freak who is cast off by his own family because he walks on all fours. He joins the religious community at Canudos in the Brazilian backlands, where he puts his literary talents to use as the messianic Counselor's official scribe. The Dwarf is a storyteller in the tradition of the ancient troubadours. In Canudos, he captivates his audience with chivalric tales that earn protection and sustenance for himself and his friends. The myopic journalist is sent to Canudos as a war correspondent. Ironically, he never actually sees the events he is supposed to cover because, before he reaches the battlefront, his glasses are broken, rendering him all but blind. Although merely an observer in the epic conflict, the myopic journalist voices a central theme of the novel, which is that the slaughter at Canudos is the result of a complete and total misunderstanding. Although by no means unmitigated successes, these three narrators may be viewed as more positive figures by virtue of their service to their communities.[4] Furthermore, by including this set of narrators in *The War of the End of the World,* Vargas Llosa shows us that his interest in storytellers carries over into the 1980s, and it is in this decade that his professional narrator characters take center stage and command our full attention.

Without a doubt, Vargas Llosa remains quite taken with the figure of the storyteller because, in his next novel after *The War of the End of the World,* he returns to the character of the novelist-narrator. This time, however, the successful Peruvian writer that resembles the real author makes more than a cameo appearance in the coda as he did in *Aunt Julia and the Scriptwriter.* In *The Real Life of Alejandro Mayta* the unnamed narrator is dramatized from the outset as the central figure in the story. We first catch up with him while he is out jogging in Barranco, his well-to-do neighborhood in Lima. In addition to being health-conscious and a man of means, the narrator is a concerned citizen. He runs past piles of trash, and this causes him to reflect on his nation's problems—poverty, corruption, insecurity, and the politically motivated violence that is tearing

Peru apart. Not only does this thoughtful individual possess a social conscience, he has a strong work ethic. After completing his run, the narrator gets right down to work on his next novel.

The first nine chapters of *The Real Life of Alejandro Mayta* feature the narrator conducting interviews in the narrative present with relatives, acquaintances, and former comrades of Alejandro Mayta, an obscure leftist revolutionary who, twenty-five years earlier, failed in his attempt to ignite a class war in the Peruvian highlands. These conversations are interspersed with excerpts from the work in progress that portrays the fictional Mayta involved in the planning and execution of that aborted rebellion. These fragments also present engrossing scenes from Mayta's private life as a closeted homosexual. The transitions between what is fictionally real (the interviews conducted in 1983) and what is fictionally false (the passages featuring Mayta's public and private life in 1958) are masterfully seamless. Thanks to these smooth temporal shifts we glide from one narrative plane to the other as we watch the novelist spin documentary evidence into an intriguing portrait of a political fanatic.

The informants give partial and inconsistent testimonies. For example, according to his godmother, Doña Josefa, Mayta was a pious innocent until he was corrupted by the fiendish Lieutenant Vallejos, the real mastermind behind the uprising. However, Vallejos' sister, Juanita, blames Mayta for having manipulated her young and impressionable brother into an evil endeavor that resulted in his early death. Despite these contradictions, the portrait of the revolutionary that emerges in the embedded narrative is consistent and convincing. In the excerpts, Mayta comes across as a well-intentioned, but utterly irrational, ideologue. He identifies with the poor and clearly wants to end their suffering. A lapsed Catholic, he puts his faith in Marxism's promise of an egalitarian utopia on earth. Mayta knows that the political left in Lima is splintered and that the Trotskyists and the Stalinists are too busy fighting one another to organize against the capitalists. And he might never have made the switch from revolutionary theory to practice had he not met Vallejos, the attractive young officer with socialist sympathies, a penchant for action, and a cache of weapons. Mayta's political fanaticism blinds him to the fact that he and his comrade lack the broad support necessary for a successful uprising. Nevertheless, he presses ahead with his absurd plan to initiate a rebellion in the highland city of Jauja. Likewise, Mayta knows he is ill-suited to the role of armed insurgent in the sierra. He is a middle-aged man who has read all the leftist literature, but who has never fired a gun before in his life. He has flat feet, a physical limitation that should render him unfit for combat. And he is fluent in French, a linguistic skill that will not help him explain to the Quechua speakers in the Andes why he and his handful of comrades are rebelling on their behalf. Mayta, in the embedded narrative, is on a collision course with failure, and as the impact approaches, it is hard for us to look away. The narrator, however, insists that we do by repeatedly interrupting the excerpts to shift our attention back to the narrative present, where he is still trying to extract information from eyewitnesses.

The novelist reminds his informants that they should not be afraid to share with him their recollections of Mayta because, in the end, it is not a biography or a history that he will publish, but a novel. He explains that he wants to uncover the truth about the leftist revolutionary, so that he can use it as a basis for his own lies: "Because I'm a realist, in my novels I always try to lie knowing why I do it . . . That's how I work. And I think the only way to write stories is to start with History—with a capital H" (67). Curiously, although he has a lot to say on the subject of how his novel gets written, the narrator does not really have an answer to the question of why it should be written at all. When asked why he bothers to write a novel as Peru, in the mid 1980s, slides into the abyss, he explains rather feebly that "No matter how ephemeral it is, a novel is something, while despair is nothing" (79). In the destruction that surrounds him, he finds impetus for his art, but he has trouble articulating how that art is a form of social engagement. However, we can appreciate that his efforts are more socially responsible than Mayta's. At least his obsession with his novel will not result in the death of anyone.

The country in the narrative present is indeed on the edge of the apocalypse. The Cold War has heated up and foreign forces are preparing to engage on Peruvian soil.[5] As a result, most Peruvians that can leave have left. Nevertheless, despite having the resources to flee, the narrator stays put to finish his project, and he manages to do so with a remarkable conclusion. In chapter ten, we learn that the former revolutionary is now living in a shantytown on the outskirts of Lima. In the final interview with the real Mayta, the narrator explains that he has taken some liberties with his character in the novel. For example, he admits to having made his fictional character a homosexual, a startling revelation that causes some consternation. The real Mayta is upset because, with a wife and children and some biases left over from his prison days, he resents the characterization. And readers are discomfited to learn that, since the real Mayta is a heterosexual, then much, if not all, of what we have taken for fact in the previous nine chapters was actually fiction. Indeed, the conversation with Adelaida, the embittered former wife of the closeted homosexual, cannot possibly have occurred. And if that one interview was the narrator's invention, perhaps they all were. Clearly, we have been duped, but why?

As the novel seems to erase itself before our eyes, we scramble to make sense of it all. Have we just lent our imaginations to an incompetent or unscrupulous novelist-narrator, who does not know or does not respect the rules of the game of fiction? Turning on him at this point seems unfair, given that he has been upfront with us all along about his intent to invent. We should have seen this coming when he promised that his novel would be a pack of lies. A more satisfying explanation of the unnerving ending is that it serves to underscore the success of this storyteller. By allowing the two narrative planes to collide and crumble in the final chapter, the narrator shows us what he has been telling us all along, that his novels are fantasies constructed over a flimsy foundation of facts. At the same time, he reminds us that a novel is not a window through which we see an objective representation of the real world, but rather an alternative world contingent upon in its author's imagination. Thus, any truths we glean from the novel—truths about the dangers revolutionary socialism, for example—are products of that imagination.

So what is the real story of Alejandro Mayta? The novelist-narrator gave us a convincing portrait of a militant Marxist, and then he snatched it away, leaving us with a bit of a blur. However, this does not mean his novel fails because, in the end, the work's political lessons are subsumed under its literary ones. Yes, the novel is a damning portrait of the political fanatic, but it is also an exploration of how this novelist creates and how his creation communicates meaning. And, by juxtaposing the figures of the revolutionary and the writer, Vargas Llosa helps us see the latter more clearly. In fact, the narrator's success seems all the more apparent when measured against Mayta's failure. The powerful storyteller ultimately overshadows the weak, contradictory revolutionary and thus emerges as the real protagonist of *The Real Life of Alejandro Mayta*.

Evidently, Vargas Llosa felt there was unexploited potential in the figure of the novelist-narrator, since he returned to it just four years later in his fifth novel, *The Storyteller*. This work presents us with two professional narrators, both successful Peruvian storytellers, albeit very different ones. The first is a novelist sojourning in Florence, and the second is an *hablador*, a traditional Amazonian storyteller. These two take turns narrating the novel's six main chapters. Their alternating voices create a counterpoint that invites us to compare written and oral forms of narration and serves as a metaphor for Peru, a nation divided between modern Western and archaic indigenous cultures. The brief first and last chapters are narrated by the novelist and frame the story.

We meet the novelist in the opening chapter, and, although he never shares his name, it does not take us long to recognize the familiar figure that appeared throughout *The Real Life of Alejandro Mayta*.[6] He is spending the sweltering summer in Florence, where he looks forward to reading masterpieces of the Western canon and forgetting about his homeland. However, despite his best efforts, he cannot escape Peru. In a gallery, he sees a photograph that portrays a group of Amazonian Indians listening in rapt attention to a partially obscured figure. After some consideration, the narrator concludes that this figure must be an *hablador*, and he soon abandons his reading of Dante in favor of a new writing project about these traditional storytellers. What follows in the even-numbered chapters is his memoir of how he learned about the *habladores* and why they matter so much to him. It all started with his college friend Saúl Zuratas.

As we learn in chapter two, Saúl is something of an outsider in Lima. The son of a Christian mother and a Jewish father, he was born with a large birthmark that covers half his face, earning him the nickname 'Mascarita' (Mask Face). He keeps a pet parrot named Gregorio Samsa, after the character in Kafka's *Metamorphosis*, his favorite book. Despite his parentage and his pet, Mascarita has little time for religion or literature. A student of ethnology, his one and only interest is a small, nomadic Amazonian tribe, the Machiguenga. Since Mascarita can speak of nothing else, conversations between the friends invariably focus on the Machiguenga. The narrator enjoys provoking his pal in lively debates about the Peruvian government's responsibility toward its most primitive populations. An admirer of Western culture, he naturally argues in favor of assimilation:

> If the price to be paid for development and industrialization for the sixteen million Peruvians mean[s] that those few thousand naked Indians would have to cut their hair, wash off their tattoos, and become mestizos—or, to use the ethnologists' most detested word, become acculturated—well, there [is] no way round it (22).

Saúl counters him calmly with the preservationists' defense:

> Do our cars, guns, planes, and Coca-Colas give us the right to exterminate them because they don't have such things? Or do you believe in 'civilizing the savages,' pal? How? . . . By forcing them to change their language, their religion, and their customs, the way the missionaries are trying to do? What's to be gained by that? Being able to exploit them more easily, that's all (28).

Although these conversations take place in the mid-1950s, the land rights of forest peoples are still very much a matter of debate, something that contributes to the contemporary relevance of the novel.

In chapter four, the narrator recalls his first to visit Amazonia in 1958. There, he meets the Schneils, a couple of American missionaries who work with the Machiguenga, and they inform him of the existence of the *habladores*: "Their mouths [are] the connecting links of this society that the fight for survival [has] forced to split up and scatter to the four winds. . . the hablador not only brings current news but also speaks of the past. He is probably also the memory of the community" (92–93). The narrator is utterly enthralled by this description of the *habladores* because, as he explains to his friend: "They're the tangible proof that storytelling can be something more than mere entertainment. . . Something primordial, something that the very existence of a people may depend on" (94). In the tribal storytellers, the narrator finds validation of his own budding vocation, that of writer. After college, the two pals' paths diverge. Unexpectedly, Saúl turns down a scholarship to pursue graduate studies in ethnography in Europe and then drops out of sight in Lima. The narrator accepts the same opportunity and leaves Peru to study literature abroad on the way to becoming a writer.

More than two decades elapse between the events of the fourth chapter and the sixth. By now, the narrator has become an accomplished novelist, and he remains obsessed with the *habladores*. On his second trip to Amazonia in 1981, he seeks out the Schneils in hope of obtaining more information. They tell him of a strange *hablador* with whom they have come in contact, a fair-skinned man with a large birthmark. This revelation suggests to the narrator that his friend has undergone a startling metamorphosis by transforming himself into a Machiguenga *hablador*. This revelation also confirms what the reader by now suspects, that the narrator of the odd-numbered chapters is in fact Saúl.

Chapters three, five, and seven are structured differently from those narrated by the novelist. Rather than a chronologically ordered memoir punctuated with precise dates and proper names, they offer us a tangle of tales that is as difficult to navigate as any jungle thicket. This makes sense, given that lengthy narrative in oral cultures is handled through episodic structure. The *hablador,* who speaks for hours at a time without running out of material, rattles off creation myths, etiological tales, parables, health advice, tribal prohibitions, snippets of gossip, humorous anecdotes, history lessons, and more. He speaks with the collective voice of the community, and his authority rests on his ability to repeat what he has been told by others, as he reminds listeners after each episode: "That, anyway, is what I have learned." However, as the narration progresses, the anonymous speaker begins to reveal clues to his identity. In the final chapter of his narration (chapter seven) he tells the rambling, fanciful tale of his own transformation from one on the margins of the wandering tribe of Israel to one who sits in the center of the tribe that wanders, the Machiguenga, and he concludes his story by revealing the name of the parrot perched on his shoulder: "Mas-ca-ri-ta."

Saúl's transformation is quite an achievement for one of Vargas Llosa's narrator characters. We recall that his earlier professional narrators either stayed put in Peru and failed, or emigrated to achieve success abroad. Saúl, however, does not flee Peru as part of his professional formation. Instead, he renounces Western civilization and sets off to find himself in the interior. In so doing, he becomes Vargas Llosa's first successful storyteller to be fully formed in Peru. As the *hablador*, Saúl is the most cherished member of the tribe. His visits are eagerly anticipated and greeted with delight by an enthusiastic public. More than an entertainer, the storyteller is the repository of the tribe's identity. His stories are the powerful cultural adhesive that holds the nomadic people together over the many miles and years of wandering.[7] The *hablador* demonstrates that storytelling is the most essential form of social engagement because without it, Machiguenga society itself ceases to exist.

Of course, the *hablador* is not fictively real in the way that the novelist-narrator is. Writing alone in Florence, the novelist fashions a fiction for his ideal alter ego, a Peruvian storyteller surrounded by an adoring audience, and we should not overlook the irony here. As literacy and the technology of print appear, listeners are transformed into readers, and oral storytellers become obsolete. Thus, it was the novelist who supplanted the prehistoric bard for whom he now pines.

---

Does the *hablador*'s fictional status undercut his success? Not entirely. As we were reminded in *The Real Life of Alejandro Mayta,* all characters are, of course, products of their creator's imaginations. Like Mayta in the excerpts, the *hablador* in chapters three, five, and seven is a fictional character in an embedded narration. And like that Mayta, he is a memorable character that sticks in readers' imaginations after the story has ended. The *hablador* is unforgettable, as much for his enchanting stories as for his incredible transformation. However, it is also fair to observe that in the end the novelist's voice overpowers that of his creation. The writer gets the last word in chapter eight of *The Storyteller,* he and uses it to assert his authority as creator of this text: "I have decided that it is [Saúl] who is the storyteller in [the] photograph" (240). And on the basis of this decision he constructed the incredible and improbable story of Saúl's conversion. As the novel's title suggests, there is one storyteller here, and he is the novelist-narrator who controls this narration from beginning to end.

Since after *The Storyteller* Vargas Llosa has not returned to the figure of the professional narrator, this completes our retrospective. Over the trajectory of Vargas Llosa's career, the professional narrator has evolved from a weaker to a stronger figure as the early utter failures were followed by moderate successes that then gave way to fully realized individuals. Concurrently, the fate of the professional narrator has gradually broken free of that of his nation. He was first a failure stuck in Peru, then a success, thanks in part to time spent abroad, and finally a success from the very heart of his homeland. This evolution has been accompanied by a shift in focus on the fate of the professional narrator from peripheral to central concern of the works in which he appears. Not surprisingly, the major themes of the work shift to an examination of the creative process itself and to an analysis of the nature and function of narrative fictions. Clearly Vargas Llosa's professional narrators have evolved, but we have yet to account for this development in the context of their creator's own professional development. My conclusion will suggest a link between the two.

If we consider the broader context of Vargas Llosa's literary production, we see that *The Real Life of Alejandro Mayta* and *The Storyteller* appear midway through a career that spans some fifty years. Furthermore, these two novels, in which the professional narrators are portrayed as major successes, appear sandwiched chronologically between two major extra-literary events of the author's life, his split with the Cuban government in 1971 and his fight against Peruvian president Alan García's plan to nationalize the banks in 1987. The first event marked the beginning of the end of Vargas Llosa's allegiance to the political left, and the second marked the beginning of his association with the neoliberal free-marketeers. Thus, the novels were written during a time of transition, when the author was ideologically adrift. During this period, he turned inward to examine his own predicament, that of the successful Peruvian writer, and he did this in the medium he knows best, the novel. Twice, he represented himself as a writer at work, struggling to define and defend his role in his nation.

After finishing his storyteller cycle, the author determined that he could best serve his country by abandoning his pen for politics, and in 1990, he made his unsuccessful bid for the presidency of Peru. Thus, Vargas Llosa's ideological transformation in the 1980s was accompanied by the development of the character of the storyteller, and his efforts to make a positive place for himself in his novels preceded his attempt to take on a new role for himself in his nation.

## Notes

1. Throughout this essay publication dates refer to the first edition in Spanish.
2. Santiago Zavala later reappears as the ghostwriter in the play *Kathie and the Hippopotamus* (1983). However, because of space limitations, this essay considers only storytellers that appear in novels.
3. On the "invisible narrator," see Vargas Llosa's *The Perpetual Orgy* (167–68).
4. As Dick Gerdes observes, these three writers fulfill the three functions of narration by providing the public with entertainment, an objective

historical record, and a meaningful interpretation of that history (193).

5.   The portrayal of foreign intervention is not accurate. In the mid eighties, Peru was involved in a bloody war between leftist Shining Path guerrillas and government forces that cost some seventy thousand lives, but that did not involve international forces.

6.   This novelist-narrator that first appeared dramatized in the final chapter of *Aunt Julia and the Scriptwriter* and then throughout *The Real Life of Alejandro Mayta* is the same forty-something, successful Peruvian writer who bears an unmistakable resemblance to the real author, Mario Vargas Llosa. Like Vargas Llosa, he studied literature in the University of San Marcos in Lima in the 1950s and then lived in Europe in the 1960s, where he launched his literary career. Although technically speaking, we have before us a series of three separate novelist-narrators, it seems more in keeping with the reader's experience to speak of a single novelist-narrator who appears in a series of three novels.

7.   According to the anthropological record—which Vargas Llosa studied, but did not follow faithfully—the Machiguenga are not nomadic, and, more importantly, they do not have *habladores* (Kristal 164–168).

## Works Cited

Gerdes, Dick. *Mario Vargas Llosa.* Boston: Twayne, 1985.

Kristal, Efraín. *Temptation of the Word.* Nashville, TN: Vanderbilt UP, 1998.

Vargas Llosa, Mario. *The Perpetual Orgy: Flaubert and Madame Bovary.* Trans. Helen Lane. New York: Farrar, Straus & Giroux, 1986.

_____. *The Real Life of Alejandro Mayta.* Trans. Alfred MacAdam. New York: Farrar, Straus & Giroux, 1986.

_____. *The Storyteller.* Trans. Helen Lane. New York: Farrar, Straus & Giroux, 1989.

_____. *A Writer's Reality.* Syracuse, NY: Syracuse UP, 1991.

# Pessimism and Detection in Vargas Llosa's *Who Killed Palomino Molero?*

Miguel Rivera-Taupier

During the 1980s, Mario Vargas Llosa experimented with genre fiction with his detective novel *¿Quién mató a Palomino Molero?*, 1986 (*Who Killed Palomino Molero?*, 1987) and his erotic narrative *Elogio a la madrastra*, 1988 (*In Praise of the Stepmother*, 1990).[1] In particular, the detective genre, interested in the solution of crimes, is generally associated with mass literature. This type of literature stands opposite to the total novel that had obsessed Vargas Llosa during his early years as an author. However, the Peruvian novelist used the detective genre for his own purposes by writing a novel in which the police investigation is less important than the representation of the society that made the crime possible. This essay argues that the social pessimism characteristic of Vargas Llosa's earlier narratives is deepened in this detective novel given that, unlike what happened in his previous novels, the attempt at rebellion against the established social order is, at best, very limited.

Critics have noted that in *Who Killed Palomino Molero?* the detective action takes a background to the inequalities of the society depicted. For instance, Arnold M. Penuel argues that the novel is not interested "in establishing the identity of the perpetrators of the crime but rather in exposing the prejudices that culminate in the murder and lead to another murder and suicide" ("Uses of Literary Perspectivism"). Brent J. Carbajal points out that the novel "is ultimately less a tale of complicated sleuthing than it is a commentary on collective corruption, social injustice and base human nature" (267). Ana María Hernández de López states "racism undergirds the narration" (127).[2] One can, therefore, say that even though Vargas Llosa is working in what is for him a new genre, he is still faithful to the topics that have always obsessed him.

The novel, based on a real-life murder case that took place in 1978,[3] is set in the small northern Peruvian city of Talara in 1954.

Talara, like all of Peru, is characterized by great social inequality. The social elites are constituted by the *criollo* (Euro-Peruvian) Air Force officers at the local base and the (US) American employees of the International Petroleum Company, though these latter are barely mentioned in the novel. At the bottom of society, one finds the mostly mestizo and poor majority. In the outskirts of the city, the tortured and mutilated corpse of Palomino Molero, a young airman, is found. Lieutenant Silva and police officer Lituma take charge of the investigation.[4] When Colonel Mindreau attempts to intimidate the investigating officers, it becomes clear that he is hiding something and that the solution to the murder is to be found in the air force base which, however, has immunity from being investigated by the regular police force. Thanks to the lead provided by an anonymous letter—we later find out it was written by Alicia Mindreau, the Colonel's daughter—the police officers discover that Palomino Molero had begun a secret affair with Alicia, and that both had escaped to the village of Amotape with the intention of getting married. There, Colonel Mindreau and Lieutenant Dufó, Alicia's fiancé, caught up with them. Even though the police officers cannot determine who the actual authors of the crime were, there is no doubt that the order was given by Mindreau and that Dufó participated in its execution. The Colonel justifies himself by arguing that he had to punish a conscripted airman who, despite the social abyss between them and Alicia's purported mental illness, had dared to elope with his daughter. However, Alicia Mindreau's testimony implies a more sordid reason, jealousy, given that the Colonel would have had an incestuous relationship with her. When Silva sends his report to his superiors with this conclusion, Colonel Mindreau kills his daughter and commits suicide. Ironically, the labor of the policemen will not be recognized because the people of Talara do not trust their investigation and the solution of the crime makes Silva's and Lituma's superiors uncomfortable. At the end of the novel, they are transferred to a remote outpost as punishment.

Silva's and Lituma's dilemma reminds one of a recurring situation in Vargas Llosa's novels: that in which characters "faced with the opportunity to acquire power, . . . prefer to evade corruption by destroying their own personal aspirations" (Kristal 66). The punishment of the investigating policemen, presented by the authorities as a reassignment, reminds one of what happens to Gamboa in *La ciudad y los perros*, 1963 (*The Time of the Hero* 1966) and Pantaleón Pantoja in *Pantaleón y las visitadoras*, 1973 (*Captain Pantoja and the Special Service*, 1978).

Nevertheless, there is a key difference between Vargas Llosa's major novels and *Who Killed Palomino Molero?*: the almost complete lack of alternatives to corruption and power in the latter novel. Rebellion against an intolerable reality is one of the recurring topics in the Peruvian novelist's works, and is often expressed by the presence of transgressive characters, who may be revolutionaries, artists, intellectuals, etc. Critics have noted that these characters are reacting against a literal or symbolic father. As José Miguel Oviedo notes: "rebelliousness . . . can be seen as a coded parricide" (74). Thus, in *Conversación en La Catedral*, 1969 (*Conversation in The Cathedral*, 1975), Santiago Zavala deviates from the example set by his father, even if this implies becoming mired in mediocrity; and Alberto, the "Poet" of *The Time of the Hero*, rejects the orders of his father and the school authorities. In *Who Killed Palomino Molero?*, instead of the parricidal rebel, one finds a young orphan searching to establish a nearly filial relationship with the novel's most powerful character.

In this novel, one finds two socially unacceptable love affairs. The first, between Palomino Molero, a poor mestizo high school dropout and the white daughter of the officer in charge of the Air Force base, disregards all social norms. The second is an affair that threatens the most basic of prohibitions: the incest taboo. Even though Colonel Mindreau is seen in Talara as a defender of the established order, according to his daughter, privately, he sings a different tune: "He says love knows no bounds. The world wouldn't understand . . . Love is love, a landslide that carries all before it" (112). Mindreau, of course, has no interest in openly challenging society's norms. No one suspects he has sexual relations with his daughter until she informs the police. Mindreau hypocritically states in private that love knows no limits, while, at the same time, he believes that the relationship between his daughter and Palomino Molero is unacceptable due to their social differences.

One cannot consider Palomino Molero a rebel either. It is true that he elopes with Alicia, thus challenging social norms and Mindreau's express prohibition, but Palomino also attempts to make use of these same norms on his behalf. In Amotape, Molero is confident that, given that he has had sexual relations with Alicia Mindreau, social differences are no longer relevant. He tells her: "No, sweetheart, remember, you're mine now. We've spent two nights together, you're my wife. Now nobody can come between us" (75). He believes that the Colonel now has no choice but to accept the relationship. Underlying his reasoning is the belief that Alicia has been "dishonored" and that now no one else would want to marry her. Molero is thus resorting to a ploy frequently used by lovers who have been rejected by their girlfriends' families. Vargas Llosa reminisces that in the Piura of his childhood: "suitors who met with parental opposition abducted their girlfriends; they would carry them off to a *hacienda* for a few days and would then—happy ending, reconciled families—celebrate the religious ceremony, with all splendour, in the cathedral" ("The Country of a Thousand Faces" 4). Molero challenges a specific social norm, but, instead of rejecting or questioning the establishment, aims to ultimately join it. Naively, he trusts the Colonel when he tells Palomino and Alicia in Amotape that they need to return to the base so that Molero's AWOL status can be erased. In other words, Molero believes he is about to begin enjoying the privileges of being the son-in-law of the head of the military base. Significantly, Palomino Molero is an orphan. He is not a parricide. Instead, he is seeking to establish a new filiation. His name already seems to imply that the author does not expect us to feel sympathy for him. Molero includes the verb *moler* (grind, crush, beat) that reminds us that he was *beaten* to death, and the main meaning of *palomino* (in Spanish) is that of pigeon chick, perhaps an allusion to his naiveté.

Alicia, for her part, shares the racism characteristic of her social class. When she speaks with the policemen, she asks them if Molero's mother was "a *chola*, a half-breed" (99). According to

Alicia, Palomino "didn't look like a *cholo* . . . His hair was very fine, even blondish. And he had the best manners of any man I've ever known" (99). She tells the investigators that she met him at a birthday party: "All the girls were saying how beautifully he sang. . . he doesn't look like a *cholo*. It's true he didn't" (100). Curiously, no one else describes Palomino as white. The narrator describes the cadaver impaled on the carob tree saying "around his face, his hair glistened, black and curly" (3). And, when Lituma is at his mother's house, he looks at a photo "of the dark-skinned boy" (11). If, moreover, we take into account that Molero was a good singer of boleros and Peruvian *criollo* music, the possibility of his being a descendant of blacks has to be taken into account given the connections between this ethnic group and Peruvian music. Which is Palomino's correct description? The contradiction can be explained by noting that, in mestizo nations, an individual's ethnic identity is not easily discerned and can give rise to contradictory opinions. But this contradiction can also be explained by Alicia's refusal to see herself as the lover of a *cholo*. Palomino Molero, therefore, could be non-white, perhaps of black origin. Thus Alicia, without rejecting racism, would have been able to overcome an uncomfortable reality for herself by whitening Palomino in her mind.

One need not turn to psychoanalysis in order to recognize the emasculation of the power figure in the coded parricide mentioned by Oviedo. There are numerous allusions to castration and impotence in the novel. The sexual organ obviously symbolizes power, but in *Who Killed Palomino Molero?* phalli and testicles are presented in a degraded manner when referring to both elite and popular characters.

As we have seen, in Amotape, Molero is confident that, once having had sexual intercourse with Alicia Mindreau, social differences have been abolished. Given his view of social normativity, one can argue that it is his own sexual organs that permit him to seal his relationship with Alicia. It is, therefore, significant, then, that his corpse exhibits the evidence of an attempted castration. Palomino Molero had overvalued the importance of the nights he had spent with Alicia Mindreau.

---

For her part, Doña Adriana, the owner of the restaurant where the policemen eat, insinuates that her husband Matías is impotent by saying he is "sort of cold" (24). This leads Silva to use the opportunity to boast "I'm like a house afire" (24). The passion Silva experiences for Doña Adriana goes from seduction to harassment, but culminates in impotence when Doña Adriana, fed up, challenges him to perform: "...are you ashamed to show it to me? Is it that small, daddy? . . . Give it to me five times in a row, that's what my husband does every night" (147). Silva loses confidence and has no other recourse but to let her alone.

Another character who displays his sexual organs is Lieutenant Dufó, who on a countertop in a brothel, challenges all the men present: "Ashamed someone's gonna see your balls? Maybe you don't have any?" (47). He then pulls down his pants. Silva points out the danger implicit in the Lieutenant's behavior: "If you went on showing off your balls like that, someone might have cut them off. Do you want to end up a capon?" (48–9). What has Dufó beside himself is that, following her father's orders, Alicia has broken up with him. He realizes that he has been used by Colonel Mindreau. He laments that Mindreau is "[a] monster who's treated me like some damn nigger, get me?" (52). In other words, even though Dufó thought himself superior to Molero, both end up resembling each other since they have been defeated by a father obsessed with his daughter, even if Molero's punishment is much more severe.

There is no mention of Colonel Mindreau's sexual organs. The novel, however, establishes a clear contrast between his public image as the most powerful man in Talara, and that presented by his daughter as almost a masochist: "He gets down on the floor like a dog and kisses my feet. . . when he does those things, when he cries and asks me to forgive him, I hate him" (112). Curiously, the more deserving of Alicia's hatred Mindreau becomes, the weaker he appears to be. She hates him more when he voluntarily submits to her than when he violently abuses her.

The references to castration and impotence point to a characteristic of the fictional world: the dominant class has lost much of its power. Even though the novel stresses the injustice of social divisions, it also makes clear that the dominance of the upper class is much less solid than it appears. If one compares *Who Killed Palomino Molero?* with the hard-boiled detective novel, a genre concerned with denouncing corruption, one finds that, while in this the detectives run great risks, Silva and Lituma suffer nothing more than the insults of Dufó and Mindreau. No one tries to kill or bribe them. Their superiors, who are never shown, do not threaten them. The "big guys," who the inhabitants of Talara imagine as those really responsible for the death of Palomino, have lost their power. Mindreau confesses to be the intellectual author of Molero's murder, but also acknowledges he was disobeyed: "A single bullet between the eyes would have been enough. And a discreet grave. Those were my orders. The stupid bloodbath, naturally, was not my idea" (127). The base commander cannot control Lieutenant Dufó's sadism. This disobedience leads to the investigation, which, in turn, causes Mindreau's fall. In this world, the power of the privileged is shaky. Moreover, they are resisted by the people of Talara.

This novel presents the charade of a portentous masculinity behind which there is nothing. One also finds a dominant class that acts as if the social structures were unchanged, when, in reality, the bases of its power have been weakened. This erosion is not the result of a popular social mobilization, but rather of the dominant class' inability to properly organize state institutions to defend its interests. In the novel, the police are inefficient. An example of its lack of professionalism is that, when Lituma is about to lower the Palomino Molero's body from the carob tree, he suddenly exclaims: "Wait, Jerónimo, I just remembered we can't touch him until the judge comes and holds his inquest" (5). Moreover, it is clear that the police have to do their job with very limited means. The police station is described as "a run-down little house with peeling paint" (135). The poverty of this building contrasts with the relative comfort of the Air Force base, only comparable in Talara to the gated neighborhood where the engineers and managers of the International Petroleum Company live. The police have no car, so they have to make use of Don Jerónimo's taxi, the only one available in the city. They pay him for the gasoline used, but not for his services. Don Jerónimo is not happy to help them and, in one occassion, when they exit the Air Force base, they discover he is not waiting for them, forcing them to walk back to town.

The police force's lack of resources explains the low esteem in which they are held. One is not surprised that the police are disrespected by those who consider themselves to be their superiors. However, it is noteworthy that they are also humiliated by those who would seem to be socially inferior. From the start, the inhabitants of Talara repeatedly state that the police are going to cover up the crime because the real culprits are *big shots*. A subofficer states to Lituma and Silva: "if you don't discover who the murderers are, everyone's going to think you were bribed by the big shots" (39); and the taxi driver repeats the rumor that they are "covering up because the murderers are big shots" (25). Towards the conclusion of the novel, Lituma answers these unfounded accusations, but, as he is leaving Doña Adriana's restaurant, "he heard the old taxi driver mutter, 'Fucking cop,' and for and instant he considered going back. He didn't" (149–50). Lituma and Silva are in a peculiar bind: because of their social origins and income, they are despised by the members of the upper classes, but their role as policemen make the common folk distrust them.

Although critics have pointed out the centrality of racism in *Who Killed Palomino Molero?*, there has not been any mention of the resemblance of the crime to the lynchings that took place in the US South. As we have seen, Molero "had been both hung and impaled on the old carob tree" (3). The body exhibited signs of torture and attempted castration. If one adds to this that racism played a role in the reasons for the murder, the parallel between Molero's killing and the lynchings of African Americans in the South is clear. These crimes were committed near "bodies of water, bridges, and landmark trees" (Allen et al. 170). Many of the victims were accused of having raped white women. In these cases, the lynchings were justified by many as a way of saving the women from the public shame of a trial. This explains another common trait found in lynchings: the castration of the victims. This had the symbolic function of punishing the man though the same organ by which he had supposedly committed the crime. Lynchings were a threat and example of what could happen to African Americans. This is the reason why the corpses were often paraded before black neighborhoods. In order for the lynching to be effective as a social threat, both the reasons for it and the identities of those responsible needed to be made public. This is why the victimizers gladly posed next to the victims in the numerous photographs with which these events were commemorated. The resemblance of Palomino Molero's death and a lynching explains why Mindreau and Dufó appear more interested in exhibiting their power than in simulating innocence. If, in the lynchings, the identity of the guilty was no secret, in this novel, the mystery is, as we have seen, weak and is revealed long before the conclusion of the book.

Even though there is no active rebellion against the powers that be, there is a hidden resistance by the people of Talara. We have already seen how the police force inspires distrust and even disrespect. Towards the end of the novel, the people of Talara refuse to accept the solution to the crime provided by the police. There is a rumor that Mindreau had discovered a lucrative smuggling enterprise—one of the most serious social ills faced by Peru during the years the novel was published—and he and his daughter were murdered in reprisal. Another version posited that Palomino Molero was murdered because he had discovered that the Colonel was spying and that Mindreau, in turn, was executed by Ecuadorian operatives. Finally, without providing a complete explanation, some claimed that the crime "might have something to do with queers" (148), since according to popular wisdom, for them, things necessarily ended badly.

Popular rumors provide information about those who repeat them. They attempt, from a specific view of reality, to provide an explanation for apparently incomprehensible events. One can thus agree with Aldo Panfichi and Víctor Vich—who have studied the conspiracy theories that attempted to explain the 1987 Alianza Lima air disaster, in which the players of the most popular soccer team in Peru died—that popular fantasies cannot simply be discarded, since "they articulate both vital experiences and unconscious desires that have real importance within the social space" (120). The different stories these authors study coincide in their granting importance to specific characters (in this case, soccer players, mostly from poor backgrounds) until they are seen as heroes, as well as in expressing a deep distrust towards the state, which is perceived as corrupt.

We can thus ask if something similar takes place with the rumors disseminated towards the end of *Who Killed Palomino Molero?* We have seen three different stories. They resemble those studied by Panfichi and Vich in their view of the state as corrupt. But unlike the ones related to the Alianza Lima air disaster, those circulating in Talara are inconsistent in their assignation of positive and negative roles. While the fantasies regarding the air disaster contrast the solidarity and honesty of the soccer players with the corruption of the armed forces, in *Who Killed Palomino Molero?* all characters are assigned a negative role in at least one of the stories. In the first, as absurd as it may seem, Colonel Mindreau is an enemy of the *big shots*. In the second, Mindreau is a traitor and Molero acts heroically. And, in the third, the men are described as homosexuals involved in crimes of passion. What all of these stories share is their pessimism and pettiness. For the people of Talara, the police only serve to protect the privileged—even if their report accuses Mindreau and Dufó—corruption always triumphs, and only the dead deserve special consideration, although with exceptions. The character seen as heroic in one rumor, becomes corrupt (or homosexual) in the other. Although Silva and Molero have acted honorably, all the rumors see them as helping to protect the criminals. If Colonel Mindreau and Molero receive in some of the rumors the praise that Silva actually deserves, it is because Silva is still alive. One cannot both be alive and face up the powerful. One is either corrupt or a martyr.

Many of Vargas Llosa's novels can be considered pessimistic in that, while there is in them a character who challenges the paternal figure who represents the established order, his destiny "is not to replace the father; it is to go under with him, as the sources of his rebellion go on the merry way" (Cueto 17). The manner in which all his characters seemed to be trapped by corruption led some left-wing intellectuals, such as Ariel Dorfman, to see in his novels a critique of Peruvian bourgeoisie, but to note that they lacked "the necessary components to overcome the problems that were presented from a socialist perspective" (Kristal 68). In *Who Killed Palomino Molero?* Vargas Llosa seems even more pessimistic since, instead of the coded parricide, we have its reverse, an attempt at arriviste filiation and because the people of Talara—even though they are the main victims of an unjust social system—do not recognize the actions of the two honest policemen. Instead, they prefer to believe incredible and contradictory stories. This is evidence that they can also marginalize others, as evidenced in their homophobic comments.

The white elite of Talara is condemned for their discrimination towards the majority of the people. However, unlike other novels by Vargas Llosa, the dominant class is shown to be weak because, while they own the repressive forces, they have lost control of what Louis Althusser calls the ideological state apparatuses, which include the media, family, social clubs, churches, and educational institutions. For Althusser, repression is indispensable, but, in the long run, it is impossible for a class to maintain control of the state without the ideological control provided by the state apparatuses. However, in Talara, social divisions are so enormous—one could argue that there are moments when the bourgeoisie and the rest of the population seem to be speaking different languages—that the dominant class has no means by which to impose its ideas among the masses. Therefore, social institutions are in such a state of ruin that they seem to be on the verge of collapse.[5] Nevertheless, the popular sectors seem unable to offer a coherent enough discourse to become a true alternative towards a more just country. This is why it is difficult to experience sympathy towards the victims of the crime—Palomino Molero and Alicia Mindreau. The first is a naive conformist. The second is a pampered girl who never questions her class privileges. Moreover, the people of Talara, instead of representing an alternative, are shown to be narrow-minded and petty and unable to recognize Silva's honesty as a sign of progress. Although the novel denounces an unjust social order, it presents the masses in such negative terms that it is impossible to imagine them ever representing a more just alternative.

This pessimism, even greater than that which has been identified in Vargas Llosa's masterpieces of the 1960s, can be explained, at least in part, by the political situation faced by Peru at the time the novel was written. As is well-known, Peru had descended into an internal armed conflict, unleashed by the Maoist group the Shining Path. The conflict, which began in 1980 in the department of Ayacucho, had, by the middle of the decade, expanded to much of the country and threatened the democratic system. Vargas Llosa had direct participation in one of the best-known episodes of this conflict when he was a member of the commission that investigated the death of eight journalists in Uchuraccay, in the department of Ayacucho.[6]

In 1986, the same year in which *Who Killed Palomino Molero?* was published, Vargas Llosa wrote a much more optimistic text about the future of Peru, the "Foreword" to Hernando de Soto's *The Other Path*. In this text, the poor who migrate from the country to the city are presented as the vanguard of a popular capitalism that could lead to the full establishment of a free market economy in Peru. Although Vargas Llosa sees in the informal economy the way out of a particularly dark moment in the history of his country, his optimism is expressed in his essays, not in his fiction, and not, particularly, in his first detective novel.

## Notes

1. The essay will use the titles of the translation after the first mention of a Vargas Llosa novel.
2. In this case, as in that of all works in Spanish in the Works Cited list, the translation is by the author of this essay.
3. See Franco 131.
4. Lituma is also a character in *La casa verde,* 1966 (*The Green House*, 1968), *La tía Julia y el escribidor*, 1977 (*Aunt Julia and the Scriptwriter*, 1982), *Historia de Mayta*, 1984 (*The Real Life of Alejandro Mayta,* 1985), *Lituma en los Andes*, 1993 (*Death in the Andes*, 1996), and *El héroe discreto*, 2013 (*The Discreet Hero*).
5. In a 1983 interview, Vargas Llosa argues that "in Peru institutions are defective . . . Why aren't the armed and police forces unimpeachable

and exemplary institutions? They share the same vices born of underdevelopment and the lack of a democratic tradition" ("El terrorismo en Ayacucho" 135).

6. Critics have noted the possibility that Vargas Llosa is exorcising his experience in the Uchuraccay comission in *Who Killed Palomino Molero?* See Kristal 187–93.

## Works Cited

Allen, James et al. *Without Sanctuary. Lynching Photography in America.* Santa Fe, NM: Twin Palms, 2000.

Boland, Roy C. "Demonios y lectores: Génesis y reescritura de *¿Quién mató a Palomino Molero?*" *Antípodas* 1 (December 1988): 160–82.

Carbajal, Brent J. "Love and Sex in Mario Vargas Llosa's *¿Quién mató a Palomino Molero?*" *Hispanic Review* 68.3 (Summer 2000): 267–78.

Cueto, Alonso. "Reality and Rebellion. An Overview of Mario Vargas Llosa's Literary Themes." *The Cambridge Companion to Mario Vargas Llosa.* Eds. Efraín Kristal & John King. Cambridge, UK: Cambridge UP, 2012. 9–21.

Franco, Fabiola. "*¿Quién mató a Palomino Molero?* Una lectura vindicativa." *Castilla. Boletín del Departamento de Literatura Española, Universidad de Valladolid* 20 (1995): 125–38.

Hernández de López, Ana María. "Que el racismo mató a Palomino Molero no es la verdad de las mentiras." *Mario Vargas Llosa: Opera omnia.* Ed. Ana María Hernández de López. Madrid: Pliegos, 1994. 125–31.

Kristal, Efraín. *Temptation of the Word. The Novels of Mario Vargas Llosa.* Nashville, TN: Vanderbilt UP, 1998.

Oviedo, José Miguel. *Mario Vargas Llosa. La invención de una realidad.* Barcelona: Barral, 1970.

Panfichi, Aldo y Víctor Vich. "Rumores y fantasías sociales. La tragedia de Alianza Lima, 1987." *Íconos. Revista de Ciencias Sociales* 25 (May 2006): 111–21.

Penuel, Arnold M. "The Uses of Literary Perspectivism in Vargas Llosa's *¿Quién mató a Palomino Molero?*" *Hispania* 73.4 Cervantes Virtual. Web. 19 Dec. 2013.

Vargas Llosa, Mario. "The Country of a Thousand Faces." *Making Waves: Essays.* Trans. John King. New York: Penguin, 1998. 1–15.

---

_____. "El terrorismo en Ayacucho." Interview with Uri Ben Schmuel. *Contra viento y marea, III (1964–1988).* Barcelona: Seix Barral, 1990. 129–40.

_____. "Foreword." *The Other Path: The Invisible Revolution in the Third World.* Hernando de Soto. New York: Harper Collins, 1987. xiii–xxii.

_____. *Who Killed Palomino Molero?* New York: Farrar, Straus & Giroux, 1987.

# Reflections on the Absurd: A Comparative Reading of *Death in the Andes* and *The Time of the Hero*

Haiqing Sun

The 2010 Nobel Prize in Literature was awarded to Mario Vargas Llosa, in the words of the Swedish Academy, "for his cartography of structures of power and his trenchant images of the individual's resistance, revolt, and defeat." This description of his novelistic oeuvre can also be a useful starting point for an analysis of two of his best-known novels written thirty years apart: *La ciudad y los perros*, 1963 (*The Time of the Hero*, 1966) and *Lituma en los Andes, 1993* (*Death in the Andes*, 1996).[1] These novels come at the beginning and end of the period during which the Peruvian novelist was most engaged with his own country, both personally and literarily.[2] In fact, the publication of *Death in the Andes* coincided with Vargas Llosa establishing his main residence in Spain and assuming that country's citizenship.[3]

Winner of the Novela Breve Prize granted by the Spanish press Seix Barral, which provided the novel publicity and distribution throughout the Spanish-speaking world, *The Time of the Hero* is generally seen as the starting point for the writer's global success, as well as for that of the Latin American Novelistic Boom of the 1960s, which included such notable writers as Carlos Fuentes, Julio Cortázar, and Gabriel García Márquez. Although it was published long after the Peruvian novelist had become acknowledged as one of greatest writers in the Spanish language, *Death in the Andes* can, in fact, be considered another milestone in Vargas Llosa's literary career. Towards the end of the 1980s, Vargas Llosa had become actively involved in Peruvian politics, even standing as a presidential candidate on a free-market platform for the elections of 1990.

Perhaps, in response to his growing political participation, Vargas Llosa's writings were often not well accepted by critics during this period. For instance, in his review of *¿Quién mató a*

*Palomino Molero?*, 1986 (*Who Killed Palomino Molero?*, 1987), Julio Ortega, once a vocal admirer of the novelist, noted the disappearance of the brilliant author of novels *The Time of the Hero* and other masterpieces of the 1960s, by asking "who killed Vargas Llosa?" (978).[4] The publication of *Death in the Andes*, therefore, not only proved that Vargas Llosa had not "died," but signaled both the end of a literary period in the Peruvian novelist's work and the beginning of a new one after his defeat in the presidential elections. Noticeably, after *Death in the Andes*, Vargas Llosa's novels would be more scholarly, stemming from his research, and no longer focused on current social issues in Peru. *The Time of the Hero* and *Death in the Andes* represent the beginning and the end of his critical examination of Peruvian sociopolitical conditions through fiction.[5]

Set in the Military Academy Leoncio Prado, outside Lima, the capital of Peru, the narrative of *Time of the Hero* develops around three key events. The first is the theft of the "chemistry exam" by Cava, a member of the group of cadets knows as the "Circle," which leads to Ricardo Arana (the Slave) to inform on them to the school authorities. The second is the military maneuver during which the Slave is killed. Alberto, also known as the Poet, accuses the Jaguar, the leader of the Circle, of murder. These two events are narrated in the first part. The third event, the investigation of the possible murder by Lieutenant Gamboa, generates much of the plot of second part. The search of the student barracks, ordered by Gamboa as part of the investigation, leads the cadets to attack the Jaguar, whom they suspect has informed on their use of alcohol and tobacco and who goes from being their feared leader, to a pariah. Gamboa's investigation of the Slave's possible murder fails due to the intervention of the Colonel, who is in charge of the military academy and tries to protect its reputation. Finally, it leads to Gamboa's reassignment to a remote Andean post, as revealed in the epilogue. In addition to passages centered on these three events, the novel includes sets of retrospective passages dealing with the personal lives—both in and out of the academy—of the Jaguar, the Slave, Alberto, and monologues by Boa (another member of the Circle).

The three central events, and those that arise as consequences of them, arguably form the "stem" of a detective story, representing, respectively, the motive, execution, and investigation of the crime. In other words, this novel, with its complex narrative techniques that forge so many subtexts into a whole, is undergirded by a lineal representation of a crime mystery. Even though *The Time of the Hero* represents different aspects of Peruvian life beyond those explicitly linked to the possible crime, it can be approached as a "diluted" crime mystery, with elements of the genre functioning as a cohesive force or meta-structure throughout its narrative.

*Death in the Andes* is also composed of two parts and an epilogue. It follows much more clearly the patterns and structures of traditional detective fiction, including the presentation of the crime, the investigation, and, of course, the solution. Set in the fictional Andean town of Naccos, during the height of the Shining Path insurgency,[6] it features police Corporal Lituma, a character in several of Vargas Llosa's novels, including *Who Killed Palomino Molero?* The crime in question is the disappearance of three people: Pedro Tinoco, a mute and handicapped youth who used to help the police; the albino Casimiro Huarcaya; and highway foreman Demetrio Chanca. Several potential solutions are proposed and examined— Doña Adriana, a barkeeper, and her husband, Dionisio, argue that the victims might have been killed by the Shining Path guerrillas, or alternatively have been devoured by the mythical Andean *pishtacos* (white humanoids who devour human fat)—by the end of the novel, Lituma discovers that the three missing people had been sacrificed to the Andean mountain gods in order to propitiate prosperity. However, the solution of the crimes only makes Lituma, who had been assigned to Naccos from the coastal city of Piura, feel more vulnerable and spiritually lost in the culturally foreign Andes, which has become, for him, an unsolvable mystery. Unlike the detective in a traditional whodunit, when Lituma is recalled to the coast, he leaves Naccos without having reinstated order, at least from a Western perspective.

As we have seen, Lieutenant Gamboa, who fulfills the function of the detective in *The Time of the Hero*, is also sent to a physically remote Andean location, in this case, Juliaca in Puno. Despite being a real town, Juliaca functions in the novel as a symbolic locale, far from the center of the conflicts. Gamboa's banishment becomes a handy solution for the military school, by which it pacifies its internal turmoil. In Vargas Llosa's fiction, the Andes function as the location of punishment.[7] Thus, the transfer to the highlands does not necessarily bring peace to the crime investigator, as seen in Lituma's experience in *Death in the Andes*. In this novel, the Andean world is both the setting of the main story and a mystery itself. It is a much more chaotic than the military academy in *The Time of the Hero*, which may reflect Vargas Llosa's own point of view on the evolution of Peruvian society during the thirty years lapsed between both novels.[8]

In *The Time of the Hero*, the Military School is presented as a rigid hierarchic social order. This order is constituted by the school authorities—with the colonel at the top, followed by the officers according to their rank—and the cadets. This represents a simple and lineal form of governance: the school has the force of control and punishment, while the cadets are under surveillance and at its mercy. Although the cadets mock the disciplinary system and attempt to undermine it with their mischiefs, they only replicate the hierarchical structures that characterize the school and, by implication, the military and society as a whole. For instance, the Circle, founded by the Jaguar and other cadets, follows the law of the jungle and creates a supplementary hierarchical structure at the blind spots of the school's surveillance. Moreover, the murder of the Slave Ricardo, its investigation, and final cover-up, shows that no challenge to the hierarchical school system is tolerated. Even Gamboa, one of the most respected officers in the school, is punished when his investigation brings the military handbook into conflict with the actually existing military institution.

In *Death in the Andes*, one finds, however, no power structure at all, at least in terms of ruling efficiency. Andean society is shown as having been driven into chaos by different forces: the state represented by the police and military troops; the Shining Path; community leaders blinded by superstitions; and even Nature itself, whose disasters can abolish all human endeavors. Each of these forces is distrusted, and often misinterpreted, by the others, and none of them can become a constructive factor in the Andean society.

The leadership of the military school in *Time of the Hero* is hypocritical, selfish, and corrupt—yet the hierarchical system it leads is capable of defending itself, as evidenced by its handling of the Slave's death and investigation, and by it being supported and replicated by the students both within and later without the school. But in the Andes, the social system malfunctions completely. There is no longer any social order, and there is no leadership capable of guiding society in times of crises. The local people believe both in the guerrillas' infinite capacity for destruction and in the Andean spirits' power to protect or punish human beings. For instance, according to Doña Adriana: "All these mountains are full of enemies . . . They live inside. Day and night they weave their evil schemes. They do endless harm. That's why there are so many accidents" (34). Meanwhile, the military atrocities worsen the situation, leading to the loss of social confidence, and the police—another representative of government—is perplexed, alienated and lost in the midst of the distrust, fear, or indifference exhibited by the local community. In the novel, Lituma exemplifies this alienation: "he felt the oppressive, crushing presence of the immense mountains, the deep sky of the sierra. Everything here moved up-ward. With every cell of his body he longed for the deserts, the endless Piura flatlands studded with carob trees, flocks of goats, white sand dunes. What are you doing here, Lituma?" (86). The only function of governmental authority is alluded to in the epilogue—if this is considered a function—when the police officers are ordered by the higher authorities to abandon their post.

In *The Time of the Hero*, class and ethnic difference are consciously represented in the cadets' stories. Alberto belongs to the upper-class, while Ricardo comes from a middle-class family. Jaguar and members of the "Circle" come from the lower social classes. Cava, who steals the exam, is of indigenous background and comes from the Andean highlands. His expulsion from the school dooms his chances at making it in the city, and he has no choice but to return to his humble origins. This ignites the Circle's anger and, possibly, leads to the Slave Ricardo's murder. Naomi Lindstrom doubts that the education offered at Leoncio Prado will "have any value in their subsequent life" (173). In the epilogue of the novel, Jaguar "heads towards a stagnation of a clerk-level job," and Alberto follows a family-arranged plan to study in the US, "fantasizing avidly about the soft, easy and hypocritical life . . . as a member of the professional class" (Lindstrom, 174–75). Both of them are thus carried away by the prospect of banal middle-class routines. Their stories end in disappointing social stagnation.

In *Death in the Andes*, the author describes complex social groups in conflict. Social stagnation is replaced by economic recession and violence. But social classification appears in its plot, particularly as an ideological weapon of the communist guerrillas. The Shining Path use a Marxist division of social classes to identify their enemies and to justify their killing innocent people.[9] By such a critical representation of social classification, Vargas Llosa makes the reader face the failure of Peruvian society as a whole. This change in the representation of class between the two novels in fact coincides with the transformation of the author's own ideological position. He has noted his "disillusionment with Marxism and socialism—in theory on the one hand, but above all in reality" (*A Fish in the Water* 216).

In *Death in the Andes*, every social group faces injustice, and this creates what could be called "a circle of victims." This is a situation in which there are no winners and no hope of ever winning. Although this "circle" is also present in *The Time of the Hero*, the underlying social situations are different. In the latter novel, most of the conflicts are found at the personal level and are brought to life by the Slave Ricardo's death. In the end, by shelving the case, the school authorities victimize Ricardo a second time. In *Death in the Andes*, the circle of victims actually stems from the perplexing social condition of "the internal boundary" for post-colonial Latin American countries, as Silvia Rosman has suggested (21). The struggles for survival often take place with unavoidable recklessness. This is caused by social disaggregation in ideology, culture, and ethnicity, as well as the unbalanced economic development from region to region. Vargas Llosa has observed such a situation in the Peru of the 1990s: "beneath all this [modernity and progress] lies an atavistic force, belonging to a certain tradition that is not easily uprooted. In the event of any collective crisis or insecurity, it erupts with great force and violence" ("Demons and Lies" 21). In the novel, as indicated previously, the guerrillas, the police, the local residents, and the highway workers all have their fates intertwined, but no one represents social progress. The military torture those they believe to be subversives in as barbaric a way as their opponents. The guerrillas kill innocents and bring fear and the abandonment of villages instead of "liberation." The local residents lose their belief in the ability of the state to protect them. They rely, instead, in their belief in Andean spirits and in the effectiveness of human sacrifice, but ultimately, they receive no supernatural help. The policemen fulfill their duty to protect the community, only to find their own lives, like that of other civilians, at the mercy of terrorists and natural disasters. When the huayco (avalanche) demolishes the road construction site, Corporal Lituma and policeman Tomás Carreño cannot do anything but passively wait for orders for them to leave the Andes.

Moreover, in both novels, the author shows the corruption of Peruvian society and how it sacrifices an individual's well-being for the benefit of the hierarchically superior groups. For example, members of the Circle force the Slave Ricardo to aid in the theft of the exam. But not only is the students' shadow hierarchy corrupt, the school authorities sacrifice Lieutenant Gamboa's career in order to cover up a scandal (the possible murder of the Slave) that may damage their reputation. The level of corruption at the school renders any notion of justice absurd.

But an even more absurd situation is present in *Death in the Andes*. In this novel, intolerance and corruption lead to the destruction of the natural environment, of villages, and even innocent lives, undermining social confidence and placing survival itself in peril. Even the solution of the crime does not set society right. Lituma, after finding out that the cause of the disappearances had been ritual human sacrifices, laments discovering the truth: "I swear, I wish I didn't know. Because what happened to them is the most stupid and perverse of all the stupid and perverse things that happen here" (228). Lituma is demoralized and seems to have had his beliefs in rationality itself undermined: "I don't care anymore . . . I am glad the apus [mountain gods] sent the huayco down on Naccos. I'm glad they stopped the work on the highway . . . I've never been so miserable in my life as I was here" (268).

Lituma's attitude may thus be identified as anti-heroic. In this novel, the crime investigator is vulnerable, reluctant, and finally defeated in his attempt at reestablishing law and order. Compared to *The Time of the Hero*, the violence in *Death in the Andes* is presented as even a greater obstacle against social progress, blocking the public's access to reason and justice.

The main characters in *The Time of the Hero*, Alberto, the Jaguar, and Gamboa, have at least elements of the tragic hero, since they courageously and unselfishly challenge the higher powers. Their failures constitute a vigorous social criticism against the oppressive power system. By contrast, in *Death in the Andes*, Lituma's detective work is reduced to a journey of disillusionment, identifying crises and absurdities in a disoriented society to which he never belongs. As Lituma comments to his partner: "You and I are the only suckers who don't know what's going on. Don't you feel like an asshole up here in Naccos . . . ?" (123). In both novels, the solution to the crime does not help serve justice, and the notion of justice is interpreted in different ways. Such a situation may help the reader observe how the author envisions the political conditions of Peru at different stages of his own social experience. In *The Time of the Hero*, justice loses in the end, but its meaning is not blurred. The main characters have all acted similarly against the mistreatment of a victim: Alberto steps up for Ricardo and Jaguar for Gamboa. In *Death in the Andes*, on the other hand, different social groups perceive justice differently, according to their location in the social hierarchy, cultural background, or needs. For both the government troops and the guerrillas, justice means the exercise of force against their enemy. Even human sacrifice is justified by Dionisio and Doña Adriana in the name of protecting the wellbeing of the community.

Deborah Cohn indicates that reason, which should be the guiding force for society, is absent in *Death in the Andes* (99). Raymond Leslie Williams, too, suggests that the novel presents Peru as a "postmodern country" that escapes rational understanding (150). But "Reason" is in fact represented in the novel through the character of the Danish anthropologist Paul Stirmsson who, while helping lead Lituma to the solution of the crimes, laments that no ancient community can pass the test of civilization. In other words, Lituma, as a detective, has to depend on a foreigner's insights to uncover some profound truths about his home country.

Lituma, like Gamboa in *Time of the Hero*, finds himself in the dilemma of having to fulfill his duty while being rendered incapable of serving justice. Despite all the negative factors that prevent him from carrying through the investigation, Lituma himself lacks two key traits necessary to fulfill his obligation: self-confidence and social intelligence. He not only lives under the threat of terrorist attack, but is also beset by homesickness and a feeling of estrangement from the Andes. In compensation, Lituma passionately immerses himself in what Madison Smart Bell calls the "absurdly naive" love story of his partner Tomás Carreño with a prostitute (27). This story helps Lituma maintain his sense of self as a coastal man despite his feeling of isolation. At the same time, this story also involves him in another investigation: tracking the identity of Tomás' lover. During the investigation of the case of disappearance, he has followed the different assumptions proposed by locals, misled by the Dionisio's and Doña Adriana's false stories, and affected by concerns over his own safety. Only after he is enlightened by Stirmsson can he begin to understand the nature of the crime. Ironically, during his service in the Andes, the identity of Tomás' lover—a trivial mystery—is the only case that Lituma solves with certainty. Unlike Gamboa, who accepts his reassignment, Lituma expresses a strong determination to retreat from the harsh Andean territory: "I don't care anymore. . . . I'll go to the Upper Marañón and forget about the sierra" (268). Lituma's situation implies that, if in a closed and oppressive social

---

space like Leoncio Prado, one can only be a tragic hero; in the Andes, where social order is lost, reason is thin on the ground, and if the social power system is malfunctioning, one can only be an absurd anti-hero.

Critics such as Cohn and Juan E. De Castro have studied *Death in the Andes* as a political novel. Indeed, the text's main plots on Peru's sociopolitical-economic crises are all of a critical nature consistent with the author's own neoliberal positions. However, the depiction of the Andes as a chaotic location resistant to improvement can also be interpreted as implying the impossibility of politics. Therefore, the novel may also be read as a "de-politicizing" text, especially regarding the case of the anti-hero Lituma. His desperation when confronted by a disastrous and uncontrollable reality; his dislike not only of Andean society, but of the degradation it has experienced in its contact with Western civilization; his persistent feeling of being a helpless stranger in the Andes; and his strong hope to leave this space and return to his familiar land; all seem to make political activity moot.

*Death in the Andes* is, until now, Vargas Llosa's last novel dealing with Peru's social problems. It reflects the author's experiences as a politician throughout the 1980s until his defeat in the presidential election of 1990. It marked a turning point in Vargas Llosa's life, when he decided to quit politics and removed himself to Europe. As mentioned previously, Vargas Llosa ended *The Time of the Hero* with the crime investigator's transfer to the Andes. In *Death in the Andes*, another investigator, Lituma, faces crises and chaos, and then leaves the Andes with no intention of ever returning. Similarly there is no hope for Vargas Llosa ever to return to active politics, as implied by the fact that he not only critically depicts the complexity of Peruvian society in this novel but also expresses his own disappointment and political disillusionment through the anti-heroic image of Lituma. In this sense, the 1993 novel may be the author's elegiac critical portrait of Peruvian society, a poetic farewell, not to the Andes but to the social writing he initiated with *The Time of the Hero*.

# Notes

1.  The essay will use the titles of the translation after the first mention of a Vargas Llosa novel.

2.  In his memoir *A Fish in the Water* (1993), the writer recalls his life as a young student in Leoncio Prado during 1950's, and his visits to the Andes as a politician and presidential candidate during late 1980's and early 1990.

3.  Vargas Llosa became a Spanish citizen in 1993, after the government of Alberto Fujimori, the winner of the 1990 elections in Peru, threatened to take away his passport. (Vargas Llosa, however, has not renounced his Peruvian citizenship). The same year, he won the Cervantes Prize, the most important award that can be granted to a Spanish-language writer.

4.  In this case, as in that of all works in Spanish in the Works Cited list, the translation is by the author of this essay.

5.  Vargas Llosa had published *La guerra del fin del mundo* in 1981 (*The War of the End of the World*, 1984). Thematically, by being set outside Peru, in late nineteenth-century Brazil, and methodologically, given that it is the result of significant archival and historical research, this novel predicts the kind of writing Vargas Llosa would practice during the 1990s and 2000s. Although Vargas Llosa has continued as a keen social critic for Peru in the past twenty years, he has limited his social commentary to his essays and articles. Even though two of his novels written since *Death in the Andes* are set in Peru—*Los cuadernos de don Rigoberto*, 1997 (*The Notebooks of Don Rigoberto*, 1997*)* and his most recent novel, *El héroe discreto,* 2013 (*The Discreet Hero*)—these do not embrace a critical perspective on sociopolitical conditions, as was the case with those written before 1993.

6.  The Shining Path (*Sendero Luminoso*) was a brutal Maoist revolutionary group led by Abimael Guzmán that started a guerrilla war in the 1980. While there are still sporadic actions by groups claiming to be the Shining Path, the violence waned after the capture of Guzmán in 1992. Approximately seventy thousand people died due to the violence and its repression.

7.  The Andes appear in the dénouement of two other novels by Vargas Llosa. In *Pantaleón y las visitadoras,* 1973 (*Captain Pantoja and the Special Service*, 1978), Pantaleón Pantoja is also punished by being sent to the Andes (the village of Pomata in Puno), after the public

---

exposure of the military brothel that he had been ordered to organize. *Who Killed Palomino Molero?* ends with Corporal Lituma's transfer to the Andes after his work on a murder case that involves military scandals. Therefore, *Death in the Andes* is in fact a sequel to this novel.

8.   Vargas Llosa critically observed the social crisis and the failure of political leadership of Peru from 1960s to 1990s and laments: "[e]ntire families were fleeing, abandoning everything, driven half mad with desperation because of the violence and the wretched poverty, to go off to swell the armies of unemployed in the cities [...] I often thought: A country can always be worse off. Underdevelopment is bottomless. And for the last thirty years Peru had done everything possible to ensure that there would be more and more poor people and that its poor would each day be more impoverished still" (*A Fish in the Water* 216).

9.   Vargas Llosa commented on the guerrillas' acts as an "intolerance totally conditioned by [Marxist] ideology" ("Demons and Lies" 20). Also see the killings of tourists and scientists in *Death in the Andes* (44, 102).

## Works Cited

Bell, Madison Smartt. "Mountains of the Mind." *The New York Times Book Review* 18 Feb. 1996. Gale General OneFile. Web. 19 Jan. 2014.

Boland, Roy. "Demonios y lectores: Génesis y reescritura de *Quién mató a Palomino Molero?*" *Antípodas* Dec. (1988): 161–82.

Cohn, Deborah. "The Political Novels: The Real Life of Alejandro Maita and Death in the Andes." *The Cambridge Companion to Mario Vargas Llosa*. Eds. Efraín Kristal & John King. Cambridge, UK: Cambridge UP, 2012. 88–101.

De Castro, Juan E. "Mario Vargas Llosa Versus Barbarism." *Latin American Research Review*. 45 (2010): 5–26.

Lindstrom, Naomi. *Twentieth-Century Spanish American Fiction*. Austin: U of Texas P. 1994.

"The Nobel Prize in Literature 2010: Mario Vargas Llosa." *NobelPrize. Org*. 2010. Web. Dec. 2013.

Ortega, Julio. "García Márquez y Vargas Llosa, imitados." *Revista iberoamericana* 137 (1986): 971–78.

Rosman, Silvia N. *Being in Common: Nation, Subject, and Community in Latin American Literature and Culture*. Lewisburg, PA: Bucknell UP, 2003.

Vargas Llosa, Mario. *A Fish in the Water: A Memoir*. Trans. Helen Lane. New York: Farrar, Straus & Giroux, 1994.

_____. *Captain Pantoja and the Special Service*. Trans. Gregory Kolovacos & Ronald Christ. New York: Farrar, Straus & Giroux, 1978.

_____. "Coloquio/Respuestas." *Semana de autor: Mario Vargas Llosa*. Madrid: Instituto de Cooperación Iberoamericana, 1985. 30–35.

_____. *Death in the Andes*. Trans. Edith Grossman. New York: Penguin, 1996.

_____. "Demons and Lies: Motivation and Form in Mario Vargas Llosa." Interview with Luis Rebaza-Soraluz. *The Review of Contemporary Fiction*. 1 (1997): 15–24.

_____. *The Time of the Hero*. Trans. Lysander Kemp. New York: Farrar, Straus & Giroux, 1986.

_____. *Who Killed Palomino Molero?* Trans. Alfred MacAdam. New York: Farrar, Straus & Giroux, 1987.

Williams, Raymond Leslie. "Los niveles de la realidad, la función de lo racional y los demonios: El hablador y Lituma en los Andes." *Explicación de textos literarios*. 25 (1996–1997): 141–54.

# Colonialism as a Smoke Screen: Anti-Nationalist Discourse in Vargas Llosa's *The Dream of the Celt*

Ignacio López-Calvo

In a first reading, it is easy to assume that Mario Vargas Llosa's historical novel *El sueño del celta*, 2010 (*The Dream of the Celt*, 2012), deals mainly with colonialism and Western modernity.[1] The characters' engagement in open criticism of Joseph Conrad's *Heart of Darkness* (1902; Conrad is one of the characters in the novel) may lead the reader to think that Vargas Llosa's novel is a reaction to Conrad's, perhaps an outcome of what Harold Bloom has called "the anxiety of influence." Irish historian Alice Stopford Green, for instance, tells her friend, Roger Casement, the novel's protagonist based on the real-life British-diplomat-turned-Irish-revolutionary Sir Roger David Casement (1864–1916), that Conrad's view of human beings in *Heart of Darkness* is misguided:

> That novel is a parable according to which Africa turns the civilized Europeans who go there into barbarians. Your Congo report showed the opposite. That we Europeans were the ones who brought the worst barbarities there. Besides, you were in Africa for twenty years without becoming a savage. In fact, you came back more civilized than when you left here believing in the virtues of colonialism and the Empire (54).

Casement responds by stating that while Conrad claimed that Congo brought out the worst possible moral corruption from both blacks and whites, he was convinced that *Heart of Darkness* actually describes an apocalyptic vision of hell, rather than Congolese reality or history. Paradoxically, the protagonist seems to prove Conrad right through his constant fear that if he stays in Congo any longer, he will end up going insane and punishing the Congolese, like the other Europeans, "because that is what happens to Europeans in this damned country"

(80). One may argue, however, that the topics of colonialism and Western modernity, while important in the novel and in themselves (as Nicholas Birns has keenly demonstrated), are a sort of smoke screen for the main thrust in the novel: the discussion of the flaws of nationalist discourse, particularly in its most radical form.

In numerous interviews, Vargas Llosa has described nationalism of all kinds as a catastrophe, a disease, and an aberration. He considers it the biggest challenge to a culture of freedom and democracy: "Nationalism is the culture of the uneducated, an ideological entelechy constructed in a manner as obtuse and primitive as racism (to which it is closely related) that makes belonging to a collectivist abstraction—the nation—the supreme value and the privileged credential of an individual" ("Razas, botas, y nacionalismo").[2] Likewise, in his article "The Culture of Liberty," Vargas Llosa denounces the dangers of nationalist perspectives' "parochial, exclusionary, and confused vision" for cultural life and personal freedom: "Seeking to impose a cultural identity on a people is equivalent to locking them in a prison and denying them the most precious of liberties—that of choosing what, how, and who they want to be" (*Foreign Policy*). The author often links nationalism, even when it "plays" democracy, to violence, populist dictatorship, and totalitarianism. In an interview with Tulio Demicheli, for instance, Vargas Llosa, referring to nationalist parties and terrorist groups in Spain, argues:

> I believe that it is a disease; in practice, a rejection of the Other because it is the completely utopian aspiration of moving toward racially, religiously or ideologically homogenous societies. This is not democratic or realistic, because all societies have evolved and diversified . . . if you dig the ideological roots of nationalism, they are a rejection of democratic forms, a rejection of coexistence in diversity, which is the essence of democracy (11).

Juan E. De Castro has associated Vargas Llosa's rejection of nationalism as an ideological fiction based on collective identity with his fondness for neoliberalism, globalization, modernization, and the free market: "Vargas Llosa has also become a passionate critic of nationalism and any version of local or regional identity that is opposed to 'a world citizenship'"(66). "One of the logical consequences of neoliberalism is a celebration of globalization—which is after all the result of the expansion of free-markets across the globe" (38).

Like many of Vargas Llosa's protagonists, Roger Casement, the protagonist of *The Dream of the Celt*, is a fanatic, a man who allows his obsessions and his "personal and social demons" (to use Vargas Llosa's own terms) to ruin his life. As Efraín Kristal points out, in the novels published in the twenty-first century,

> Vargas Llosa remains as concerned with the mindset of those disposed to fight for their utopias, but he no longer deplores them—as he did in the 1990s—as hopeless fanatics or misguided utopians with grotesque convictions... His focus has shifted from the dreadful consequences of fanaticism, to an empathetic exploration of the traumas and suffering that turn some individuals into enemies of the world ("From Utopia to Reconciliation" 131).

Indeed, the author's empathy and compassion for Roger Casement, despite his being described as a "radical nationalist" (19), is apparent throughout the plot and especially in the novel's epilogue. This, however, does not prevent Vargas Llosa from using the historical character as an exemplum of the dangers of radical nationalism.

## Nationalism, Madness, and Religion
With this goal in mind, the narrator resorts to two efficient comparisons that run throughout the plot: he sometimes identifies nationalism/patriotism with madness, other times with the fanatic religious fervor of medieval crusaders and the first Christian martyrs. Casement often describes his mission in religious terms, vowing to make amends and to redeem his sins of youth (his collaboration in the colonization of the Congo) by documenting the abuses committed by Europeans in Congo. The same religious vocabulary is used to analyze patriotism and nationalism. Casement realizes, for example, that the saint and the warrior embody two of the main prototypes of the Irishman. In Amazonia, he likewise declares that evil "can

reveal itself openly and perpetrate the worst monstrosities without the justifications of patriotism or religion" (234). Other characters, such as the Irish nationalist Robert Monteith, also highlight the fellowship between religion and patriotism: "To die fighting for your homeland is a death as honorable as dying for your family or your faith. Don't you agree?" (342).

Paradoxically, while the evocation of blind religious faith is used to discredit nationalistic discourse, all religious characters in *The Dream of the Celt* are admirable. As stated, it is not their religious practices and beliefs that Vargas Llosa compares with radical nationalism, but those of the crusaders and other religious zealots. To leave no doubt about the pathological downturn that the protagonist's obsession with nationalism, patriotism, and Ireland's independence has taken, he admits on four different occasions his fear of losing his sanity. We find the first hint of Casement's obsessive or fanatic leanings at the end of the second chapter when, after three trips to Africa, he announces with such fervor that he will move there that his uncle Edward compares it to that of Medieval crusaders. Later, the subjective narrator also compares other Irish nationalists, such as Patrick Pearse, the founder of two Gaelic-language schools who wants this language to be the official language of Ireland again, with crusaders: "Roger came to feel a great affinity for the radical, intransigent crusader for Gaelic and independence that Pearse was" (306–07). These analogies become increasingly negative, as can be seen when Father Crotty compares the Irish radical nationalist Joseph Plunkett with the crusaders:

> His Christianity is that of the Christians who died in Roman circuses, devoured by wild beasts. But also of the Crusaders who reconquered Jerusalem by killing all the ungodly Jews and Muslims they encountered, including women and children. The same burning zeal, the same glorification of blood and war. I confess, Roger, that people like him, even though they may be the ones who make history, fill me with more fear than admiration (330).

Even Casement is alarmed by "The somewhat mad romanticism of Joseph Plunkett and Patrick Pearse" (328) and the latter's ominous description of Irish patriots as the contemporary version of the first Christian martyrs. The use of the word "mad" in this quotation is yet another link between nationalism and madness. In one of his essays, Pearse had written that Irish patriots' blood would be the seed of their country's freedom. Casement will later realize that, although Pearse and Plunkett are aware of the inevitability of a defeat against the military might of the British Empire, they still dream that their own patriotic immolation and martyrdom will one day inspire a long-lasting Irish rebellion that will ultimately lead to independence: "It's a question of a hundred revolutionaries being born for each one of us who dies. Isn't that what happened with Christianity?" (331). The Irish nationalists, therefore, take, once again, a page out of the history of religion. In the end, Casement ends up not only understanding their will to become the symbol that will energize Irish rebellion, but also wishing he could have joined this rebellion of "Poets and mystics" (279). In consonance with the constant links between religious faith and nationalist fanaticism in the novel, Pearse and Plunkett openly declare the mystic nature of their struggle and the sculptor Herbert Ward lightheartedly calls his friend Casement a mystic.

## Nationalism and Indigenism

In *La utopía arcaica. José María Arguedas y las ficciones del indigenismo*, 1996 (The Archaic Utopia: José María Arguedas and the Fictions of Indigenismo), Vargas Llosa presents indigenist discourse as a "historical-political fiction" (68) and dismisses Inca Garcilaso de la Vega's foretelling that Quechua culture and language would be preserved throughout the centuries, waiting for the right moment to be restored:

Luis E. Valcárcel is the first Peruvian intellectual of the twentieth century to develop in such an explicit and coherent way the Andeanist discourse against the coast and Lima. He was also the one who revived in the most influential way the archaic utopia inaugurated by Inca Garcilaso de la Vega in his *Royal Commentaries of the Incas* about a Quechua race and culture metaphysically preserved throughout history, waiting for its moment to restore, in a great crash—an

Andean storm—in modern times, that remote society of beings, equal, healthy, and free from greed and commercial calculations, which the Inca Empire embodied and that the Conquest had undone (7).

Similarly, in *The Dream of the Celt*, the author shows his skepticism about the nationalist Gaelic League's goal of getting rid of English language and culture to restore Irish language, sports, and traditions: "They dreamed of a separate Ireland, safe from destructive modern industrialism, living a bucolic, rural life, liberated from the British Empire" (90). This evokes the romanticized fictions and the utopian overtones in both nationalist and indigenist discourses that Vargas Llosa often derides. Even Casement himself wonders whether his friends Eoin MacNeill and Pearse's dream of making Gaelic the mother tongue of all Irish people again is feasible and realistic:

> English had become the way to communicate, speak, be, and feel for an immense majority of the Irish, and trying to renounce it was a political whim whose only result would be a Babelic confusion that would culturally transform his Ireland into an archaeological curiosity, isolated from the rest of the world. Was it worth it? (302–03)

In this novel, therefore, Vargas Llosa carries out an ideological appropriation of a nationalist leader's voice, in order to criticize nationalist discourse itself.

This disparaging skepticism, albeit of a more veiled nature this time, resurfaces when the narrator mentions a poem written by Casement, which lends its title to the novel: "in September 1906, before leaving for Santos, he wrote a long epic poem, "The Dream of the Celt," about the mythic past of Ireland" (110). Behind the guise of a seemingly innocuous statement, we must note the emphasis on an ahistorical, mythical past that suggests the collective fantasy, the dangerous and anti-democratic ideological fictions on which, according to the author, both nationalism and indigenism are founded. To continue with the comparison between Vargas Llosa's anti-indigenist and anti-nationalist arguments: whereas *La utopía arcaica* criticizes the Peruvian Marxist José Carlos Mariátegui's ignorance of indigenous culture, even though, according to Vargas Llosa, he appropriated their plight for his own political goals, *The Dream of the Celt* presents a hardly veiled mockery of Casement's futile attempts at learning Gaelic, becoming more familiar with Irish culture, and understanding the *seanchaí* (traditional, Irish, itinerant storytellers). In several passages, Casement, who ends up converting to Catholicism seemingly because he associates it with Irish nationalism, confesses his lack of familiarity with either Catholicism or Irish history, culture, and language. Here, it is no coincidence that patriotism and religion go hand in hand again.

Following up with his argumentation against indigenism in *El hablador,* 1987 (*The Storyteller*, 1989) and *Lituma en los Andes*, 1993 (*Death in the Andes*, 1996), in *The Dream of the Celt*, Vargas Llosa continues to wrestle with the issue of the incorporation of indigenous people into the westernized national life of the rest of Peru. Kristal maintains that the author "has not resolved his own dilemmas about the preservation or eventual modernization of indigenous cultures" (*Temptation of the Word* 157). Yet it seems quite clear in these three novels that he does support the incorporation of Amazonian and Andean indigenous people into Western modernity. As a case in point, in a conversation between Casement and Víctor Israel, a Jewish Maltese rubber plantation owner, the latter mocks the idea of allowing Amazonia to continue existing in the Stone Age, instead of using its raw material wealth to modernize Peru and to improve Peruvians' living standards. Casement's response seems to turn him into Vargas Llosa's alter ego, as he justifies the economic exploitation of Amazonia and the incorporation of its indigenous people into western culture: "'Amazonia is a great emporium of resources, no doubt,' Roger agreed, without becoming agitated. 'Nothing more just than that Peru should take advantage of it. But not by abusing the natives, or hunting them down like animals, or forcing them to work as slaves. Rather, by incorporating them into civilization by means of schools, hospitals, and churches'" (162).

In keeping with the polyphonic approach of the novel, in Congo Casement had already bemoaned the cruel customs and religious practices of "those men from another time" (43) who "seemed mired in the depths of time" (42), including cannibalism, the sacrifice of twins and harelipped babies, as well as the killing of servants and slaves to bury them along with their masters. For the same reasons, several characters, including Casement and the Baptist missionary Theodore Horte, at one point or another praise the "civilizing" potential of colonialism to free African natives from primitivism, superstition, slavery, cannibalism, lack of hygiene, and other scourges. They often claim that local populations live in the past and therefore need to be brought up to par with present time, always represented by Western modernity. Once the protagonist realizes the big lie that is colonialism, however, he begins to encourage others to see the world from the point of view of the indigenous victims. More importantly, unlike the perspective offered in *The Storyteller* and *Death in the Andes*, now the narrative voice, using free indirect style and avoiding any sort of ontological ambiguities, ironically condemns Pablo Zumaeta's and other rubber plantation chiefs' habit of justifying "the worst atrocities against pagans who, of course, were always cannibals and killers of their own children" (133). As seen in this quotation, the narrator presents the oppressors' accusations as a mere excuse for conquest, inhumane treatment, and brutal exploitation. There is no doubt in the narrator's or the protagonist's minds that the particular brand of western "civilization" that colonizers and rubber plantation owners are trying to impose in Congo and in the Amazonian region of Putumayo will only bring massive genocides.

## Nationalism and the Irrational Side of Human Nature

Vargas Llosa vindicates and restores the memory of this historical character as a freedom-fighter, who gave his life and savings to the struggle against colonialism, for the defense of indigenous rights, and for Ireland's emancipation. The author tries to elicit his readers' empathy by warning early, through an epigraph taken from the Uruguayan essayist José Enrique Rodó's *Motivos de Proteo*, 1909 (*Proteus' Motivations*), about the ambiguities of human nature. Casement's complex psychology turns him into an ideal literary character for Vargas Llosa, whose opus has often dealt with the leitmotif of the irrational side of human nature and humans' need to create fictions. *The Dream of the Celt* lets us know that, like all human beings, Casement had weaknesses and personal flaws. Besides his tendency to radicalism and fanaticism, he may have been a pedophile. Among the many contrasts and contradictions of his personality, he went from admiring the British Empire and working tirelessly on its behalf to conspiring against it and seeking Germany's assistance for his separatist aspirations during World War I. In fact, the British diplomat Sir Roger Casement devotes part of his life to Ireland's independence, while concomitantly serving the British government in Africa and South America so well that he attains British knighthood. Thus, in the last paragraph of chapter six, we learn that he was awarded with the Companion of the Order of St. Michael and St. George for foreign and diplomatic service only one day after declaring his hatred for the British Empire in an argument with his uncle Roger. Casement also went from abhorring the ominous fanaticism of the Irish nationalists he meets to becoming as radical as them. Along with the warning in the epigraph, Vargas Llosa offers a veiled justification of his protagonist's actions by reminding us that "politics, like everything else connected to power, at times brought to light the best in a human being—idealism, heroism, sacrifice, generosity—but also the worst—cruelty, envy, resentment, pride" (308).

The reader can observe Casement's progressive political radicalization through the eyes of his friend Herbert Ward. At first, we are told, he found a certain charm in Casement's "conversion" to nationalism (note the religious connotations of the term). Yet in his letters, Ward would warn his friend about the potential dangers of this ideology: "he joked about the dangers of 'patriotic fanaticism' and reminded him of Dr. Johnson's phrase, according to which 'patriotism is the last refuge of the scoundrel'" (141). Still not taking his friend's new ideological turn seriously, Ward continues to mock glitzy jingoism, whose love for flags, hymns, and uniforms is indicative of its provincial outlook, exhorting him to "return to reality and leave 'the dream of the Celt' into which he had retreated" (210; incidentally, this sentence reveals the negative connotation of the novel's title). With time, however, the tone of his warnings changes dramatically: Ward begins to condemn Casement's fanaticism and extremism. He criticizes, in particular, his increasing intolerance and his tendency to resort to yelling, instead of reasoning. Much to Casement's chagrin, as a result one day Ward sends him a letter that ends their long-lived friendship. Paradoxically, Casement notices that this letter exudes the same patriotic sentiment that his former friend had always despised as provincial. However, he also begins to wonder whether Ward is right: "*Am I turning into a fanatic?* He would ask himself from then on, at times with alarm" (305). The Irish historian Alice Stopford Green and the Irish-born playwright George Bernard Shaw also encourage their intellectual friends to avoid falling into an empty patriotism that may become a substitute for reason, lucidity, and intelligence.

Casement is, therefore, a Quixotic figure, who ends up in poverty because he donated most of his savings to humanitarian and nationalist organizations. Blinded by his hatred of the British Empire and determined to fight for justice in Congo, Peru, and Ireland, he fearlessly defies death on several occasions. Yet, as forewarned in the epigraph, the protagonist also has a darker side: like the other fanatic protagonists in Vargas Llosa's novels, he knows no limitations in the fulfillment of what he considers his duty. For example, when the other members of the British commission argue that it is time to return to England because they have accumulated enough information, Casement insists on staying in Putumayo to gather new data that may make his report more exhaustive and convincing. In reality, however, his desire to stay has to do with his new obsession with meeting Armando Normand, the most sadistic and cruel of all the Peruvian Amazon Company's chiefs. In the narrator's words, "He was rather perversely curious to meet him" (182).

During his trips to Africa, Casement loses his innocence upon discovering the true nature of colonization. Later, he claims to have discovered his own country by comparing Ireland's subjugation to England to the situation of the Congo Free State under the colonization of King Leopold II's Belgium. After denying it for years, the protagonist finally admits that Ireland, like the Congo Free State, is also a colony. Now, his greatest fear and obsession is that, unless his compatriots rebel soon enough against British colonization, they will end up, like the native people in Amazonia and Congo, losing their soul, becoming fatalistic automatons, and suffering the same process of moral disintegration that will render them helpless. During his stay in Africa, there is also a process of self-discovery through which he finds his own sexual orientation. While neither the plot nor the epilogue present Casement's homosexuality as a negative trait, there is a hint at a truly dark side of the protagonist, his possible pedophilic behavior: "a gloomy aureole of homosexuality and pedophilia surrounded his image throughout all of the twentieth century" (354), states the author in the epilogue. The British government takes revenge on Casement for his conspiracy against the Empire not only by hanging him, but also by making his personal diaries public, which ruins his reputation even more. In them, the usually mild-mannered protagonist uses lewd and obscene language to describe his personal encounters with young men and, although this is purposely unclear in the novel, perhaps also with boys. According to both the narrative voice in the plot and Vargas Llosa in the epilogue, many of the scenes described in the diary, specifically where he pays young men to have sex with him, were probably only exaggerations or described his sexual desires rather than his life experiences. In any case, they affected public opinion for decades, not only in England but also in Ireland, where his contribution to the struggle for independence was not acknowledged until much later.

## Conclusion

*The Dream of the Celt* underscores the difficulties of reconstructing historical events and of judging historical figures. In fact, the discipline of history is described in the novel as "a branch of fable-writing attempting to be science" (215) and disparaged as a colonizing tool used by the British to make Irish students believe that their country had no history worth remembering. Casement himself bemoans that history will condemn him for leading the Easter Rebellion of April 24, 1916, even though, considering it a suicidal enterprise, he actually tried to stop it. The reason he was unsuccessful was precisely his lack of power and influence within the Irish separatist movement. By contrast, it is not too difficult to figure out the author's unambiguous stand for the westernization of indigenous cultures and against nationalist discourse, discredited (like indigenism in other novels) as a dangerous ideology and an anachronistic, naïve fiction.

Vargas Llosa's harshest criticism in this historical novel is not truly addressed at his flawed, yet still heroic protagonist, but rather, indirectly, at present-day nationalist discourses in Europe and Latin America. *The Dream of the Celt* is not an accusation against Casement, but an exploration of the personal, societal, and cultural traumas that led this epic hero to turn into a pathologically fanatic nationalist. In this sense, Birns has rightfully praised "Vargas Llosa's masterful ability to be at once objective and empathetic about a character without endorsing that character's ideology at all" (18). The protagonist, therefore, is an excuse to expose the dangers of nationalism in previous decades as well as today. Paradoxically, the novel ends up acknowledging that the romantic heroism of those "radicals" who gave their life for their country's freedom during the Easter Rebellion did achieve their objective of raising awareness among their compatriots and spurring them into anti-colonialist action. Today, it is widely acknowledged by historians that this uprising spawned events that led to the establishment of the Irish Free State in 1921, a fact that seems to undermine Vargas Llosa's arguments against nationalism.

## Notes

1. The essay will use the titles of the translation after the first mention of a Vargas Llosa novel.

2. In this case, as in all quotations from texts in Spanish in the Works Cited list, the translation is mine.

## Works Cited

Birns, Nicholas. "Tricontinental Modernities: Vargas Llosa's Late Turn against Imperialism in El sueño del celta." *Transmodernity* 2.2 (2012): 14–32.

De Castro, Juan E. *Mario Vargas Llosa: Public Intellectual in Neoliberal Latin America*. Tucson: U of Arizona P, 2011

Demicheli, Tulio. "Mario Vargas Llosa: El PSOE se ha vuelto el caballo de Troya de los nacionalismos." *ABC* 20 May 2007: 10–12

Kristal, Efraín. "'From Utopia to Reconciliation: *The Way to Paradise, The Bad Girl, The Dream of the Celt*." *The Cambridge Companion to Mario Vargas Llosa*. Ed. Efraín Kristal & John King. New York: Cambridge UP, 2012. 129–47.

_____. *Temptation of the Word. The Novels of Mario Vargas Llosa.* Nashville, TN: Vanderbilt UP, 1998.

Vargas Llosa, Mario. "The Culture of Liberty." *Foreign Policy* 122 (Jan. –Feb. 2001): 66–71.

_____. *The Dream of the Celt.* New York: Farrar, Straus & Giroux, 2012.

_____. "Raza, botas y nacionalismo." *El País* 15 Jan. 2006. Web. 1 Sep. 2013.

_____. *La utopía arcaica: José María Arguedas y las ficciones del indigenismo*. Mexico City: Fondo de Cultura Económica de México, 1996.

# Dissonant Worlds: Mario Vargas Llosa and the Aesthetics of the Total Novel

Mark D. Anderson

The young Mario Vargas Llosa searched during the 1960s and early 1970s for his own style, drawing on myriad sources to inform his thinking on the subject. As this style materialized in novels like *La casa verde*, 1966 (*The Green House*, 1968) and *Conversación en La Catedral*, 1969 (*Conversation in The Cathedral*, 1975), he penned a series of pieces of literary criticism on a vast and seemingly incongruous body of texts, ranging from Joanot Martorell's fifteenth-century chivalric novel *Tirant lo Blanc* and Flaubert's *Madame Bovary* to fellow Peruvian José María Arguedas' *Los ríos profundos* (*Deep Rivers*), not to mention his monumental doctoral dissertation on contemporary Colombian novelist Gabriel García Márquez's entire ouevre up to that point, published as *García Márquez: historia de un deicidio*, 1971 (García Márquez: The Story of a Deicide).[1] Common themes run through this literary criticism despite contextual distances, laying out his conceptualization of the novel as a genre.

The terms *novela total* (total novel), *ambición totalizadora* (totalizing ambition), and *afán totalizante* (totalizing desire) appear frequently in these texts, leading literary critics to identify the aesthetic of the "total novel" with Vargas Llosa in particular and the other writers of the Spanish-American literary "Boom" of the 1960s: especially García Márquez, Carlos Fuentes, and Julio Cortázar, but also Ernesto Sábato and Fernando del Paso. Although the total novel is primarily associated with these authors' early works, it has resurfaced in recent years in discussions of maximalist works, such as Roberto Bolaño's massive *2666,* 2004 and even North American David Foster Wallace's *Infinite Jest*, 1996. Extrapolating from the Boom authors' novels as much as what Vargas Llosa says about the genre, critics usually view the *total novel* as a distinctly Latin American strain of literary modernism that combines structural experimentation similar to that of Faulkner and Dos Passos and stylistic singularity under the sign of Proust and Joyce with postcolonial concerns arising from the Latin American context. Such concerns include the construction of more inclusive, democratic modes of cultural and political representation; the critical reappraisal of the relationships between oral and written histories; and cosmopolitanism as an approach to transcending the center-periphery dialectic at the heart of colonialism. These novels are identifiable by their vast scale; an encyclopedic but "anthropophagic" range of cultural references; multiple, entwined narrative strands recounted by polyphonic voices; synchronistic representations of time and space; and, not least, by their massive volume.[2] One might add the rejection of allegory as a means to apprehending social relations, since the multiple narrative strands are designed to preserve individual, class, and ethnic specificities, while simultaneously portraying their emplacement within systematic social relations. In this sense, most novels that critics describe as *total* take a predominantly realist approach to representation, although they often incorporate mythological or fantastical elements that bring into relief the horizons of the real by exceeding its bounds.

Paradoxically, given that critics usually view the *total novel* as a product of the Spanish American Boom, Vargas Llosa appears to have borrowed his terminology from Franco-Lithuanian novelist Romain Gary, who opposed the "roman total" (total novel) to the "roman totalitaire" (totalitarian novel) in his own meditations on crafting literature in *Pour Sgagnarelle*, 1965 (For Sgagnarelle). In this work, Gary developed many of the key concepts that resurface in Vargas Llosa's reflections on the total novel, including: those concepts regarding the autonomy of art from ideological stances, since ideological art "subjects the world to itself" in totalitarian fashion; that the novel should constitute a total "fictional universe" that does not claim to represent faithfully the real world (as in the ideological novel) and yet rivals it in scope, thus questioning the hegemony of what we take collectively for the real; and that the novelist "plays God" within this fictional world, displacing in the Freudian sense his own ideological pretensions to absolute truth and totalitarian world interpretation (and, by extension, to world domination, the implicit *telos* of all ideology) to the realm of explicitly fictional authority, only to abandon the fictional world to its own devices in the same way that God is absent from his creation (22–24).[3] Gary, in turn, drew inspiration from nineteenth-century French poet Stéphane Mallarmé's frustrated desire to write an infinitely open and endless book that he simply called "le Livre." Of course, Vargas Llosa was also shaped by prior Latin American thinking on the topics of artistic representation and literary craft, even when he didn't always acknowledge his sources: especially the work of Jorge Luis Borges and Chilean avant-garde poet Vicente Huidobro (both of whom were certainly familiar with Mallarmé's project), but one could also cite as antecedents authors as diverse in style as Martín Adán, Macedonio Fernández, Leopoldo Marechal, Juan Carlos Onetti, Guimarães Rosa, and Juan Rulfo.[4]

## Novel as Dissonance

Critics have often expressed frustration with the ambiguities present in Vargas Llosa's rather spotty theory of the total novel, even when many of them have employed the terminology that he popularized in Spanish America. He formulated his thoughts on the topic most coherently in "Carta de batalla por *Tirant lo Blanc*," 1969 ("Going to Battle for *Tirant lo Blanc*"); *García Márquez. Historia de un deicidio*, 1971; and *La orgía perpetua. Flaubert y* Madame Bovary, 1975 (*The Perpetual Orgy: Flaubert and* Madame Bovary, 1986), but never as an autonomous theory. His writing on the topic was always interspersed throughout his works of literary criticism. His theory of the total novel thus remained maddeningly inconclusive, resurfacing inconsistently and incompletely throughout his essays and interviews dealing with literary craft. This apparent inconclusiveness may derive in part, of course, from its referential position with respect to Romain Gary's more comprehensive exploration of the topic, a referentiality that Vargas Llosa felt no need to acknowledge, since nearly all of his critical works are addressed to writers rather than critics. He is primarily interested in the liberating possibilities of literature for the individual as self-creator, not in consolidating a coherent theory of aesthetics. Many critics nevertheless found his failure to establish a convincing explanation of the connections between artistic creation and social representation (beyond including social injustices among the "demons" that can haunt a writer and compel him or her to produce literature) quite paradoxical given the realist mode within which he writes. Indeed, he has consistently and unapologetically privileged the author's creative autonomy over commitment to social representation or political engagement, a situation that critics, interested in the relationships between art, social justice, and political change, have found particularly vexing, since his works seem to foreground precisely these social and political themes. Given his recent Nobel Prize, however, the time seems ripe for a second look at Vargas Llosa's thinking on the aesthetics of social representation as well as an assessment of whether or not it retains any relevance to our current moment in cultural history.

Vargas Llosa often states in interviews that writing comes from a position of fundamental dissatisfaction or unhappiness with reality. This dissatisfaction drives the author to annihilate or abolish reality by substituting it for the symbolic:

> Writing novels is an act of rebellion against reality, against God, against God's creation, which is reality. It is an attempt to correct, change, or abolish real reality, to substitute it with a fictional reality created by the novelist. He is a dissident: he creates illusory life, he creates worlds of words because he doesn't accept life and the world the way they are (or as he believes them to be). The root of his vocation is a feeling of dissatisfaction with life; every novel is a secret deicide, a symbolic assassination of reality (*García Márquez. Historia de un deicidio* 85).

For Vargas Llosa, writing is an inherently deconstructive activity. By replacing reality with a vast scale model of itself (he compares the total novelist to Borges' demented cartographers, who wished to create a 1:1 scale map of the real world), the author draws attention to the symbolic nature of "life and the world" as they are or "as he believes them to be."[5] If what we take as the real can be displaced even momentarily by a fictional "world of words" that seems equally real within its own context or may even appear to constitute a deeper reality than that which can be observed empirically, the notion of the real itself comes into question. It becomes a matter of precedent (how one envisions the past) rather than present (what can be observed empirically at any given moment), and, therefore, it also becomes a matter of imagination, "belief," interpretation, or ideology.

Upon emerging from a purely imaginary world that nevertheless seems real during the event of reading, the reader is drawn into a dialectical confrontation between two realities: the explicitly fictional one, constituted in his or her imagination, and the one that seems external and therefore objective, yet only persists as an imagined whole assembled from perceptions and memories that are fragmented, both temporally and spatially. The fictional world thus enters into a relationship of dissonance with the real world, and the reader is forced to come to grips with the fact that, irrespective of the existence of an objectively measurable reality, worlds are always assembled and interpreted within the mind. The fiction/reality dialectic is thus negative, since it cannot transcend itself. Its synthesis is the negation of the dialectic itself because the reconciliation of opposites results in a paradox: the postulation of an immaterial fictional component to material reality. In this way, the ideological transcendence of reality is shown always to be irreal—a fiction.

Vargas Llosa avoids the "there is nothing outside the text" aporia of deconstructionism, however, because he believes that there is a fundamentally real, material reality, even if we are ultimately only able to perceive it through the distortions of culture. The goal of culture, then, becomes self-erasure: it must get as close as possible to the real in order to be able to transform it more efficiently, to make reality ever more amenable to human habitation through material development and the implementation of universal human rights, and thus render its own fantastic (fictional), trauma-mediating aspects unnecessary. In this rather reductionist scenario, the fiction/reality dialectic serves to unmask ideology (and idealism of any kind) as what distances culture from reality, frustrating the project of development.

In order for this dialectical confrontation to occur, however, the fictional world must seem real, not symbolic: thus, the importance for Vargas Llosa of using realist modes of representation. As he stated in an interview, "The raison d'être of all fiction is to be experienced, lived, not as a lie, but as truth. Paradoxically, because of its own nature, fiction is and can only be a lie" ("Demons and Lies" 17). A work that draws attention to its language—to its own symbolic nature—could never aspire to supplement for reality as a whole; it would always seem ancillary to it, subordinated in the same way that language appears empirically subordinate to the material objects it describes. Likewise, more specialized genres, like the fantastical novel or the psychological novel, also subordinate themselves to reality by disassociating themselves explicitly from it: since they claim no pretension to objectivity, they appear to be exclusively subjective, partial interpretations, or even pure fiction, with no relation to the real world. The total novel, on the contrary, "plagiarizes real reality," taking all of its elements from it, but configuring them in a closed order that never appears in nature (*García Márquez* 11–13). As he writes about Martorell's *Tirant lo Blanc*, the total novel attempts to "impose itself as the only total reality that is at the same time a representation of total reality, which it mirrors illusorily in all of its enormities and minutiae and at all of its scales—it has its replica or equivalence in the essential parts that compose it" ("Carta de batalla por *Tirant lo Blanc*" 38–39).

This is true in the quantitative, material sense, since the total novel models its broad array of characters, settings, and plots on real life, but it also encompasses subjective aspects of human experience, becoming a "verbal object that communicates the same sensation of plurality as the real, it is, like reality, act and dream, objectivity and subjectivity, reason and wonder. In this consists its 'total realism,' the supplanting of God" ("Carta de batalla por *Tirant lo Blanc*" 26). The subjective does not detract from the total novel's autonomy from the real world, however, since it acquires the appearance of objectivity due to its scalar relationship to the realistic fictional world as a whole: "because of Flaubert's maniacally materialistic style, the subjective reality in Madame Bovary is possessed of a solidity, a physical weight, as palpable as that of physical reality" (*The Perpetual Orgy* 11). It is this vast interplay between scales that endows the fictional world with its own, autonomous existence within the mind of the reader, an autonomy that is absolutely necessary to compete with and destabilize the worldviews that we take for unquestionable reality.

Unlike the chaotic real world, however, the total novel imposes structure and plot over all of the elements that compose it, making its reality legible in a way that objective reality could never be. As the totality of real world phenomena, material reality can never exceed or transcend itself as interpretation; in the absence of God or some other metaphysical entity capable of endowing reality with uniform, absolute meaning, there is nothing outside of reality. The total novel, on the other hand, presents itself as a body that is "more than the sum of its parts" (*The Perpetual Orgy* 30). That excess, that exceeding of the bounds of reality, is what Vargas Llosa calls the "elemento añadido" (added element)—the explicitly supplementary, interpretative component that only a God can endow to his creation. Order is thus originality, and it is always exterior to empirical reality:

> The representation of total reality that a novel can give is illusory, a mirage: qualitatively identical, it is quantitatively a minute, imperceptible particle compared to the infinite vertigo that inspires it. It gives the impression of being a chaos as vast as the original, but it is not that chaos; it represents reality because it took from it all the atoms that compose its being, but it is not that reality. Its difference is its originality ("Carta de batalla por *Tirant lo Blanc*" 33).

The added element is, thus, what makes visible and inescapable the supplementarity of the total novel to objective reality: the explicit fictionality that prevents it from being taken as non-fiction or real truth.

This is the crux of Vargas Llosa's notion of deicide. As Romain Gary pointed out, "one never plays God legitimately" (24). By playing God within the fictional world in an explicitly supplementary way (Vargas Llosa favors the term "suplantador de Dios" [imposter of God]), the author of the total novel supplants God (absolute truth) in his position in the real world, but occupies only illegitimately that position, effectively "killing" or invalidating it. The order of the fictional world calls attention to the absence of the author, since it is only that absence that makes the fictional world simultaneously ordered and autonomous or self-sustaining. In contrast, the disorder of empirical reality (which becomes evident through contrast with the fictional order of the novel) exposes not the absence, but the death of God (in the Nietzschean sense). For Vargas Llosa, order is a purely human creation.

The author of the total novel is not really a god-like lone creator situated beyond society, however; the added element is a response to a provocation, a possession, a haunting in the sense in which Derrida used the word in *Specters of Marx*. For Vargas Llosa, the drive to create an autonomous world that frees the author from the horror of unordered, chaotic reality derives from the need to exorcize "demons"—individual and collective traumas that possess the author, forcing him to respond obsessively to the imperative that they place on him or her:

> The point of departure of the novelistic calling, the vocation of creating with words and with the imagination worlds that are distinct from the real world, is born of a certain conflict, some incompatibility with lived experience that induces a person, generally in an obscure, nonrational manner, to seek out the alternative offered by fiction. The imagination does not work in a vacuum, it is not a gratuitous movement of the spirit, it operates drawing upon that conflict, trauma, interdict, enmity. [...] I call all of this "demons," metaphorically ("Demons and Lies" 15).

In psychoanalytical terms, of course, Vargas Llosa's evocation of the "demon" recalls the threat that the "Other" poses to the Self—as Sartre proclaimed famously in the final lines of *No Exit*, "Hell is other people," which is as likely a source for Vargas Llosa's terminology as the more commonly cited Goethean demonic.[6] The author attempts to expel others' haunting, "demonic" presences from his consciousness through narrative, incorporating them into his self-narrative (identity) as sameness or expelling them through testimony or other biographical modes of representation. However, since those presences always exceed the words used to represent them, indelible traces—loose memories—remain. Furthermore, Vargas Llosa appears to agree with Levinas that the Other places ethical exigencies on the Self. Those internalized traces of the Other continually demand that we represent them, that we testify on their behalf, even when symbolization will always be inadequate. This situation cannot be resolved definitively even by becoming a god within the fictional world:

> No novelist can free himself of that fixation, the weight of that moment of rupture [with reality and/or identity] that cumbers the practice of the impersonator of God. [...] The exercise of his vocation is a palliative, not a remedy. He will never triumph in that vertiginous, almost unconscious drive to substitute: every novel will be a failure, every story a letdown (*García Márquez* 95).

Those demons from the novelist's past will thus endlessly compel him or her to produce symbolic substitutions, to testify to their existence and externalize them as distinct, dialogic voices within his or her own narrative. There is never the possibility of permanent closure.

Furthermore, the fundamental incompatibility or break with reality that Vargas Llosa insists on as the origin of fiction recalls Lacan's notion of the horrifying and traumatic nature of the encounter with the unmediated, undifferentiated real—that which resists symbolization and order. Indeed, it is precisely this chaotic undifferentiation that the novelist attempts to overcome by imposing fictional structure, creating a symmetrical world in which everything is neatly categorized in binary oppositions:

> In this binary world, one is two, that is to say, everything is itself and its replica, at times itself, at times deformed; almost nothing exists for itself alone, since almost everything is duplicated in something that confirms and denies it. . . The fictitious reality, unlike the real

one, does not give the impression of increasing and multiplying freely, chaotically, but, rather, of doing so within the framework of an inflexible overall plan, obeying an imminent law or universal virtuality (*The Perpetual Orgy* 146).

Vargas Llosa thus coincides with poststructuralism in critiquing the imposition of arbitrary symmetries over real reality, which he equates to a magical rather than rational thought process. He is careful to point out, however, that this fictional structure of binaries is necessary to create the impression of totality, but it cannot be dialectical if it wishes to preserve the autonomy of the fictional world; the oppositions are complementary or contradictory, but no synthesis transcending the opposition can be made (*The Perpetual Orgy* 147). In this way, the total novel uses structure to mitigate the traumatic chaos of undifferentiated reality, but it maintains, within the fictional world, the traces and appearance of that reality by rejecting synthetic resolution.

On the other hand, Vargas Llosa explicitly rejects a psychoanalytical explanation of his concept of the "demon" due to its pathologizing of creativity: "I did not want to use the word *trauma* so as not to give an orthodox Freudian explanation; nor do I believe that it can be explained as merely stemming from neurosis. It is a type of conflict that can be infinitely broader than that determined purely pathologically" ("Demons and Lies" 15). For Vargas Llosa, this fundamental unhappiness or dissatisfaction with reality, this haunting by demons becomes a productive experience, as it is the only way to conceive of alternate realities. If one were content with real reality, one would be unable to develop a critical stance towards it, and there would be no need for fiction at all. And if there were no creation, there would be no self-creation either; those demons are the traces of others in us, traces that can never be exorcized fully, as that would imply the dissolution of the self as a fundamentally dialogic construct.

While Vargas Llosa flirts with psychoanalysis in his own attempts at unveiling the demons that motivated Flaubert and García Márquez to write, he recognizes the ultimate impossibility of establishing causality, which could only be a reductive enterprise. Much more important to his theory is this analysis of the process whereby fictions are created subjectively, yet take on their own life, seeming real. As much as he esteems literature, he is more concerned about "fiction that doesn't recognize itself as such, that has pretensions of being an objective reading of reality" ("Demons and Lies" 18). His meditations on literature thus become reflections on the construction of ideology, of Marx's "false consciousness," that is, on the way in which intellectual constructs, leading to a particular worldview, are naturalized and then become self-evident or autonomous for their readers—often leading to catastrophic results. It is noteworthy that the ideological fiction, to which Vargas Llosa refers in that particular quote, is not that which his detractors would likely expect, given his political orientation: he is alluding to nineteenth-century liberalism (a philosophy with which his critics often associate him) as it manifested itself in the 1897 massacre of peasants in Canudos by the troops of the Brazilian Republic, the subject of his novel *La guerra del fin del mundo*, 1981 (*The War of the End of the World*, 1984). In this scenario, literature's explicit fictionality unmasks the fictionality of ideologies of all stripes, even those close to the author ("Demons and Lies" 18).

## The Total Novel in Context
Initially, leftist critics, who viewed literature primarily as a vehicle for social truths, were able to sidestep the problematic relations between Vargas Llosa's theorization of the total novel as a fundamentally deconstructive genre and his novelistic practice because his narrative represented social relations in unambiguously realist fashion and because he himself supported, in word and deed, the 1959 Cuban revolution, even serving on the governing board of revolutionary Cuba's most prominent cultural organization, the Casa de las Américas. During this period, Vargas Llosa's resounding proclamation that literature was a "permanent insurrection" against reality was assumed to be an attack against only a certain reality, that of neocolonial, exploitative capitalism (De Castro & Birns 2–3). His insistence on the autonomy of literary creation could thus easily be

associated with Marxist literary critic Georg Lúkacs' formulation of the realist novel as an "organic" work of art that achieved autonomy from its creator's bourgeois worldview by reproducing reality objectively. Following Vargas Llosa's so-called "neoliberal turn" in the 1970s, however, his emphasis on creative liberty came to be viewed by Marxist critics as a bourgeois validation of individualism that conflicted with movements for collective social justice, even when they continued to view many of his novels as exemplary representations of systematic social relations. Ironically, Vargas Llosa was not particularly well received by literary autonomists either, perhaps due to the social content of his works: Borges, for example, claimed disdainfully to have never bothered opening one of Vargas Llosa's novels (Interview with Soler Serrano).

Similarly, Vargas Llosa's formulation of the total novel was, at first, quite appealing to nationalistic projects of democratization and the decolonization of racial identities, whether those of the political left or the more center-right liberal democrats. In nationalistic frameworks, the novel often becomes an allegory of integration under a single form, even in the midst of tension and conflict. For critics interested in national identities and the construction of horizontal, democratic civil societies, then, works like *The Green House* and *Conversación en La Catedral* and *Conversation in The Cathedral* provided insight into how unreconciled social and racial tensions could resolve into a single, heterogeneous narrative. At the same time, *La ciudad y los perros*, 1963 (*The Time of the Hero*, 1966) and *Conversation in The Cathedral* delivered powerful indictments of authoritarian governments and their effects for civil society, which, in the novels, degenerates into a Spencerian free-for-all. Most of Vargas Llosa's novels can, therefore, be read in the negative, as advocating for democratic equality under the rule of law by rejecting authoritarianism at any scale, from the family to the nation. Indeed, this is a reading that Vargas Llosa himself has fostered in essays, interviews, and his 1990 presidential campaign, portraying himself as a champion of egalitarian democracy.

The validity of this political persona came into question, however, when he rejected explicitly *Indigenismo* as a mode for incorporating indigenous peoples into national political and cultural citizenship in several works written in the 1980s. As Ignacio López-Calvo has pointed out, Vargas Llosa's novels and essays dealing with Peru's problematic relations with its indigenous citizens paint a scenario in which indigenous identities cannot be conserved within modernity (123). His discourse on the *indio* thus seemed to mirror anachronistic nineteenth-century liberal arguments about the unfitness of indigenous cultures for modern economic and political life—a decidedly undemocratic position that threw Vargas Llosa out of synch with the multiculturalism that became the primary way of conceiving nationhood in late twentieth-century neoliberalism. He has attempted to problematize this stance in more recent years, especially in order to clarify his position in relation to U.S. neoconservativism, but he nevertheless continues to promote a view of identity in which the individual must be liberated from the constraints of any collective identity, whether ethnic, racial, or even national (De Castro 57–58). For readers sympathetic to US-style multiculturalism and identity politics, then, the total novel has come to represent an elitist attempt to encompass ethnic and social differences in a single, anachronistic grand narrative of Western universalism. The total novel would, therefore, be superseded by testimonial modes of discourse—popular self-representation—during the rise and implementation of neoliberal multiculturalism in the 1980s.

Yet another impediment to the acceptance of the total novel as a valid theory of aesthetics arises from its intimate association with the Spanish-American Boom, which many critics now view primarily as a commercial phenomenon—a marketing ploy developed by the Spanish Seix-Barral publishing house to promote its affiliated authors and to open an international market for literature in Spanish. Brett Levinson, for example, has argued that the Boom was a mechanism for incorporating the radical literary experimentation of "high modernism" into the marketplace, accompanying the shift in political power away from the elite "cultured" class toward the democratic consumerism of the bestseller, and thus playing a role in the construction of Latin America as a regional market within globalized capitalism (23). In this reading, the Boom would be inseparable from the rise of neoliberal capitalism in Latin America, an assessment that is in no way hindered by Vargas Llosa's strident support for neoliberalism.

The theory of the total novel, as laid out by Vargas Llosa, problematizes this perspective, however, provoking turbulence within the projects of the Boom and the Post-Boom to integrate Latin America into the global cultural marketplace via "World Literature." Unlike life-writing or even avant-garde technical experimentation, the total novel retains its explicitly supplementary or destabilizing position with respect to reality, even when the novels themselves are incorporated into the culture industry as material products that are bought and sold in the global marketplace. During the event of reading, at least, the realistic fictional world demands equal status as a totality, as an alternative reality that rivals in scale and scope what we take for real reality. And one totality can never modify another, becoming subordinated to it as part; since it is of the same infinite scale, it can only replace the other, never be incorporated into it. It is this showdown between two totalities that produces that dialectical confrontation, in which worldview is shown to be an ideological construct rather than empirical reality. This dialectical confrontation will occur regardless of whether or not the novel is a marketable product. It is a question of structure rather than political positioning.

This is precisely the aspect of Vargas Llosa's writing that confounds his leftist critics, whose belief in the fundamental complementarity of aesthetics and politics does not easily permit a reconciliation between the subversive realism of his novels, their market status as bestsellers, and Vargas Llosa's own "right wing" politics. Nevertheless, Romain Gary's foundational opposition between the "totalitarian novel" and the "total novel" made clear that the latter was designed precisely to disrupt the convergence of aesthetics, politics, and the marketplace in the undemocratic manufacture of consensus and consent, and thus maintain the fundamentally critical and subversive position of fiction with respect to society. The total novel may thus question the Marxist perception of the world as ordered exclusively by economic forces, but it also undermines neoliberal claims regarding the "end of history" in the triumph of capitalist "pragmatism" over utopian idealism.

Paradoxically, given Vargas Llosa's explicit support of neoliberal capitalism, his anti-authoritarian streak—that view of literature as a "permanent insurrection"—coheres with the most recent work of leftist political philosophers, such as Giorgio Agamben, Alain Badiou, and Jacques Rancière, who are concerned about the real possibilities for political action in the era of globalized neoliberal consensus under the sign of democracy. Building on theories critical of mass capitalism developed by Herbert Marcuse and Theodor Adorno following World War II, these authors argue that the civil society that ostensibly upholds democracy, providing equality through horizontal access to "political speech" (the vote), has been supplanted by a civil society rooted in the uniformity of consumerism rather than potential for political action. The governing political class neutralizes potentially dissident collective political identities by segregating them within demographic groups by age, ethnicity, race, sex, and/or other factors. These demographics are distributed in such a way as to create binary oppositions between majorities and minorities, in which the minority groups' access to political speech is always superseded by that of a majority group. People have the vote, but their votes do not count in a political sense, only in a demographic one—and those demographics are coordinated by the state to create the appearance of democratic consensus. The loss of political power is then mitigated by providing access to consumer comforts to the degree necessary in order to maintain the calm, recasting social inequalities as market segmentation: there is a product for everyone, just not the same product.

In this situation of total consensus that recognizes no exclusions (no opposition), the only truly political act is to reveal publicly the reality that the process of demographic segmentation creates minorities that are excluded from democratic political agency. This may be achieved through a variety of strategies, such as when popular movements occupy public spaces, but literature and art can also play a critical role in making visible the contradictions within the neoliberal consensus that, since it encompasses all demographics, claims to be solely pragmatic and objective, not ideological. In this climate of totalitarian material and political consensus, dissonance of any kind has become politicized. Vargas Llosa's conceptualization of the total novel as dissonance thus provides a useful tool for revealing what Rancière calls the "gaps within the sensible" in order to disrupt the manufacture of consensus. Indeed, recent total novels, such as Daniel Sada's *Porque parece mentira la verdad nunca se sabe*, 1999 (*Because it seems like a lie, the truth may never be known*) and Roberto Bolaño's *2666*, transparently draw upon the power of dissonant worlds for political ends, disrupting the seemingly implacable inertia of political pragmatism under neoliberal capitalism. The total novel's invalidation of absolute consensus can thus no longer be read as pure, disinterested deconstruction; it has become a mode of dissent or, to use Rancière's terminology, dissensus.

## Notes

1. The essay will use the titles of existing translations after the first mention of a Vargas Llosa novel or essay.

2. In line with the Brazilian modernists' use of "anthropophagy" to describe willful acts of subversive postcolonial mimicry, Vargas Llosa frames the creative process as "an act of cannibalism: these materials are digested fully by the new reality, transformed into a distinct and homogeneous substance" (García Márquez. Historia de un deicidio 481).

3. In this case, as in that of all works not in English in the Works Cited list, the translation is by the author of this essay.

4. Vargas Llosa frequently discusses his relationship with Borges, but he never mentions Huidobro's influence on his work, which seems highly likely given the language used in creacionista works, like "Arte poética," "La creación pura," and "Total." On the other hand, there is always the possibility of a common source for their shared language in French authors, like Flaubert, Hugo, Mallarmé, and Proust.

5. He references Borges' "Del rigor en la ciencia" in "Carta de batalla por Tirant lo Blanc" 11.

6. Vargas Llosa has frequently acknowledged the influence that Sartre had on him as a young writer (Williams 101–103). Regarding the Goethean notion of literary creation as an irrational process, see the

debate between Ángel Rama and Vargas Llosa in García Márquez y la problemática de la novela (25–33). Efraín Kristal provides a more complete genealogy of this line of thought in The Temptation of the Word (3–4).

## Works Cited

Borges, Jorge Luis. Interview with Joaquín Soler Serrano. *A Fondo*. Radiotelevisión Española. 23 April 1980. Web. 15 Dec. 2013.

De Castro, Juan E. *Mario Vargas Llosa: Public Intellectual in Neoliberal Latin America*. Tucson: U of Arizona P, 2011.

De Castro, Juan E. & Nicholas Birns, eds. *Vargas Llosa and Latin American Politics*. New York: Palgrave MacMillan, 2010.

Gary, Romain. *Pour Sgagnarelle: Reserche d'un personnage et d'un roman*. Paris: Gallimard, 1965.

Kristal, Efraín. *Temptation of the Word: The Novels of Mario Vargas Llosa*. Nashville, TN: Vanderbilt UP, 1998.

Levinson, Brett. *The Ends of Literature: The Latin American "Boom" in the Neoliberal Marketplace*. Stanford, CA: Stanford UP, 2001.

López-Calvo, Ignacio. "Going Native: Anti-Indigenism in Vargas Llosa's *The Storyteller* and *Death in the Andes*." *Vargas Llosa and Latin American Politics*. Eds. Juan E. De Castro & Nicholas Birns. New York: Palgrave Macmillan, 2010. 103–24.

Rama, Ángel & Mario Vargas Llosa. *García Márquez y la problemática de la novela*. Buenos Aires: Corregidor, 1973.

Rancière, Jacques. *Dissensus: On Politics and Aesthetics*. Trans. Steven Concoran. New York: Continuum, 2010.

Vargas Llosa, Mario. "Carta de batalla por *Tirant lo Blanc*." *Carta de batalla por Tirant lo Blanc*. Barcelona: Seix Barral; Mexico City: Planeta, 1992. 9–58.

_____. "Demons and Lies: Motivation and Form in Mario Vargas Llosa." Interview with Luis Rebaza-Soraluz. *Review of Contemporary Fiction* 17.1 (1997): 15–24.

_____. *García Márquez. Historia de un Deicidio*. Barcelona: Barral, 1971.

_____. *The Perpetual Orgy: Flaubert and Madame Bovary*. Trans. Helen Lane. New York: Farrar, Straus & Giroux, 1986.

_____. *A Writer's Reality.* Ed. Myron I. Lichtblau. Syracuse, NY: Syracuse UP, 1991.

William, Raymond L. *Vargas Llosa. Otra historia de un deicidio.* México: Taurus, 2000.

# Mario Vargas Llosa and His Discontents_____

Will H. Corral

Since the fifties, Mario Vargas Llosa has marshaled nonfiction to expound on his fundamental tensions with the civilization that surrounds him. His novels fine-tune those beliefs, best defined by Raymond Henry Williams' analytical concept, "structures of feeling." The Peruvian's views of the last three decades or so on the often irreconcilable cultures that civilization can encompass make his detractors relapse obdurately to his far past. His 1960s commitment to progressive Latin American ideals under Western eyes was sincere, but his opponents modulate or ignore that fidelity, concluding he is fundamentally conservative, a purist, or worse. Such verdicts focus suitably on his later opinions about politics, dystopian technological revolutions, or the dislocation of recent art.

Williams' view about cultural change actually serves to checkmate Vargas Llosa's censors:

> In most description and analysis, culture and society are expressed in an habitual *past tense*. The strongest barrier to the recognition of human cultural activity is this immediate and regular conversion of experience into finished products... relationships, institutions and formations in which we are still actively involved are converted, by this procedural mode, into formed wholes rather than forming and formative processes (128, my emphasis).

Compare that appraisal to Henry James' in an 1880 letter to William Dean Howells:

> I sympathize even less with your protest against the idea that it takes an old civilization to set a novelist in motion—a proposition that seems to me so true as to be a truism. It is on manners, customs, usages, habits, forms, upon all these things matured and established, that a novelist lives—they are the very stuff his work is made of; and in saying that in the absence of those 'dreary and worn-out

paraphernalia' which I enumerate as being wanting in American society, 'we have simply the whole of human life left,' you beg (to my sense) the question (267).

James rejects Howells' judgment that "It is not provincial for an American to be American" (267), arguing that it is extremely provincial for Europeans to be Europeans. The Peruvian and James share that credence.

When brought away from fiction to more direct human interactions and motives, change—even when conceived as the alteration of mechanisms for understanding cultural symbols or value systems—is what Vargas Llosa undergoes; his antagonists usually do not, and, therein, lays the crux for interpreting his views. That change is in numerous ongoing debates of his nonfiction compilations, from the far-reaching volumes of writings from 1962 to 2012, collected as *Piedra de toque* (*Touchstones*), to *La civilización del espectáculo* (Civilization of the Spectacle, 2012).

If civilization is a too ample and bandied-about term for a particular writer to express individual friction or address it thoroughly, it is equally true that Vargas Llosa has the mettle and experience to present substantial statements that upend the historically instinctual repression with which intellectuals of his caliber deal with civilization and its avatars. For him, discovering the implications of recent cultural shifts is finding relations with greater "past" events without losing the urgency of the present. He approaches civilization as a natural process of human evolution that is rapidly losing social unity and creative power, two characteristics Arnold J. Toynbee saw as the nature of the breakdown of civilizations in *A Study of History* (1947).

## Historicizing His Clash with Civilization
Although undefined by them or their Latin American applications, Vargas Llosa's discontents should be analyzed as contemporaneous to a Western sense of crisis (the culture of complaint), the initially US-bound culture wars of the eighties and nineties, and how technology stopped being an industry to become a substratum of urban culture. These phases and writing without a nationalist mindset contextualize

his views. A succinct account of the earlier writings that culminate in his current views on civilization is in order, and scrutinizing the *Piedra de toque* tomes provides a key but incomplete perspective on his discontents because much more is and will be available by him on myriad cultural presences.[1]

The *Piedra de toque* volumes, part of his complete works in Spanish, comprise six hundred uncollected newspaper pieces. His relations with journalism are conflicted, and *Piedra de toque* elucidates how he will not have it otherwise. Unabridged, they evince ideological consistency, generic disobedience, unconventionality, and reliably contrarian views (sometimes extended further than they can be sustained) on culture and politics. His catholic interests will be in full view with imminent miscellanea volumes, the French edition of his writings, three previously published volumes of literary essays, autobiographical and political writings, and the commentary he still publishes every other week.

That variety obviously makes it difficult to choose representative pieces. For example, volume three contains multiple notes and references to Hussein, Chávez, and Fujimori, and the full contents of his Iraq diary and a series of essays on Israel/Palestine. This tome confirms his apparently instinctive ability to connect with his times, and there are other texts, in which he spares no praise or stridency in referring to cultural, social, and even personal matters. His world, then, is not exclusively geopolitical and humanistic. It is also difficult to disassociate these writings from his fiction, such as a 1969 essay on writing of *La casa verde*, 1966 (*The Green House*, 1968) (not included), or articles on the Congo and King Leopold related to *El sueño del celta*, 2010 (*The Dream of the Celt*, 2012), all of which abundantly confirm the complexity of his intertextual practices.

But he writes for cultured general readers, and as a literary thinker, his domain is as vast as that of Balzac, Orwell, and Updike, allowing durable arguments that those writers could be read as the Vargas Llosa of their times. Opposed to relativism, jargon, and self-righteousness, the touchstone approach displays a personal edge and less than subtle ideological subtexts, and no solace to his detractors. As standards or criteria by which something is judged, the *Piedra de toque* volumes recall his tenacity and intellectual design. A half-century later, one confirms that there is nothing traditional in this dialogic, pluralistic, interdisciplinary, thoughtful, and seldom dogmatic nonfiction.

Volume one shows that, in the early sixties, journalism was a left-hand occupation (conceivably because in 1963 and 1969, he wrote two novelistic masterpieces), asserting in the prologue, also titled "Piedra de toque," that "although journalism and literature have many things in common they are essentially different, precisely because in both genres the relation of the writer with language is very distinct, as is the reality each genre relays" (xi).[2] As with journalism, any bias is reflected in the subject he chooses to cover, not in the reporting. If perceived as orthodox, how does one explain his enduring attention to the dynamism of popular culture blenders and unorthodox narrative technique? Consequently, this volume includes seminal essays on his ideological evolution, from Sartre to Camus; critiques of "cheap" intellectuals (Corral 2009) and "primitive" novels; Mickey Mouse; and analogous uncollected notes, reports, and reviews.

In volume two—which includes other uncollected essays that bring readers back to volume one—literariness is more abundant, weaving Cervantes and Borges into discussions, and continuing that mode in volume three. *Maîtres-penseurs,* like Jean François Revel, Isaiah Berlin, F. A. Hayek, and mainly Karl Popper become major influences (see *Wellsprings,* 160–200, 133–159). Contemptuous of Castro and Pinochet, he does not disdain other polemical figures and teachable moments in cultural history or world politics. Direct and timely on archaic utopias, populism, postmodernism's gospels, and modish dysfunctions that threaten cultural cohesion, from the eighties on, his journalism fuses features of articles, speeches, essays, reports, notes, prologues and introductions, book reviews, and the like. It presents an unconventional blurring of boundaries that reveals his contemporaneity and ability to contest received ideas.

*Piedra de toque* gathers what could be termed a great thinker's "meta-auto-bibliography," and critics could spend another half-century deciphering it, while other readers are delighted,

---

instructed, and annoyed. Here, with intact professional ethics, powers undiminished, and influence extant are history, stories, organized memories, aesthetic premises, contextualized polemics, and criticism that show that caring too much who agrees or disagrees is the death of thinking. Other tenets, some unavailable in English, are found in texts that complement *Piedra de toque*, such as *Diccionario del amante de América Latina* (*Dictionary of the Lover of Latin America*, 2006), which coincide with his conviction, expressed in a 2005 essay absent from *Piedra de toque*, that in order to discover Latin America, one must leave it (as he did in the sixties), concluding that Europeans and Latin Americans understand one another because their worlds are "the front and back of the same civilization" ("Dentro y fuera de América Latina" 52).

By extension, he manifests that "The order that creates literature is benign and a benefactor, like that of some philosophies—not all of course—or the arts, or the democratic system, or the market. Thanks to them we can protect ourselves from chaos, putting it at the service of our tranquility and wellbeing" ("Bienvenido, caos" 430). Compare that assertion with his economic program for Peru, aimed at dismantling discriminatory structures and expressed in his 1993 memoir *El pez en el agua* (*A Fish in the Water*, 1994): "So that millions of the poor and marginalized Peruvians could finally accede to what Hayek calls the inseparable trinity of civilization: legality, liberty and property" (527).

His love/hate relationship with Peru is constant because his "style" stirs higher symbolic nooks and crannies, surpassing patriotic sentiments and his faith in international neoliberalism. It is a bond with clear antecedents that correct various stereotypes a committed native could have regarding a "colonized" Latin America, as he states in a 1970 article on Puerto Rico's images and reality:

> The United States has modernized that Latin raw material of flavorful humanity without destroying it completely, with factories that provide jobs and high salaries to the natives, with clean housing, highways, cars, with hotels and movie casinos that draw tourists from all over the world. The result is happiness: a country that maintains the best of barbarism and civilization, maracas and deodorant, warm

and spontaneous relationships and skyscrapers, air conditioning and home cooking ("Imágenes y realidad de Puerto Rico" 484).

In the nineties, his nonfiction centered on relating foreign sociocultural events to Latin America and in seeing universal truths in those relationships. In 1996's pro-market "Robin Hood y los alegres compadres" ("Robin Hood and the Merrymen"), he concludes:

> Those societies that know how to distinguish between the rich and the thief, bent on finishing off the latter and not the former, without inferiority complexes regarding well-earned wealth, and which have overcome the Christian and collectivist prejudice that makes poverty a value *per se*, are very few. But they are the ones that have reached the highest levels of existence and are at the vanguard of civilization (982–983).

The overall tenor of the items above, their contradictions, pet peeves, irritants, and the possibilities for intermingling that are noticeable in them, beg the question why his detractors do no credit to themselves by decontextualizing them, thereby exceeding the particular issues at stake through overstating the proximity between him and orthodox views of civilization. Vargas Llosa further complicates his assessments with an intellectual sovereignty that supports correspondences and discrepancies, and if the judgment of critics and artists can be corrected by time, those of artists last longer, making the blindness of the public give way to insight. Reading fictions as if their ultimate cultural effect could be summarized by recounting inferences from plots is a conservative approach that smacks of scholarly sensationalism, assuming plots shape responses. Further, whatever intricacies Vargas Llosa finds in his discontent, they are not elucidated in Freudian terms.

Coincidentally, the Spanish *El malestar en la cultura* is closer than *Civilization and Its Discontents* to Freud's *Das Unbehagen in der Kultur*. To Deborah Solomon's "What do you have against psychoanalysis?" for a 2007 *New York Times* interview, Vargas Llosa responded "It's too close to fiction, and I don't need more fiction in my life. I love stories, and my life is principally concentrated on stories, but not with a pretense of scientific precision" (15). His references to Freud are standard; his discontents not irreparable, as Freud would have it. *Malestar*—malaise, discomfort, uneasiness, or feeling ill—sustains his bibliotherapy: turning psychology into actions, revealing how often observations are presented as proven edicts, when they are just intriguing musings about human behavior. *Malestar*, thus understood, also helps explain why he still connects with the public.

There is another aspect that makes his clash with civilization different from that of the United States neoconservatives with whom he is inaccurately associated: If his fiction (plausible plots with profound characters) conforms to his understanding of life and his feeling for characters isolated from culture or civilization, his nonfiction avoids pondering when he has to explain, which brings his writing closer to the general expectations for an essay. Both procedures, different as they are, exhibit his gift for narrative, which his opponents admit grudgingly, implicitly expecting perfection from an author they seem to dislike personally.

## Civilization as Spectacle

After the praise for the Nobel and his cultural legacy by younger writers and an older intellectual cohort, Vargas Llosa resumed his characteristic polemical stances, confirming his dynamism, or obstinacy.[3] He was then too experienced and wise to let dogmatism creep into his nonfiction. Yet *La civilización del espectáculo* (Civilizaton of the Spectacle)—despite the spectacle of a mind calibrating its every move—is perceived as engaging, but rigid. No thesis of his has met similar reactions since *La utopía arcaica: José María Arguedas y las ficciones del indigenismo*, 1996 (Archaic Utopia: José María Arguedas and the Fictions of Indigenismo), a dazzling study of long gestation (Corral 2012, 286–292) on the flaws of committed writing. That essay paralleled a bespoke turn: since 1977's *Tía Julia y el escribidor* (*Aunt Julia and the Scriptwriter*, 1982), *A Fish in the Water*, and *El héroe discreto* (The Discreet Hero, 2013) and its riffs on civilization and culture, he regularly rehearses and revises his story of himself, intertwining biographical episodes into a larger narrative.

*La civilización del espectáculo* contains opinion articles published between 1995 and 2011, some abridged, revised, or updated. Preceded by an examination of civilization's metamorphoses and followed by a final reflection, the six chapters have one or two subsections in italics called "Antecedents," four of which were published before in English. Vargas Llosa shows the unity beneath the thematic diversity by adding longer linked essays for this edition, since his *idée-mère* (Alexis De Tocqville) and "unit-ideas" (Arthur O. Lovejoy) exist in other forms in *Piedra de toque*. By restructuring prior arguments, he stresses cross readings and signposts his conceptual uniformity, self-criticism, and how his output matches his ambition.

The extensive prefatory text (13–32) examines the shaky moorings of writings about civilization, perusing the rarefied cultural sphere of literary interpretation (about which he always has much to say), and ending in the jumbled arena of popular culture, whose meaning is now much more vague, more rooted in the past, just as its criticism is based mainly on currency, without making the case that preeminent popular culture could aspire to aesthetic seriousness comparable to high art. The discontents include journalism, contemporary art, postmodernity, imposing oppressive customs on democratic systems for the sake of diversity, the erosion of eroticism's possibilities, culture's links to politics and power, religious frivolity, and information's relation to knowledge and social media. The final reflection (199–207), a gloomy appraisal of civilization's future contamination, centers on disappearing aesthetic concerns, ideas, the value of printed books, and, revealingly, the realization that his essay cannot cover all related themes.

The first two chapters, devoted to his understanding of civilization (33–59–80) and culture (65–80), are programmatic and feasibly the most conceptually problematic for the authorial development detailed above. Sharing the nostalgia for the past that Spanish-language reviews attribute to the book, Roger Atwood recognizes Vargas Llosa's honesty, lucidity, and thoughtfulness, but feels "his arguments can be sweeping, to put it mildly" (32), and the book suffused with "stagey overstatements" (32). But Atwood misses the complexity of his remark that, were the volume a novel, its cast of characters would be "pretentious, grasping denizens of art galleries, sociology departments and tabloid newsrooms with few aspirations beyond their own enrichment and fame. They would have little idea of history or ideology" (32).

The complexity lays in the hybridity of his prose, as exemplified in his most recent novel. In *El héroe discreto*, Don Rigoberto, a character from other novels, thinks about how early retirement would allow him to "spend hours in his small civilized space, protected against barbarism, staring at his beloved etchings, the art books that crammed his library, listening to good music" (26). Or, finding a composition written by his son Fonchito, he shuts himself in his study to calibrate human freedom (196–97), riffing later on the role of journalism and reality and fiction as additional proof that "the small spaces of civilization will never prevail over immense barbarism" (201–02), art (251–52), journalism (330–31), and the coming wasteland that Don Rigoberto, never the author's alter ego, perceives are mainly Western, as his son Fonchito reminds him. But the pompous insurance executive retorts there is room for Peruvian culture: "Fernando de Szyszlo's paintings. César Moro's poetry in French. And the Majes shrimp, of course" (368).

That international and Spanish American to and fro is ultimately Western, and parallels the alternating points of view with which he structures the great majority of his novels. It is a pillar to post movement that also defines *La civilización del espectáculo*, particularly in chapters three (81–103) and four (105–128), devoted respectively to cultural prohibitions based on beliefs and what he believes to be the disappearance of eroticism. This is Vargas Llosa at his most liberal, in Anglo-American terms. Atwood finds chapter four, one with a nod to Freud and briefly autobiographical (111–12), "too broad to be convincing" (32). But Atwood undervalues Vargas Llosa's belief (based on Georges Bataille's ideas on permissiveness) that "The disappearance of prejudices, something in effect liberating, cannot mean the abolition of rituals, mystery, and the forms and discretion thanks to which sex became civilized and human" (110).

No less polemical, especially since he takes on polemicists, are the fifth chapter, on "Culture, Politics, and Power" (129–56), and the sixth on "The Opium of the People" (157–198). In reading these chapters and subsections, which register their original dates of publication, one should keep in mind that the time elapsed to their appearance in book form could mean that those issues are dynamic for the public, and their cultural relevance is, thus, more limited, even considering that Vargas Llosa chose to intermingle the main texts and their corollaries. If chapter five contains an excursus on audiovisual technology and its relation to censorship in authoritarian societies (134–37), concluding that "[i]n the civilization of spectacle the most denigrating roles are perhaps reserved for politicians" (137), it becomes diffuse by the notion that "A vital aspect of our times that abets the weakening of democracy is the disregard for the law" (145–51), especially when supported by an "Antecedent" on the Julian Assange affair (152–56), which is ongoing as of this writing.

The last chapter of *La civilización del espectáculo*, "The Opium of the People," is not a defense of religion, nor an attack. Rather, he sees it as one of those cultural polemics that no side can win. His interest, given that religion gives no sign of being eclipsed and gives every sign of a long life because "it is part of all known cultures and civilizations" (164) is whether this is good or bad for culture and freedom (163). Yet, the chapter is ultimately a defense of secularization, which cannot mean "persecution, discrimination or the prohibition of beliefs and cults, but untrammeled freedom" (175) for "the survival and perfection of democracy" (176). "Righting" religion's present problems is necessary for the free and open society he has been touting for years, and not surprisingly, he lists the *maîtres-penseurs* mentioned above who "pointed out economic and political freedom only fulfilled its civilizing function, which created wealth and employment and the defense of the individual's sovereignty … only when society's spiritual life was intense and kept alive and inspired a respected hierarchy of values" (182).

Vargas Llosa has come full circle in terms of his interest of the last three decades or so mentioned at the beginning. Before going on to an "Antecedent" on veils, burkas, and hiyabs, he ends this sixth chapter arguing that "immigration is indispensable for developed countries that want to continue being so and, also for that practical reason, ought to favor it and welcome workers of different languages and beliefs" (186). It is full circle because, agreeing in *Piedra de toque* with a refutation of Samuel Huntington's *The Clash of Civilizations* as a "fallacious myth because, for example, the Islamic world offers a very diverse spectrum of political realities" ("Después del diluvio" 274), Vargas Llosa in fact celebrates cultural difference and Latin American immigration to the United States (De Castro 57). Nevertheless, he believes, with Berlin, that "absolute freedom creates inequality" (Vargas Llosa and Magris 81) and, not seeing a prompt solution to issues of immigrant cultural identity, agrees with limits to cultural expression and migration (not by putting up walls, but by instilling democratic values in the countries of origin) "because there are things that a democratic society cannot renounce." (Vargas Llosa and Magris 85).

*La civilización del espectáculo* evidently reads culture as artistically bankrupt (and thus a greater danger for civilization) and scuffles with the default perspective that shock automatically confers value. Those who pinpoint his antiquarian shoring up of civilization's ruins fail to see how his unawareness of the value of the postmodern dismantling of hegemonic cultural grand narratives may be more threatening to their interests; or that, although he does not dismiss all contemporary cultural expressions as ephemeral, he could consider that scurrilous behavior and chaos can inspire fine works of art and literature. But because his command of detail and chronology hardly wanes, his nonfiction never projects the sense that, in the aftermath of crises, coincidental details acquire a larger significance as portents of what is to come.

As stated, the reception of the original was polemical and includes a dossier on the topic in an issue of Mexico's *Letras Libres*, but there were also positive reviews too numerous for the purpose of this reading.[4] Even considering that, as Vargas Llosa admits, much remains to be said about civilization, to claim that he is idealizing the past or being apocalyptic (as some of the reviewers posit) is to avoid the issue. It is not a matter of questioning him, as shown above, but of asking if he is right. For him, *present* culture is largely trivial because its relevancy derives from its contemporaneity, blatant commercialization, and obtuse academic interpretations,[5] where distinctions in aesthetic greatness, craftsmanship, originality of concept or subject, proven artistic trajectory, or any others mean little.

A persistent problem with his pronouncements on civilization is that what makes sense to him runs into the relativism that currently rules humanistic interpretation. Where he wants to find order in experience, professor-types discover designs for imaginative disorganization and, in the worst cases, for academic conflicts of interest, Altar of the Oppressed poses, self-branding, and unctuous back-scratching.[6] Actually, any anxiety, backlash or revulsion he expresses has to be contextualized by his backing of a civilization in which business plays a defining role. If, without those criteria, culture becomes public entertainment, why not add that such developments also mean that historically great works are defined by a "high" culture, in which influential names are as important as other considerations? Beyond petty squabbles, an impartial assessment of his conception of civilization shows tremors more than seismic shifts, self-critical steadiness, and usually unassailable logic from a shape-shifting mastermind.

## Conclusion

For his avowals on civilization and culture, Vargas Llosa revisits erstwhile topics, adds deductions, fills in gaps, finds addenda and polishes them, postulates negations, and provides inversions. It is a re-writing that actually minimizes the quarrels of critics intent on finding the source of his truth in his templates. In a February 29, 1984 letter, Saul Bellow invited him to a conference, stating a kindred self-concept: "The politics of our century tend to crush imagination—to present us with spectacles and conditions which appear to make art irrelevant. At the same time, in a variety of ways, it is clear that our fragile enterprise remains one of the best hopes of humanity—if we can keep it alive" (418). No wonder then that, to unravel disputes, he ultimately makes choices and compromises that take the rhetorical punch out of opposing views.

What writers of his renown cause reflex reactions from opponents and sympathizers, or exhibit compelling sensitivity and sophistication in adding undertones to undertones, without courting favor or resorting to hackwork? These queries are crucial for reading Vargas Llosa's views and legacy as a thinker, who believes in society and wants to enhance its civilization, but not in the techno-utopian mode preferred by contemporary opinionators that has the larger public still waiting for answers.

## Notes

1. Among them, *Diccionario del amante de América Latina* (*Dictionary of the Lover of Latin America*, 2006), published first in French and not coordinated by the author. For this volume's purposes, I refer readers to the available English-language nonfiction listed in the Works Cited as representative links between past and present views, rather than linear accountings that subsume important nuances. The *Piedra de toque* volumes are extensively reviewed by David Gallagher, "Fidel, Maggie and Liv."

2. In this case, as in that of all texts in Spanish in the Works Cited list, the translation is by the author of this essay.

3. Recognition abundantly expressed in Carmen Caffarel Serra et al., *Vargas Llosa. De cuyo Nobel quiero acordarme* (Vargas Llosa Whose Nobel I Want to Remember, 2011), and the autumn 2011 issue of the Chilean journal *Estudios Públicos* 122, edited by Arturo Fontaine, devoted entirely to him. He often opines generously on new writers, as in "Leer y escribir en Latinoamérica: entrevista a Mario Vargas Llosa."

4. See "¿Alta cultura o cultura de masas?", a conversation with critic Gilles Lipovetsky, whose ideological development and writings on the ephemeral nature and individualism of contemporary culture parallel Vargas Llosa's.

5. In "Saul Bellow and Chinese Whispers," he criticizes the permanent antagonism caused by identity politics in the United States, adding

"The university has abdicated its obligation to defend culture against fraud [...] the humanities have fallen into the hands of falsifiers and sophists of every hue, who pass off ideology as knowledge and intellectual snobbery as modernity and who make young people feel an indifference or a disgust for the life of books" (308).

6. In "Making It. Stanley Fish and the Creed of Careerism," *The New Republic* 244. 14 (September 2, 2013), 35–39, Russell Jacoby avers that "Interpretation becomes the province of like-minded professionals who constitute a community with its own preconceptions, conceptions, and rules. Little or nothing exists outside these communities" (36), a tribalism sustained by how "The lax concept of 'socially constructed' flattens out cultural distinctions" (39).

## Works Cited

Atwood, Roger. "Past Glories." *The Times Literary Supplement* 5720 (16 Nov. 2012): 32.

Bellow, Saul. "To Mario Vargas Llosa." *Letters*. Ed. Benjamin Taylor. New York: Viking, 2010. 418–420.

Corral, Wilfrido H. "Discount Latin American(ist) Intellectuals." *Social Science and Modern Society* 46.2 (March/April 2009). 119–123.

_____. *Mario Vargas Llosa. La batalla* en *las ideas*. Madrid, Franfurt: Vervuert, Iberoamericana, 2012.

Gallagher, David. "Fidel, Maggie and Liv." *The Times Literary Supplement* 5775 (6 Dec. 2013): 3–4.

De Castro, Juan E. *Mario Vargas Llosa: Public Intellectual in Neoliberal Latin America*. Tucson: U of Arizona P, 2011.

Fontaine, Arturo, ed. *Estudios Públicos* 122 (Autumn 2011).

Jacoby, Russell. "Making It. Stanley Fish and the Creed of Careerism." *The New Republic* 244.14 (Sep. 2, 2013): 35–39.

James, Henry. *Henry James Letters. II 1875–1883*. Ed. Leon Edel. Cambridge, MA: Harvard UP, 1975.

Serra, Carmen Caffarel, et al. *Vargas Llosa. De cuyo Nobel quiero acordarme*. Madrid: Instituto Cervantes, 2011.

Vargas Llosa, Mario. "Bienvenido, caos." *Piedra de toque II (1984–1999)*. Ed. Antoni Munné. Barcelona: Galaxia Gutenberg/Círculo de Lectores, 2012. 426–431.

---

_____. *La civilización del espectáculo*. Madrid: Alfaguara, 2012.

_____. *Diccionario del amante de América Latina*. Ed. Albert Bensoussan. Barcelona: Paidós, 2006.

_____. "Dentro y fuera de América Latina." *Letras Libres* [Mexico] 7.84 (Dec. 2005): 48–52.

_____. "Después del diluvio." *Piedra de toque III*. Ed. Antoni Munné. Barcelona: Galaxia Gutenberg/Círculo de Lectores, 2012. 273–277.

_____. "*El corazón de las tinieblas* (1902). *Joseph Conrad: Las raíces de lo humano*." *La verdad de las mentiras*. Madrid: Alfaguara, 2002. 33–46.

_____. *A Fish in the Water*. Trans. Helen Lane. New York: Farrar, Straus & Giroux, 1994.

_____. "Imágenes y realidad de Puerto Rico." *Piedra de toque I*. Ed. Antoni Munné. Barcelona: Galaxia Gutenberg/Círculo de Lectores, 2012. 483–489.

_____. *The Language of Passion. Selected Commentary*. Trans. Natasha Wimmer. New York: Farrar, Straus & Giroux, 2000.

_____. "Leer y escribir en Latinoamérica: entrevista a Mario Vargas Llosa." Interview with Daniel Mordzinski. *Bogotá 39. Retratos y Autorretratos*. Eds. Cristina Fuentes La Roche & Rodolfo Mendoza. Xalapa, Mexico: Universidad Veracruzana, Almadía, Hay Festival, 2012. 14–21.

_____. *Making Waves: Essays*. Trans. John King. New York: Farrar, Straus & Giroux, 1996.

_____. "Piedra de toque." *Piedra de toque I (1962–1983)*. Ed. Antoni Munné. Barcelona: Galaxia Gutenberg/Círculo de Lectores, 2012. ix–xii.

_____. "Robin Hood y los alegres compadres." *Piedra de toque II*. Ed. Antoni Munné. Barcelona: Galaxia Gutenberg/Círculo de Lectores, 2012. 978–983.

_____. "Saul Bellow and Chinese Whispers." *Making Waves: Essays*. Trans. John King. New York: Penguin, 1996. 305–10.

_____. "The Storyteller: Questions for Vargas Llosa." Interview with Deborah Solomon. *The New York Times Magazine* (7 Oct 2007): 15.

_____. *Wellsprings*. Cambridge, MA: Harvard UP, 2008.

Vargas Llosa, Mario & Gilles Lipovetsky. "¿Alta cultura o cultura de masas?" *Letras Libres* 14.163 (Julio 2012): 14–22.

Vargas Llosa, Mario & Claudio Magris. "Cultura, sociedad y política." *La literatura es mi venganza.* Lima: Seix Barral, 2011. 59–86.

Williams, Raymond Henry. "Structures of Feeling." *Marxism and Literature.* Oxford, NY: Oxford UP, 1977. 128–135.

# RESOURCES

# Chronology of Mario Vargas Llosa's Life

| | |
|---|---|
| 1936 | Mario Vargas Llosa is born in Arequipa, Peru to Ernesto J. Vargas and Dora Llosa. Parents had divorced before his birth. |
| 1950 | Three years after his parents reunite, Vargas Llosa is enrolled in the military school Leoncio Prado. |
| 1952 | Vargas Llosa finishes high school in Piura, where he lives with his Uncle Luis Llosa and his wife Olga. Vargas Llosa writes and successfully stages the (now lost) play *La huida del Inca* (The Inca's Escape) set in pre-Columbian times. The play wins second place in a student competition sponsored by the Ministry of Education. |
| 1953 | Vargas Llosa returns to Lima and enrolls in San Marcos National University to study law and literature. |
| 1955 | Vargas Llosa marries Julia Urquidi, Olga Llosa's sister. |
| 1956 | Vargas Llosa publishes his first short story, "El abuelo" ("The Grandfather"), in the newspaper, *El Comercio*. |
| 1958 | His short story, "El desafío" ("The Challenge"), wins a contest sponsored by *La Revue Française*. As part of the award, Vargas Llosa travels to Paris. He graduates from San Marcos and, as the best literature student, wins a scholarship to continue his studies at the Complutense University in Madrid. |
| 1959 | Vargas Llosa travels to Madrid and publishes in Spain, *Los jefes* (The Leaders), a collection of short stories that include "The Grandfather" and "The Challenge." Later that year, he moves to Paris. |

| | |
|---|---|
| 1962 | The manuscript of *La ciudad y los perros* (*The Time of the Hero*), loosely based on Vargas Llosa's experiences at the Leoncio Prado Military School, wins the Seix Barral Biblioteca Breve Prize. |
| 1963 | *The Time of the Hero* is published. It wins Premio de la Crítica Española. |
| 1964 | Vargas Llosa divorces Julia Urquidi. |
| 1965 | Vargas Llosa marries Patricia Llosa. |
| 1966 | *La casa verde* (*The Green House*) is published. The Vargas Llosas move to London. His first son, Álvaro Vargas Llosa, is born. |
| 1967 | *The Green House* is awarded the first Rómulo Gallegos Award given by the government of Venezuela to the best Spanish-language novel published within the previous five years. His second son, Gonzalo, is born. The novella *Los cachorros* ("The Cubs") is published. |
| 1969 | *Conversación en La Catedral* (*Conversation in The Cathedral*) is published. |
| 1970 | The Vargas Llosas move to Barcelona. |
| 1971 | The Padilla Affair leads to Vargas Llosa's break with the Cuban government. He earns his doctorate in philology at the Universidad Complutense de Madrid. His dissertation is published as *García Márquez. Historia de un deicidio* (García Márquez: Story of a Deicide), the foundational study of the Colombian novelist's works. |
| 1973 | *Pantaleón y las visitadoras* (*Captain Pantoja and the Special Service*) is published. This novel signals |

what Raymond L. Williams has called Vargas Llosa's "discovery of humor."

| | |
|---|---|
| 1974 | His daughter Morgana Vargas Llosa is born. Vargas Llosa and his family return to Lima. |
| 1975 | Vargas Llosa publishes *La orgía perpetua Flaubert y* Madame Bovary (*The Perpetual Orgy Flaubert and* Madame Bovary). He is named a member of the Academia Peruana de la Lengua. |
| 1976 | Vargas Llosa is elected president of Pen Club International. He is a member of the Jury at the Cannes Film Festival. |
| 1977 | *La tía Julia y el escribidor (Aunt Julia and the Scriptwriter)* is published. |
| 1980 | Vargas Llosa is a writer in residence at the Wilson Center in Washington, D.C. |
| 1981 | *La guerra del fin del mundo (The War of the End of the World)* and the essay collection *Entre Sartre y Camus (Between Sartre and Camus)* are published. The play *La señorita de Tacna (The Young Lady from Tacna)* is published and opens in Buenos Aires. |
| 1982 | The Congress of Peru grants him their Medal of Honor in recognition of his literary production. |
| 1983 | The play *Kathie y el hipopótamo (Kathie and the Hippopotamus)* is published and staged in Caracas. Vargas Llosa is part of the committee that investigates the killing of eight journalists in Uchuraccay in the province of Ayacucho. |

| 1984 | *La historia de Mayta* (*The Real Life of Alejandro Mayta*) is published. |
|---|---|
| 1985 | The French government grants him the Legion of Honor. |
| 1986 | The first two volumes of Vargas Llosa's selected nonfiction *Contra viento y marea* are published. His play *La Chunga* (*La Chunga*) is published. It is staged in Lima. He is elected Honorary Member of the American Academy and Institute of Arts and Letters. He is awarded the Prince of Asturias Award for literature. |
| 1987 | *El hablador* (*The Storyteller*) is published. Vargas Llosa leads the protest against then Peruvian President Alan García's proposal to nationalize the banks. |
| 1988 | Vargas Llosa founds the Moviento Libertad, a free-market based political party. His erotic novel, *Elogio de la madrastra* (*In Praise of the Stepmother*), is published. |
| 1989 | Vargas Llosa becomes the presidential candidate for the Frente Democrático, the alliance of the Movimiento Libertad with the traditional center-right parties Partido Popular Cristiano and Acción Popular. |
| 1990 | The third volume of *Contra Viento y Marea* (Against Wind and Tide) is published. Vargas Llosa receives an honorary doctorate from Florida International University. Vargas Llosa loses the presidential elections to dark horse candidate Alberto Fujimori. Vargas Llosa and his wife leave Peru for London. |
| 1992 | Vargas Llosa receives honorary doctorates from Boston University and the University of Genoa. |

| 1993 | *Lituma en los Andes* (*Death in the Andes*) is published. It receives the Planeta Award. His play *El loco de los balcones* (The Madman of the Balconies) is published. It is also staged in London. The Spanish government grants him the country's citizenship. He receives honorary doctorates from Yale University, Georgetown University, and The University of Rennes II. Vargas Llosa receives the Cervantes Prize, the most prestigious award granted to Spanish language writers. He becomes a member of the Real Academia Española. The French government grants him the Ordre des Arts et des Lettres in the grade of Commandeur. |
|------|------|
| 1995 | Vargas Llosa receives the Jerusalem Prize. |
| 1996 | Vargas Llosa receives the Peace Prize of the German book trade. *La utopía arcaica: José María Arguedas y las ficciones del indigenismo* (The Archaic Utopia: José María Arguedas and the Fictions of Indigenismo) is published. |
| 1997 | *Making Waves: Essays* (1996) wins the National Book Critics Circle Award for criticism. *Los cuadernos de don Rigoberto* (*The Notebooks of Don Rigoberto*) is published. |
| 1999 | Vargas Llosa receives an honorary doctorate from Harvard University. |
| 2000 | *La fiesta del Chivo* (*The Feast of the Goat*) is published. After the fall of the regime of Alberto Fujimori, Vargas Llosa visits Peru for the first time in ten years. |
| 2001 | The Universidad Nacional Mayor de San Marcos, Vargas Llosa's alma mater, grants him an honorary doctorate. Vargas Llosa receives La Orden del Sol, Peru's highest award, at the level of Gran Cruz. The |

Universidad de Murcia awards the first annual "Vargas Llosa" Novel Award.

2002    The PEN American Center grants him the Nabokov Award. The new edition of *La verdad de las mentiras*, 2002 (The Truth of Lies) receives the Bartolomé March Prize granted in Spain to the best book of literary criticism. He is named by the Cristóbal Gabarrón Foundation to be the "greatest novelist of our time in the Spanish language." Vargas Llosa is granted honorary doctorates by the University of La Trobe (Australia), Skidmore College, the Universidad Nacional de Piura (Peru), and the Universidad Nacional Pedro Ruíz Gallo of Chiclayo (Peru). He helps found the Fundación Internacional para la Libertad (International Foundation for Liberty) in order to promote free-market policies and ideas in the Spanish-speaking world. He is named its first President, a position he has held to the present (2014). He is named president of the Biblioteca Virtual Miguel de Cervantes, the main depository of Spanish-language books on the World Wide Web.

2003    *El paraíso en la otra esquina* (*The Way to Paradise*) is published. *The Language of Passion: Selected Commentary* is published. The Peruvian Congress grants him its Great Cross Medal of Honor. Vargas Llosa travels to Iraq to interview personalities and write articles. The French Pen Club awards him the Roger Callois Award. He receives honorary doctorates from the University of Oxford, Université Catholique de Louvain, and the Universidad Nacional de Ingeniería.

2004    Vargas Llosa receives the Konex Award (Buenos Aires) "for being the most important living Peruvian man of letters." *La tentación de lo imposible. Víctor Hugo y Los miserables* (*The Temptation of the Impossible Víctor Hugo and Les Misérables*) is published.

| 2005 | Vargas Llosa receives the Mercosur 2004 Award for Letters for his trajectory. He is also granted the first Lázaro Carreter Award; the Irving Kristol Award, by the American Enterprise Institute; and the Ovidio 2005 Award, granted by the Writers' Union of Romania. His play *La verdad de las mentiras* (The Truth of Lies) is staged in Barcelona with the author and the well-known actor Aitana Sánchez Gijón as its cast. He is named one of the one hundred most influential global thinkers by the magazines *Foreign Policy* and *Prospect*. He receives honorary degrees from the Universidad Ricardo Palma (Lima), the Université Sorbonne Nouvelle (Paris), 2006 *Las travesuras de la niña mala* (*The Bad Girl*) is published; his play *Odiseo y Penélope* is staged in Mérida, Spain. Vargas Llosa and Aitana Sánchez Gijón constitute its cast. He receives the Maria Moors Cabot Award for his journalism from Columbia University. |
|---|---|
| 2007 | *Odiseo y Penélope* is published. Vargas Llosa is named an honorary fellow of King's College, London. He receives an honorary doctorate from the Université de Reims, Champagne-Ardenne. |
| 2008 | Vargas Llosa's play *Al pie del Tamésis* (By the Shores of the Thames) is staged and published. *Wellsprings* is published. He is included by *Foreign Policy* and *Prospect* in its list of the one hundred most influential public intellectuals. He is named Commandeur des Arts et Lettres by the Government of France. He is granted the Award for Freedom by the Friedrich Naumann Foundation and the Isaiah Berlin Award by the Università degli Studi di Genova. His play *Las mils noches y una noche* (The Thousand and One Nights) is staged. *El viaje a la ficción: El mundo de Juan Carlos Onetti* (Voyage into Fiction: The World of Juan Carlos Onetti) is published. He receives honorary doctorates |

from the Pontificia Universidad Católica (Lima), the Universidad de Alicante, and the Universidad Simón Bolívar (Caracas).

| | |
|---|---|
| 2009 | Vargas Llosa is elected one of the *100 Top Global Thinkers* by *Foreign Policy*. He is granted honorary doctatorates by the Universidad de Granada, Universidad Inca Garcilaso de la Vega (Lima), and the Université de Bordeaux. |
| 2010 | Vargas Llosa receives the Nobel Prize for Literature. He publishes *El sueño del celta* (*The Dream of the Celt*). The Cátedra Vargas Llosa, for the promotion of the study of his work and Spanish-language literature, is founded in Peru by the Association of University Presidents. The government of Chile grants him Orden del Mérito Docente y Cultural Gabriela Mistral. The government of the Dominican Republic grants him la Orden Heráldica de Cristóbal Colón in the degree Gran Cruz Placa de Plata. The City College of New York and the Universidad San Ignacio de Loyola grant him honorary doctorates. |
| 2011 | The Kings of Spain grant him the hereditary title of Marquis of Vargas Llosa. He is elected member of the American Academy of Arts and Letters. The government of Mexico condecorates him with order of the Águila Azteca award. The government of Panama grants him the Orden Vasco Nuñez de Balboa in the degree of Gran Cruz. He receives the Alfonso Reyes Prize from universities and institutions in the Monterrey (Mexico) area. Stamps in honor of the Nobel Prize are issued in Spain and Peru. The Military School Leoncio Prado, the setting for his first novel, *La ciudad y los perros* (*The Time of the Hero*) and its alumni association honor him in a ceremony. The Universidad Ricardo Palma begins activities related to |

the Cátedra Vargas Llosa. The Cátedra Vargas Llosa in Spain is founded in a ceremony presided over by Prince Felipe in Madrid. *Touchstones Essays on Literature Arts and Politics* is published.

| | |
|---|---|
| 2012 | *La civilización del espectáculo* (Civilization of the Spectacle) is published. Vargas Llosa is voted the third most influential Latin American intellectual by *Foreign Policy*. The Real Academia Española and the Asociación de Academias de la Lengua publish a commemorative and critical edition of *La ciudad y los perros* (*The Time of the Hero*), celebrating the novel's fiftieth anniversary. |
| 2013 | *El héroe discreto* (The Discreet Hero) is published. Vargas Llosa receives an honorary doctorate from the University of Cambridge. The City University of New York and La Sorbonne (Paris) join the Cátedra Vargas Llosa. The Cátedra Vargas Llosa and the Universidad de Ingeniería y Tecnología del Perú establish the Premio Bienal de Novela Mario Vargas Llosa. |

# Works by Mario Vargas Llosa

### Fiction

*Los jefes,* 1959 ("The Leaders," collection of short stories included in *The Cubs and Other Stories,* 1979)

*La ciudad y los perros,* 1963 (*The Time of the Hero,* 1966)

*La casa verde,* 1966 (*The Green House,* 1968)

*Los cachorros,* 1967 ("The Cubs," novella included in *The Cubs and Other Stories,* 1979)

*Conversación en La Catedral,* 1969 (*Conversation in The Cathedral,* 1975)

*Pantaleón y las visitadoras,* 1973 (*Captain Pantoja and the Special Service,* 1978)

*La tía Julia y el escribidor,* 1977 (*Aunt Julia and the Scriptwriter,* 1982)

*La guerra del fin del mundo,* 1981 (*The War of the End of the World,* 1984)

*Historia de Mayta,* 1984 (*The Real Life of Alejandro Mayta,* 1986)

*¿Quién mató a Palomino Molero?,* 1986 (*Who Killed Palomino Molero?,* 1987)

*El hablador,* 1987 (*The Storyteller,* 1989)

*Elogio de la madrastra,* 1988 (*In Praise of the Stepmother,* 1990)

*Lituma en los Andes,* 1993 (*Death in the Andes,* 1996)

*Los cuadernos de don Rigoberto,* 1997 (*The Notebooks of Don Rigoberto,* 1998)

*La fiesta del Chivo,* 2000 (*The Feast of the Goat,* 2001)

*El paraíso en la otra esquina,* 2003 (*The Way to Paradise,* 2003)

*Travesuras de la niña mala,* 2006 (*The Bad Girl,* 2007)

*El sueño del celta,* 2010 (*The Dream of the Celt,* 2012)

*El héroe discreto,* 2013 (The Discreet Hero)

### Plays

*La huida del inca,* 1952 (The Inca's Escape, lost play)

*La señorita de Tacna*, 1981 (*The Young Lady from Tacna* in *Three Plays*, 1990)

*Kathie y el hipopótamo*, 1983 (*Kathie and the Hippopotamus* in *Three Plays*, 1990)

*La Chunga*, 1986 (*La Chunga* in *Three Plays*, 1990)

*El loco de los balcones*, 1993 (The Madman of the Balconies)

*Ojos bonitos, cuadros feos*, 1996 (Beautiful Eyes, Ugly Paintings)

*Odiseo y Penélope*, 2007 (Odysseus and Penelope)

*Al pie del Támesis*, 2008 (Next to the Thames)

*Las mil y una noches*, 2010 (*The Thousand and One Nights*)

## Children's Literature
*Fonchito y la luna*, 2010 (Fonchito and the Moon)

## Memoir
*El pez en el agua*, 1993 (*A Fish in the Water*, 1994)

## Essays & Articles
*Bases para una interpretación de Rubén Darío*, 2001 (Bases for an Interpretation of Ruben Dario; written in 1958)

*García Márquez: historia de un deicidio*, 1971 (García Márquez: Story of a Deicide)

*Historia secreta de una novela*, 1971 (A Secret Story of a Novel)

*La orgía perpetua: Flaubert y* Madame Bovary, 1975 (*The Perpetual Orgy: Flaubert and* Madame Bovary, 1986)

*Entre Sartre y Camus*, 1981 (Between Sartre and Camus)

*Contra viento y marea. Volumen I (1962–1982)*, 1983 (Against Wind and Tide. Volume I [1962–1982])

*La suntuosa abundancia. Ensayo sobre Fernando Botero*, 1984 (Sumptuous Abundance: An Essay on Fernando Botero)

*Contra viento y marea. Volumen II (1972–1983)*, 1986 (Against Wind and Tide. Volume II [1972–1983])

---

*Contra viento y marea. Volumen III (1964–1988)*, 1990 (Against Wind and Tide. Volume III [1964–1988])

*La verdad de las mentiras: ensayos sobre la novela moderna*, 1990 (*The Truth of Lies: Essays on the Modern Novel*)

*A Writer's Reality*, 1991

*Carta de Batalla por* Tirant lo Blanc, 1991 (Tirant lo Blanc's Battle Letter)

*Un hombre triste y feroz. Ensayo sobre George Grosz*, 1992 (A Sad and Fierce Man: Essay on George Grosz)

*Desafíos a la libertad*, 1994 (Challenges to Liberty)

*La utopía arcaica: José María Arguedas y las ficciones del indigenismo*, 1996 (Archaic Utopia: José María Arguedas and the Fictions of Indigenismo)

*Making Waves: Essays*, 1996.

*El lenguaje de la pasión*, 2001 (The Language of Passion)

*Cartas a un joven novelista*, 1997 (*Letters to a Young Novelist*, 2002)

*Diario de Irak*, 2003 (Iraq Diary)

*La tentación de lo imposible. Ensayo sobre* Los miserables *de Víctor Hugo*, 2004 (*The Temptation of the Impossible: Victor Hugo and* Les Misérables, 2007)

*Israel/Palestina: paz o guerra santa*, 2006 (Israel/Palestine: Peace or Holy War)

*Touchstones: Essays on Literature, Art, and Politics*, 2007

*Diccionario del amante de América Latina*, 2007 (Dictionary of the Lover of Latin America)

*Wellsprings (Richard Ellman Lectures in Modern Literature)*, 2008.

*El viaje a la ficción: El mundo de Juan Carlos Onetti*, 2009 (The Voyage into Fiction: The World of Juan Carlos Onetti)

*Sables y utopias: visiones de América Latina*, 2009 (Sabres and Utopia: Visions of Latin America)

*In Praise of Reading and Fiction: The Nobel Lecture* (2011)

*La civilización del espectáculo*, 2012 (Civilization of the Spectacle)

*Piedra de toque I (1962–1983)*, 2012 (Touchstone I [1962-1983])

*Piedra de toque II (1984–1999)*, 2012 *(*Touchstone II [1984-1999])
*Piedra de toque III (2000–2012)*, 2012 (Touchstone III [2000-2012])

# Bibliography

Alonso, Carlos. "The Elementary Structure of Kinship: Vargas Llosa's *La tía Julia y el escribidor.*" *The Burden of Modernity: The Rhetoric of Cultural Discourse in Spanish America.* New York: Oxford UP, 1998. 128–151.

Anderson, Benedict. "El Malhadado País." *The Spectre of Comparison: Nationalism, South East Asia and the World.* New York: Verso, 1998. 333–59.

Armas Marcelo, J. J. *Vargas Llosa. El vicio de escribir.* Madrid: Alfaguara, 2002.

Boland, Roy. *Mario Vargas Llosa: Oedipus and the Papa State. A Study of Individual and Social Psychology in Mario Vargas Llosa's Novels of Peruvian Reality.* Madrid: Editorial Voz, 1990.

Bolaño, Roberto. "The Cubs, Again." *Between Parentheses: Essays, Articles and Speeches, 1998–2003.* Ed. Ignacio Echevarría. Trans. Natasha Winner. New York: New Directions, 2011. 319–22.

_____. "The Prince of the Apocalypse." *Between Parentheses: Essays, Articles, and Speeches.* Ed. Ignacio Echevarría. Trans. Natasha Winner. New York: New Directions, 2011. 322–24.

Birns, Nicholas. "Tricontinental Modernities: Vargas Llosa's Late Turn against Imperialism in *El sueño del Celta.*" *Transmodernity: Journal of Peripheral Cultural Production of the Luso-Hispanic World* 2.1 (2012): 14–32.

Booker, M. Keith. *Vargas Llosa Among the Postmodernists.* Gainesville: U of Florida P, 1994.

Castillo, Debra. "The Uses of History in Vargas Llosa's *Historia de Mayta.*" *Inti: Revista de Literatura Hispánica.* 24–25 (1986–1987): 375–82.

Castro-Klarén, Sara. "Monuments and Scribes: *El hablador* Addresses Ethnography." *Structures of Power: Essays on Twentieth Century Spanish-American Fiction.* Eds. Terry J. Peavler & Peter Standish. Albany, NY: State U of New York P, 1996. 39–57.

_____. *Understanding Mario Vargas Llosa.* Columbia: U of South Carolina P, 1990.

Clayton, Michelle. *"The War of the End of the World* by Mario Vargas Llosa." *The Cambridge Companion to the Latin American Novel.* Ed. Efraín Kristal. Cambridge, UK: Cambridge UP, 2005. 283–96.

Cohn, Deborah. "The Case of the Fabricated Facts: Historical Reconstruction in Faulkner's *Absalom, Absalom!* and Vargas Llosa's *Historia de Mayta." Comparatist: Journal of the Southern Comparative Literature Association* 21 (1997): 25–48.

Corral, Wilfrido (Will) H. "Cortázar, Vargas Llosa, and Spanish American LiteraryHistory." *American Literary History* 4.3 (1992): 489–516.

_____. *Vargas Llosa. La batalla en las ideas.* Madrid: Iberoamericana/ Vervuert, 2012.

De Castro, Juan E. *Mario Vargas Llosa: Public Intellectual in Neoliberal Latin America.* Tucson: U of Arizona P, 2011.

De Castro, Juan E. & Nicholas Birns, eds. *Vargas Llosa and Latin American Politics.* New York: Palgrave Macmillan, 2010.

Dunkerley, James. "Mario Vargas Llosa: Parables and Deceits." *Political Suicide in Latin America and Other Essays.* London: Verso, 1992. 139–52.

Enkvist, Inger. *On Translating Mario Vargas Llosa: The Novels of Mario Vargas Llosa in English, French and Swedish Translation.* Trans. Linda Schenck. Madrid: Vox, 1993.

Erickson, Sandra S. F. *Euclides da Cunha, Vargas Llosa and Cunninghame Graham: Thrice Told Tales.* Joao Pessoa: Universitária da Paráiba, 2006.

Feal, Rosemary Geisdorfer. *Novel Lives: The Fictional Autobiographies of Guillermo Cabrera Infante and Mario Vargas Llosa.* Chapel Hill: North Carolina Studies in the Romance Languages and Literature, 1986.

Fenwick, M. J. *Dependency Theory and Literary Analysis: Reflections on Vargas Llosa's* The Green House. Minneapolis: Institute for the Study of Ideologies and Literature, 1981.

Filer, Malva. "Vargas Llosa: The Novelist as Critic." *Texas Studies in Literature and Language* 19.4 (1977): 503–13.

Fradinger, Moira. "Mario Vargas Llosa's *The Feast of the Goat* or Sovereign Politics: We the Nation State." *Binding Violence: Literary Visions of Political Origins.* Stanford: Stanford UP, 2010. 183–238.

---

Franco, Jean. "Reading Vargas Llosa: Conversation is not Dialogue." *Critical Passions: Selected Essays*. Eds. Mary Louise Pratt & Kathleen Newman. Durham, NC: Duke UP, 1999. 233–38.

Fuentes, Carlos. "Vargas Llosa's Will to Totality." *Review: Latin American Literature and Arts* 61 (2000): 13–19.

Gallagher, David. "Mario Vargas Llosa." *Modern Latin American Literature*. Oxford: Oxford UP, 1973. 122–43.

Gerdes, Dick. *Mario Vargas Llosa*. Boston: Twayne Publishers, 1985.

Goodman, Robin Truth. "Mario Vargas Llosa and the Rape of Sebastiana." *Infertilities: Exploring Fictions of Barren Bodies*. Minneapolis: U of Minnesota P, 2000. 135–63.

Granés, Carlos. *La revancha de la imaginación. Antropología de los procesos de creación: Mario Vargas Llosa y José Alejandro Restrepo*. Madrid: Consejo Superior de Investigaciones Científicas, 2008.

Herrero-Olaizola, Alejandro. "The Writer in the Barracks: Mario Vargas Llosa Facing Censorship." *The Censorship Files: Latin American Writers and Franco's Spain*. Albany: State U of New York P, 2007. 37–70.

Kerr, Lucille. "Facing the Author: Telling Stories in Mario Vargas Llosa's *El hablador*." *Reclaiming the Author: Figures and Fictions from Spanish America*. Durham, NC: Duke UP, 1992. 134–59.

Kerr, Roy A. *Mario Vargas: Critical Essays on Characterization*. Potomac, MD: Scripta Humanistica, 1990.

Kokotovic, Mischa. "Mario Vargas Llosa Writes Of(f) the Native: Cultural Heterogeneity and Neoliberal Modernity." *The Colonial Divide in Peruvian Narrative: Social Conflict and Transculturation*. Eastborne: Sussex Academi P, 2007. 163–94.

Köllman, Sabine. *A Companion to Mario Vargas Llosa*. Woodridge: Tamesis Books, 2014.

_____. *Vargas Llosa and the Demon of Politics*. New York: Peter Lang, 2002.

Krauze, Enrique. "Mario Vargas Llosa: Creative Parricide." *Redeemers: Ideas and Power in Latin America*. Trans. Hank Heifetz. New York: Harper, 2012. 365–402.

Kristal, Efraín. *The Temptation of the Word: The Novels of Mario Vargas Llosa*. Nashville, TN: Vanderbilt UP, 1998.

Kristal, Efraín & John King, eds. *The Cambridge Companion to Mario Vargas Llosa*. Cambridge: Cambridge UP, 2012.

Larsen, Neil. "Mario Vargas Llosa: The Realist as Neo-Liberal." *Determinations: Essays on Theory, Narrative, and Nation in the Americas*. New York: Verso, 2001. 143–68.

López-Calvo, Ignacio. "The Goat, the Patriarch, and other Trujillos: Condemning or Abetting Dictatorships." *God and Trujillo: Literary Representations of the Dominican Dictator*. Gainesville: UP of Florida, 2005. 25–57.

Manguel, Alberto. "The Blind Photographer." *Into the Looking-Glass Wood: Essays on Words and the World*. New York: Random House, 2011. 109–20.

Martin, Gerald. "Mario Vargas Llosa: Errant Knight of the Liberal Imagination." *Modern Latin American Fiction: A Survey*. Ed. John King. London: Faber & Faber, 1987. 205–33.

Moraña, Mabel. *Arguedas/Vargas Llosa. Dilemas y ensamblajes*. Madrid: Iberoamericana, 2013.

Moses, Michael V. "Vargas Llosa: Apocalyptic History and the Liberal Perspective." *The Novel and the Globalization of Culture*. New York: Oxford UP, 1995. 148–92.

Muñoz, Braulio. *Storyteller: Mario Vargas Llosa Between Civilization and Barbarism*. Lanham, MD: Rowan & Littlefield, 2000.

O'Bryan-Knight, Jean. *The Story of the Storyteller:* La tía Julia y el escribidor, Historia de Mayta *and* El hablador *by Mario Vargas Llosa*. Amsterdam: Rodopi, 1995.

Oviedo, José Miguel. *Mario Vargas Llosa. La invención de una realidad*. Barcelona: Barral, 1970.

_____. *Dossier Vargas Llosa*. Lima: Taurus, 2007.

Pamuk, Orhan. "Mario Vargas Llosa and Third World Literature." *Other Color: Essays and a Story*. Trans. Maureen Freely. New York: Knopf, 2007. 168–73.

Rama, Ángel. "*La guerra del fin del mundo*: una obra maestra del fanatismo artístico." *La crítica de la cultura en América Latina*. Eds. Saúl Sosnowski & Tomás Eloy Martínez. Caracas: Biblioteca Ayacucho, 1985. 335–63.

Reagan, Patricia E. "Stories of the Other/Reflections of the Self in Mario Vargas Llosa's *El hablador*. *The Postmodern Storyteller: Donoso,*

*García Márquez and Vargas Llosa.* Lanham, MD: Lexington Books, 2012. 85–127.

Rossamn, Charles & Alan Warren Friedman, eds. *Mario Vargas Llosa: A Collection of Critical Essays.* Austin: U of Texas P, 1978.

Rowe, William. "Liberalism and Authority: The Case of Mario Vargas Llosa." *On Edge: The Crisis of Contemporary Latin American Culture.* Eds. George Yúdice, Jean Franco, & Juan Flores. Minneapolis: U of Minnesota P, 1992. 45–64.

Rushdie, Salman. "Mario Vargas Llosa." *Imaginary Homelands: Essays and Criticism 1981–1991.* London: Granta Books, 1991. 308–17.

Sa, Lucía. "*The Storyteller* (1987)." *Rain Forest Literatures: Amazonian Texts and Latin American Culture.* Minneapolis: U of Minnesota P, 2004. 251–73.

Saba, Edgardo & Alonso Cueto, eds. *Las guerras de este mundo. Sociedad, poder y ficción en la obra de Mario Vargas Llosa.* Lima: Planeta, 2008.

Sun, Haiqing. "A Journey Lost in Mystery: Mario Vargas Llosa's *Death in the Andes.*" *Detective Fiction in a Postcolonial and Transnational World.* Eds. Nels Pearson & Marc Singer. Farnhan: Ashgate, 2009.

Sommer, Doris. "About Face: The Talker Turns toward Peru." *Proceed with Caution, when Engaged by Minority Writing in the Americas.* Cambridge, MA: Harvard UP, 1999. 234–70.

Ubilluz, Juan Carlos. "The Taming of Bataille in Vargas Llosa's *Elogio de la madrastra.*" *Sacred Eroticism: Georges Bataille and Pierre Klossowski in the Latin American Erotic Novel.* Lewisburg: Bucknell UP, 2006. 180–205.

Van Delden, Maarten & Yvon Grenier. "The Private and the Public: Mario Vargas Llosa on Literature and Politics." *Gunshots at the Fiesta: Literature and Politics in Latin America.* Nashville, TN: Vanderbilt UP, 2009. 195-214.

Wasserman, Renata. "Mario Vargas Llosa, Euclides da Cunha, and the Strategy of Intertextuality." *PMLA: Publications of the Modern Language Association of America* 108.3 (1993): 460–73.

Weldt-Basson, Helene Carol. "*El sueño del celta*: Postcolonial Vargas Llosa." *Redefining Latin American Historical Fiction: The Impact of Feminism and Postcolonialism.* Ed. Helene Carol Weldt-Basson. New York: Palgrave Macmillan, 2013. 231–47.

Williams, Raymond. L. *Mario Vargas Llosa*. New York: Ungar Publishing, 1986.

_____. *Vargas Llosa. Otra historia de un deicidio*. Madrid: Taurus, 2000.

Zapata, Miguel Ángel, ed. *Mario Vargas Llosa and the Persistence of Memory*. Lima: Fondo Editorial de la U de San Marcos, 2006.

# About the Editor

**Juan E. De Castro** is an associate professor in literary studies at Eugene Lang College, The New School for Liberal Arts, New York. He is the author of *Mestizo Nations: Culture, Race, and Conformity in Latin American Literature* (2002), *The Spaces of Latin American Literature: Tradition, Globalization and Cultural Production* (2008), and *Mario Vargas Llosa: Public Intellectual in Neoliberal Latin America* (2011). He is also the editor of *Vargas Llosa and Latin American Politics* (2010, with Nicholas Birns) and *The Contemporary Spanish American Novel: Bolaño and After* (2012, with Will H. Corral and Nicholas Birns). He is currently working on a book-length study on the pioneer Peruvian Marxist thinker and activist José Carlos Mariátegui.

# Contributors_____

**Mark D. Anderson** is associate professor of Latin American literatures and cultures at the University of Georgia. He wrote his doctoral dissertation on the total novel in Mexico and has published several articles on the subject. He is the author of *Disaster Writing: The Cultural Politics of Catastrophe in Latin America* (2011).

**Gene H. Bell-Villada**, professor of Romance Languages at Williams College, has authored six books, including *García Márquez: The Man and his Work* (1990, revised 2010), *Art for Art's Sake & Literary Life* (1996), and *On Nabokov, Ayn Rand and the Libertarian Mind: What the Russian-American Odd Pair Can Tell Us About Some Values, Myths and Manias Widely Held Most Dear* (2013). He is also the author of two books of fiction and a memoir: *Overseas American: Growing Up Gringo in the Tropics* (2005). His latest edited collection, with Nina Sichel, is *Writing out of Limbo: International Childhoods, Global Nomads, and Third Culture Kids* (2011).

**Nicholas Birns** teaches at the New School. His books include *Understanding Anthony Powell* (2004), *Theory After Theory: An Intellectual History of Literary Theory from 1950 to the Early 21$^{st}$ Century* (2010), and *Barbarian Memory: The Legacy of Early Medieval History in Early Modern Literature* (2013). He has co-edited *The Contemporary Spanish American Novel* (2013) with Juan E. De Castro and Will H. Corral.

**Jeff Browitt** is a senior lecturer in the Faculty of Arts and Social Sciences at the University of Technology, Sydney. He has published on cultural theory, Central American literature, Latin American popular culture, and Colombian political economy. He is the author of *Contemporary Cultural Theory* (Routledge, 2002, with A. Milner), co-editor of *Rubén Darío: cosmopolita arraigado* (IHNC, 2010, with W. Mackenbach), and translator of Carlos Monsiváis' *A New Catechism for Recalcitrant Indians* (FCE, 2010, with N. Castrillón).

**Sara Castro-Klarén**, professor of Latin American literature and culture at John Hopkins University, is the author of *Understanding Mario Vargas Llosa* (1990), one of the central studies on the Peruvian novelist. She is also the author of *El mundo mágico de José María Arguedas* (1973), *Escritura sujeto y transgresión en la literatura latinoamericana* (1989), and *The Narrow Pass of our Nerves: Writing, Coloniality and Postcolonial Theory* (2011). As an editor, she has published *Women's Writing in Latin America: An Anthology* (1992, with Sylvia Molloy and Beatriz Sarlo), *Beyond Imagined Communities: Reading and Writing the Nation in 19th Century Latin America* (2003, with John Charles Chasteen), *Narrativa femenina en América Latina: Prácticas y perspectivas teóricas/Latin American Women's Narrative: Practices and Theoretical Perspectives* (2003), *A Companion to Latin American Literature and Culture* (2008), and *Entre Borges y Conrad: Estética y territorio en William Henry Hudson* (2012, with Leila Gómez).

**Will H. Corral** received his PhD from Columbia University and has taught at the University of Massachusetts, Amherst, and Stanford University. His most recent books are *The Contemporary Spanish American Novel: Bolaño and After* (2013, with Juan E. De Castro and Nicholas Birns), *El error del acierto (contra ciertos dogmas latinoamericanistas)* (2013, rev. and expanded), *Vargas Llosa: la batalla en las ideas* (2012), *Bolaño traducido: Nueva literatura mundial* (2011), and *Cartografía occidental de la novela* (2010). In 2014, he held the "Cátedra Abierta Roberto Bolaño" in Chile.

**Alonso Cueto** is the author of nine novels, in addition to novella and short story collections, essays, and plays. His novel *The Blue Hour* (2005) won the Herralde Prize, and *El susurro de la mujer ballena* (*The Whisper of the Whale Woman* 2007) was the runner-up to the Planeta Prize. He is also a professor of the Pontificia Universidad Católica and a member of the Academia Peruana de la Lengua. His most recent publication is the novel *Cuerpos secretos* (2012).

**Carlos Granés**, an anthropologist and essayist, is the author of *La revancha de la imaginación. Antropología de los procesos de creación: Mario Vargas Llosa y José Alejandro Restrepo* (2008) and *El puño* *invisible. Arte, revolución y un siglo de cambios culturales* (2011), which received the Isabel Polanco International Essay Award. He edited and wrote the introduction for *Sables y utopias. Visiones de Latinoamérica* (2009), the collection of Vargas Llosa's articles on political issues. He is also the Secretary of the Cátedra Vargas Llosa.

**Ignacio López-Calvo** is a professor of literature at University of California, Merced. He has published *Dragons in the Land of the Condor: Writing Tusán in Peru* (forthcoming); *The Affinity of the Eye: Writing Nikkei in Peru* (2013); *Latino Los Angeles in Film and Fiction* (2011); *Imaging the Chinese in Cuban Literature and Culture"* (2007); *"God and Trujillo": Literary and Cultural Representations of the Dominican Dictator* (2005); *Religión y militarismo en la obra de Marcos Aguinis 1963–2000* (2002); and *Written in Exile: Chilean Fiction since 1973* (2001).

**Jean O'Bryan-Knight** is a lecturer in Spanish at the University of Pennsylvania, where she enjoys teaching Latin American literature to undergraduates. Her courses cover a variety of topics including Andean authors, major works of the "boom," narratives of the *selva*, and coming of age stories. In all of these courses she covers, works by Mario Vargas Llosa and his novels never fail to excite her students. She is also the author of *The Story of the Storyteller: La tía Julia y el escribidor, Historia de Mayta, and El hablador by Mario Vargas Llosa* (1995).

**Miguel Rivera-Taupier** is an assistant professor of Spanish at Missouri Western State University. He has published articles on contemporary Latin American literature. His research focuses on the detective novel, mental maps, and the representation of megalopolises in contemporary Latin American fiction.

**Haiqing Sun** received her BA and MA in Spanish from Peking University, China, and PhD in Spanish from University of Southern California. Her research interests and publications are on Hispanic American narrative and comparative study of Chinese and Latin American fiction. She is associate professor of Spanish at Texas Southern University.

**Raymond Leslie Williams**, distinguished professor of Spanish at the University of California, Riverside, has written fifteen books on the modern Latin American novel. Among these are *Gabriel García Márquez* (1984), *Mario Vargas Llosa* (1987), *The Colombian Novel: 1844–1987* (1991), *The Postmodern Novel in Latin America* (1995), *The Writings of Carlos Fuentes* (1996), *Vargas Llosa: Otra historia de un deicidio* (2001), *The Twentieth-Century Spanish American Novel* (2003), *The Columbia Guide to the Latin American Novel since 1945* (2007), and *A Companion to Gabriel García Márquez* (2010). He is currently completing a book on environment, trauma, and politics in the complete fiction of Vargas Llosa.

# Index

Marechal, Leopoldo 203
Mariátegui, José Carlos 193, 257
Markee, Patrick 48
Márquez, Gabriel García xii, 3,
    21, 41, 47, 69, 117, 175,
    201, 262
Martínez, Tomás Eloy 48, 254
Martorell, Joanot 201
Marxism 7, 10, 151, 180, 234
Marx, Karl 7
masculinity 31, 98, 167
Mask Face 155
*Massive Novel of Peruvian*
    *Realities, A* 53
Mayer, Dora 86
McCanon, Shreve 126
McMurray, George R. 53
Mendoza, Rodolfo 233
Menem, Carlos Saúl 14
Merceditas, Doña 96
*Metamorphosis* 155
Mignolo, Walter 87
military 4, 5, 10, 11, 12, 19, 29,
    30, 31, 58, 59, 92, 97, 106,
    114, 117, 119, 120, 122,
    128, 132, 134, 146, 164,
    176, 178, 179, 181, 186,
    192, 237
Millones Santagadea, Luis 80
Mindreau, Alicia 162, 164, 165,
    171
Miraflores 96, 100
Mississippi 126
modernity, modernization 7, 57,
    63, 66, 71, 72, 73, 82, 83,
    85, 86, 87, 132, 133, 143,
    181, 188, 189, 194, 195,
    213, 232

Molero, Palomino xi, 46, 96, 161,
    162, 163, 164, 165, 167,
    168, 169, 170, 171, 172,
    173, 174, 176, 177, 186,
    187, 247
Monteith, Robert 191
Monte Santo 135
Moquegua 82
moral code 108, 112, 113
Morales, Evo 14, 22
Moraña, Mabel 88, 254
Moro, César 227
*Motivos de Proteo* 195
*Mountains of the Mind* 186
Movimiento Libertad 21, 41, 240
Munné, Antoni 232, 233
Musil, Robert 128

*N+1* 3, 17
Nabokov, Vladimir 44
narrative point of view 126
nationalism xii, 148, 189, 190,
    191, 192, 193, 194, 196, 199
*Nations, Fictions* 143, 145
*Nation, The* xii, 62, 73, 83, 84, 99,
    143, 189, 212
naturalism 9, 21
nature 31, 56, 57, 58, 59, 60, 61,
    63, 65, 66, 67, 73, 78, 134,
    158, 161, 183, 184, 192,
    193, 195, 196, 197, 204,
    206, 209, 220, 231
*Nature and the Discourse of*
    *Modernity in Spanish*
    *American Avant-Garde*
    *Fiction* 69
*Nature in the Twentieth-Century*
    *Latin American Novel* 69,
    70